English Phonetics and Phonology
A practical course

Third edition

PETER ROACH

Emeritus Professor of Phonetics
University of Reading

CAMBRIDGE
UNIVERSITY PRESS

CAMBRIDGE UNIVERSITY PRESS
Cambridge, New York, Melbourne, Madrid, Cape Town, Singapore, São Paulo

Cambridge University Press
The Edinburgh Building, Cambridge CB2 2RU, UK

www.cambridge.org
Information on this title: www.cambridge.org/9780521786133

First published 1983
Third edition 2000
10th printing 2006

Printed in the United Kingdom at the University Press, Cambridge

A catalogue record for this publication is available from the British Library

ISBN-13 978-0-521-78613-3 paperback
ISBN-10 0-521-78613-4 paperback

ISBN-13 978-0-521-79798-6 set of two cassettes
ISBN-10 0-521-79798-5 set of two cassettes

ISBN-13 978-0-521-79799-3 set of two audio CDs
ISBN-10 0-521-79799-3 set of two audio CDs

Contents

Preface to the third edition   vii
List of symbols   ix
Chart of the International Phonetic Alphabet   xi
How to use this book   xii

1 **Introduction**   1

2 **The production of speech sounds**   8
   2.1 Articulators above the larynx
   2.2 Vowel and consonant
   2.3 English short vowels

3 **Long vowels, diphthongs and triphthongs**   19
   3.1 Long and short vowels
   3.2 Diphthongs
   3.3 Triphthongs

4 **Voicing and consonants**   27
   4.1 The larynx
   4.2 Respiration and voicing
   4.3 Plosives
   4.4 English plosives
   4.5 Fortis and lenis

5 **The phoneme**   38
   5.1 The phoneme
   5.2 Symbols and transcription
   5.3 Phonology

Contents

6 Fricatives and affricates   48
6.1 Production of fricatives and affricates
6.2 The fricatives of English
6.3 The affricates
6.4 Fortis consonants

7 Nasals and other consonants   58
7.1 Nasals
7.2 The consonant l
7.3 The consonant r
7.4 The consonants j and w

8 The syllable   70
8.1 The nature of the syllable
8.2 The structure of the English syllable
8.3 Syllable division
8.4 Practical conclusions

9 Strong and weak syllables   81
9.1 Strong and weak
9.2 The ə vowel ("schwa")
9.3 Close front and close back vowels
9.4 Syllabic consonants

10 Stress in simple words   93
10.1 The nature of stress
10.2 Levels of stress
10.3 Placement of stress within the word

11 Complex word stress   104
11.1 Complex words
11.2 Suffixes
11.3 Prefixes
11.4 Compound words
11.5 Variable stress
11.6 Word-class pairs

12 Weak forms   112

13 Problems in phonemic analysis 121

13.1 Affricates
13.2 The English vowel system
13.3 Syllabic consonants
13.4 Clusters of s plus plosives
13.5 Schwa (ə)
13.6 Distinctive features
13.7 Conclusion

14 Aspects of connected speech 134

14.1 Rhythm
14.2 Assimilation
14.3 Elision
14.4 Linking

15 Intonation 1 156

15.1 Form and function in intonation
15.2 Tone and tone languages
15.3 Complex tones and pitch height
15.4 Some functions of English tones

16 Intonation 2 162

16.1 The tone-unit
16.2 The structure of the tone-unit
16.3 Pitch possibilities in the simple tone-unit

17 Intonation 3 171

17.1 Fall–rise and rise–fall tones followed by a tail
17.2 High and low heads
17.3 Problems in analysing the form of intonation
17.4 Autosegmental treatment of intonation

18 Functions of intonation 1 183

18.1 The attitudinal function of intonation

19 Functions of intonation 2 193

19.1 The accentual function of intonation
19.2 The grammatical function of intonation

19.3 The discourse function of intonation
19.4 Conclusions

20 Further areas of study in phonetics and phonology 204
20.1 Laboratory phonetics
20.2 The study of variety

Recorded exercises 214
Unit 2: English short vowels 215
Unit 3: Long vowels. Diphthongs and triphthongs 216
Unit 4: Plosives 218
Unit 5: Revision 221
Unit 6: Fricatives and affricates 223
Unit 7: Further consonants 225
Unit 8: Consonant clusters 227
Unit 9: Weak syllables 229
Unit 10: Word stress 232
Unit 11: Complex word stress 234
Unit 12: Weak forms 236
Unit 13: Revision 238
Unit 14: Elisions 239
Unit 15: Tones 240
Unit 16: The tone-unit 241
Unit 17: Intonation 243
Unit 18: Intonation: extracts from conversation 244
Unit 19: Transcription of connected speech 245
Unit 20: Further practice on connected speech 247

Answers to written exercises 248
Answers to recorded exercises 260
Recommendations for general reading 270
Bibliography 273
Index 280

Preface to the third edition

The second edition of this book was published in 1991, and since then a number of important books and papers in the field have appeared. My first task, therefore, has been to update thoroughly the recommendations for further reading and, where possible, to incorporate some new ideas. I have tried to avoid recommending works which are no longer in print, although this has not always been possible. The structure of the book remains virtually unchanged except that I have moved the discussion of distinctive features from Chapter 20 to Chapter 13, and shortened it. I feel it now fits more naturally with the discussion of other phonological issues in that chapter, which I have simplified a little. I have given up the use of the name *Received Pronunciation* (*RP*) for the accent described in the book: it is a term which I have always disliked, and I have chosen to refer instead to *BBC pronunciation*. I have attempted to improve the treatment of word stress, and have added some more modern ideas about the analysis of intonation.

Since the publication of the second edition, I have worked on the 15th edition of the *Daniel Jones English Pronouncing Dictionary* (Jones, 1997; edited and revised by Roach and Hartman), and I have made a number of changes to transcriptions in the present book in order to avoid disagreements with what I would regard as a companion volume. I have made a large number of minor changes to the text in an attempt to make it clearer to read, and I have removed a number of errors. I wish I could believe that I have removed all of them. The recorded exercises have been kept unchanged in order to retain continuity with the earlier editions, and these are now also available on audio CD.

In the previous editions I thanked the many people who had given me help, and I remain grateful to all of them. This third edition has had the benefit of advice from many more people who have used the book for teaching or study and who have suggested improvements. I would like to thank everyone who has helped me in this way, although there are too many for me to name all of them. Takeshi Shimaoka and Hiroshi Miura translated the book into Japanese, and passed on to me many valuable observations as a result of their careful work. Snezhina Dimitrova has given me very useful feedback from her experience with using the book. At the University of Reading my colleagues Erik Fudge, Paul Kerswill and Linda Shockey have provided me with helpful advice and ideas. I am grateful to Jane Setter for helpful advice and discussion on many points. She and James Hartman were co-editors of the 15th edition of the *Daniel Jones English Pronouncing Dictionary*, and their collaboration has also been helpful in the revision of the present book. I would like to thank Mickey Bonin of Cambridge University Press for his editorial work and guidance. I remain grateful, as ever, to my wife Helen, who has helped in the work of revising the book and supported me while I was trying to finish the work.

List of symbols

1 *Symbols for phonemes*

ɪ	as in 'pit' **pɪt**	iː	as in 'key' **kiː**
e	as in 'pet' **pet**	ɑː	as in 'car' **kɑː**
æ	as in 'pat' **pæt**	ɔː	as in 'core' **kɔː**
ʌ	as in 'putt' **pʌt**	uː	as in 'coo' **kuː**
ɒ	as in 'pot' **pɒt**	ɜː	as in 'cur' **kɜː**
ʊ	as in 'put' **pʊt**		

ə   as in 'about, upper'
    əbaʊt, ʌpə

eɪ	as in 'bay' **beɪ**	əʊ	as in 'go' **gəʊ**
aɪ	as in 'buy' **baɪ**	aʊ	as in 'cow' **kaʊ**
ɔɪ	as in 'boy' **bɔɪ**		

ɪə	as in 'peer' **pɪə**
eə	as in 'pear' **peə**
ʊə	as in 'poor' **pʊə**

p	as in 'pea' **piː**	b	as in 'bee' **biː**
t	as in 'toe' **təʊ**	d	as in 'doe' **dəʊ**
k	as in 'cap' **kæp**	g	as in 'gap' **gæp**
f	as in 'fat' **fæt**	v	as in 'vat' **væt**
θ	as in 'thing' **θɪŋ**	ð	as in 'this' **ðɪs**
s	as in 'sip' **sɪp**	z	as in 'zip' **zɪp**
ʃ	as in 'ship' **ʃɪp**	ʒ	as in 'measure' **meʒə**
h	as in 'hat' **hæt**		
m	as in 'map' **mæp**	l	as in 'led' **led**

n	as in 'nap' **næp**		**r**	as in 'red' **red**
ŋ	as in 'hang' **hæŋ**		**j**	as in 'yet' **jet**
			w	as in 'wet' **wet**

tʃ	as in 'chin' **tʃɪn**		**dʒ**	as in 'gin' **dʒɪn**

2 *Non-phonemic symbols*

i	as in 'react', 'happy' **riækt, hæpi**
u	as in 'to each' **tu iːtʃ**
ʔ	glottal stop
ʰ	aspiration, as in 'pin' **pʰɪn**
ˌ	syllabic consonant, as in 'button' **bʌtn̩**
ˇ	shortened vowel, as in 'miss' **mɪ̆s**
.	syllable division, as in 'differ' **dɪf.ə**

3 *Stress and intonation*

|	tone-unit boundary
||	pause
ˈ	primary stress, as in 'open' **ˈəʊpən**
ˌ	secondary stress, as in 'ice cream' **ˌaɪsˈkriːm**

Tones: ˎ fall

ˏ rise

ˇ fall–rise

ˆ rise–fall

‾ level

ˈ	stressed syllable in head, high pitch, as in 'please ˎdo
ˌ	stressed syllable in head, low pitch, as in ˌplease ˎdo
·	stressed syllable in tail, as in ˌmy ·turn
↑	extra pitch height, as in ↑ˌmy ·turn

Chart of the International Phonetic Alphabet (revised 1993, updated 1996)

CONSONANTS (PULMONIC)

	Bilabial	Labiodental	Dental	Alveolar	Post alveolar	Retroflex	Palatal	Velar	Uvular	Pharyngeal	Glottal
Plosive	p b			t d		ʈ ɖ	c ɟ	k g	q ɢ		ʔ
Nasal	m	ɱ		n		ɳ	ɲ	ŋ	N		
Trill	B			r					R		
Tap or Flap				ɾ		ɽ					
Fricative	ɸ β	f v	θ ð	s z	ʃ ʒ	ʂ ʐ	ç ʝ	x ɣ	χ ʁ	ħ ʕ	h ɦ
Lateral fricative				ɬ ɮ							
Approximant		ʋ		ɹ		ɻ	j	ɰ			
Lateral approximant				l		ɭ	ʎ	L			

Where symbols appear in pairs, the one to the right represents a voiced consonant. Shaded areas denote articulations judged impossible.

CONSONANTS (NON-PULMONIC)

Clicks	Voiced implosives	Ejectives	
ʘ Bilabial	ɓ Bilabial	ʼ	Examples:
ǀ Dental	ɗ Dental/alveolar	pʼ	Bilabial
! (Post)alveolar	ʄ Palatal	tʼ	Dental/alveolar
ǂ Palatoalveolar	ɠ Velar	kʼ	Velar
ǁ Alveolar lateral	ʛ Uvular	sʼ	Alveolar fricative

OTHER SYMBOLS

ʍ	Voiceless labial-velar fricative	ɕ ʑ	Alveolo-palatal fricatives
w	Voiced labial-velar approximant	ɺ	Alveolar lateral flap
ɥ	Voiced labial-palatal approximant	ɧ	Simultaneous ʃ and x
ʜ	Voiceless epiglottal fricative		
ʢ	Voiced epiglottal fricative	Affricates and double articulations can be represented by two symbols joined by a tie bar if necessary.	k͡p t͡s
ʡ	Epiglottal plosive		

VOWELS

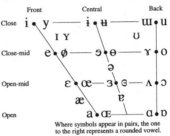

Where symbols appear in pairs, the one to the right represents a rounded vowel.

DIACRITICS   Diacritics may be placed above a symbol with a descender, e.g. ŋ̊

̥	Voiceless	n̥ d̥	̤	Breathy voiced	b̤ a̤	̪	Dental	t̪ d̪
̬	Voiced	s̬ t̬	̰	Creaky voiced	b̰ a̰	̺	Apical	t̺ d̺
ʰ	Aspirated	tʰ dʰ	̼	Linguolabial	t̼ d̼	̻	Laminal	t̻ d̻
̹	More rounded	ɔ̹	ʷ	Labialized	tʷ dʷ	̃	Nasalized	ẽ
̜	Less rounded	ɔ̜	ʲ	Palatalized	tʲ dʲ	ⁿ	Nasal release	dⁿ
̟	Advanced	u̟	ˠ	Velarized	tˠ dˠ	ˡ	Lateral release	dˡ
̠	Retracted	e̠	ˤ	Pharyngealized	tˤ dˤ	̚	No audible release	d̚
̈	Centralized	ë	̴	Velarized or pharyngealized	ɫ			
̽	Mid-centralized	e̽	̝	Raised	e̝ (ɹ̝ = voiced alveolar fricative)			
̩	Syllabic	n̩	̞	Lowered	e̞ (β̞ = voiced bilabial approximant)			
̯	Non-syllabic	e̯	̘	Advanced Tongue Root	e̘			
˞	Rhoticity	ɚ a˞	̙	Retracted Tongue Root	e̙			

SUPRASEGMENTALS

ˈ	Primary stress
ˌ	Secondary stress
	ˌfoʊnəˈtɪʃən
ː	Long eː
ˑ	Half-long eˑ
̆	Extra-short ĕ
ǀ	Minor (foot) group
‖	Major (intonation) group
.	Syllable break ɹi.ækt
‿	Linking (absence of a break)

TONES AND WORD ACCENTS

LEVEL			CONTOUR		
e̋ or	˥	Extra high	ě or	˩˥	Rising
é	˦	High	ê	˥˩	Falling
ē	˧	Mid	e᷄	˦˥	High rising
è	˨	Low	e᷅	˩˨	Low rising
ȅ	˩	Extra low	e᷈	˧˦˨	Rising-falling
ꜜ	Downstep		↗	Global rise
ꜛ	Upstep		↘	Global fall

How to use this book

The first thing to remember about this book is that it is intended to be a *course*. It is designed to be read from beginning to end, and is therefore different from a reference book. Most readers of the book are expected either to be studying in a college or university, or to be practising English language teachers. The readers can be divided into groups as follows:

- Firstly, they will be either (a) students using the course under the direction of a tutor in charge of their course, or (b) working through the course as individuals.
- Secondly, they will be either (a) native speakers of a language other than English, or (b) native speakers of English.
- Finally, they will be either (a) teachers of English (or being trained to be such), or (b) students of English or linguistics and phonetics.

The course is intended to be used by all of these groups (if you multiply them together you get eight categories, and you should be able to place yourself in one of them); most of the material in the course has at some time or other been used by people of all eight categories, but it is necessary to use the course differently in these different circumstances.

Each chapter is followed by short additional sections, which you may choose not to use. Firstly, there is a section of notes on problems and further reading: this tells you how you can go further in studying the areas discussed in the chapter. Secondly, where relevant, there are brief notes for teachers about pronunciation teaching and the use of the taped practice material. Finally, there are some written exercises which test your understanding of the material in the chapter. Answers to the questions are given near the end of the book (pages 248–59).

The course includes recorded material (available on audio CD and on cassette) which comprises practical exercise material. There are 19 Audio Units (AU) which correspond to Chapters 2–20 of this book. When there is a relevant recorded exercise the following symbol is placed in the margin with a reference to the exercise: ⌒ AU1, Ex 1 indicates Audio Unit 1, Exercise 1. If you are a non-native speaker of English, every unit ought to be relevant to you, although the relevance of any particular exercise will depend on your particular native language. If you are a native speaker of English, only some of the exercises will be relevant: those on intonation are the most likely to be worth studying. The CD version of the material can be used in a domestic CD player or personal CD stereo, and also on a computer with a CD drive. The cassette version was designed for use in a language laboratory, but such a facility is hard to find these days. However, the cassettes can be used conveniently in an ordinary cassette recorder. The material is the same in both cases. The way in which this book is designed for students using the course under the direction of a tutor is as follows:

i) All the students in the class read a chapter of this book.
ii) The students then have a class with the tutor in charge of this part of their course. This provides an opportunity to discuss the material in the chapter, and for the tutor to check if difficult points have been understood, to provide additional explanation and examples if necessary and possibly to recommend further reading.
iii) If the students are not native speakers of English it is expected that they will then have a session working on the Audio Unit corresponding to the chapter they have read and discussed.
iv) The group then goes on to the next chapter.

If you are working through the course individually you will of course arrange your own way of proceeding; the only important point here is that it would not be advisable to use the Audio Units without first reading the relevant chapters in the book.

The book begins with Chapter 1 which is an Introduction, and there is no Audio Unit corresponding to this. Please read the Introduction, whichever category you come into, since it explains the purpose of the course and presents a number of basic points that are important for understanding the material that follows.

1 Introduction

You probably want to know what the purpose of this course is, and what you can expect to learn from it. An important purpose of the course is to explain how English is pronounced in the accent normally chosen as the standard for people learning the English spoken in England. If this was the only thing the course did, a more suitable title would have been "English Pronunciation". However, at the comparatively advanced level at which this course is aimed it is usual to present this information in the context of a general theory about speech sounds and how they are used in language; this theoretical context is called **phonetics and phonology**. Why is it necessary to learn this theoretical background? The same question arises in connection with grammar: at lower levels of study one is concerned simply with setting out how to form grammatical sentences, but people who are going to work with the language at an advanced level as teachers or researchers need the deeper understanding provided by the study of grammatical theory and related areas of linguistics. The theoretical material in the present course is necessary for anyone who needs to understand the principles regulating the use of sounds in spoken English.

The nature of phonetics and phonology will be explained as the course progresses, but one or two basic ideas need to be introduced at this introductory stage. In any language we can identify a small number of regularly used sounds (vowels and consonants) that we call **phonemes**; for example, the vowels in the words 'pin' and 'pen' are different phonemes, and so are the consonants at the beginning of the words 'pet' and 'bet'. Because of the notoriously confusing nature of English spelling, it is particularly important to learn to think of English pronunciation in terms of phonemes rather than letters of the alphabet; one must be aware, for example, that the word 'enough' begins with the same vowel phoneme as that at the beginning of 'inept' and ends with the same consonant as 'stuff'. We often use special symbols to represent speech sounds; using the symbols chosen for this course, the word 'enough' would be written (**transcribed**) as ɪnʌf. A list of the symbols is given on p. ix, and the International Phonetic Alphabet (IPA) on which the symbols are based is reproduced on p. xi.

The first part of the course is mainly concerned with identifying and describing the phonemes of English. Chapters 2 and 3 deal with vowels and Chapter 4 with some consonants. After this preliminary contact with the practical business of how some English sounds are pronounced, Chapter 5 looks at the phoneme and at the use of symbols in a theoretical way, while the corresponding Audio Unit revises the material of Chapters 2–4. After the phonemes of English have been introduced, the rest of the course goes on to look at larger units of speech such as the syllable and at aspects of speech such as **stress** (which could be roughly described as the relative strength of a syllable) and **intonation** (the use of the pitch of the voice to convey meaning). It would be a mistake to think that phonemes are studied first because they are the most important aspect of speech; the reason is simply that, in my experience, courses which begin with matters such as stress and intonation and deal with phonemes later are found more confusing by the students who use them. You will have to learn a number of technical terms; you will find that when they are introduced in order to be defined or explained, they are printed in bold type. This has already been done in this Introduction in the case of, for example, **phoneme**, **phonetics** and **phonology**. Another convention to remember is that when words used as examples are given in spelling form, they are enclosed in single quotes (see for example 'pin', 'pen', etc.). Double quote marks are used where quote marks would normally be used; see, for example, "English Pronunciation" above.

Languages have different **accents**: they are pronounced differently by people from different geographical places, from different social classes, of different ages and different educational backgrounds. The word "accent" is often confused with **dialect**. We use the word "dialect" to refer to a variety of a language which is different from others not just in pronunciation but also in such matters as vocabulary, grammar and word order. Differences of accent, on the other hand, are pronunciation differences only.

The accent that we concentrate on and use as our model is the one that is most often recommended for foreign learners studying British English. It has for a long time been identified by the name **Received Pronunciation** (usually abbreviated to its initials, **RP**), but this name is old-fashioned and misleading. Since it is most familiar as the accent used by most announcers and newsreaders on BBC and British independent television broadcasting channels, a preferable name is **BBC pronunciation**. This should not be taken to mean that the BBC itself imposes an "official" accent – individual broadcasters all have their own personal characteristics, and an increasing number of broadcasters with Scottish, Welsh and Irish accents are employed. However, the accent described here is typical of broadcasters with an English accent, and there is a useful degree of consistency in the broadcast speech of these speakers.

This course is not written for people who wish to study American pronunciation. The pronunciation of English in North America is different from most accents found in Britain. There are exceptions to this – you can find accents in parts of Britain that sound American, and accents in North America that sound English. But the pronunciation that you are likely to hear from most Americans does sound noticeably different from BBC pronunciation.

In talking about accents of English, the foreigner should be careful about the difference between **England** and **Britain**; there are many different accents in England, but the range becomes very much wider if the accents of Scotland, Wales and Northern Ireland (Scotland and Wales are included in Britain, and together with Northern Ireland form the **United Kingdom**) are taken into account. Within the accents of England, the distinction that is most frequently made by the majority of English people is between **Northern** and **Southern**. This is a very rough division, and there can be endless argument over where the boundaries lie, but most people on hearing a pronunciation typical of someone from Lancashire, Yorkshire or other counties further north would identify it as "Northern". This course deals almost entirely with BBC pronunciation. There is, of course, no implication that other accents are inferior or less pleasant-sounding; the reason is simply that BBC is the accent that has always been chosen by British teachers to teach to foreign learners, and is the accent that has been most fully described and has been used as the basis for textbooks and pronouncing dictionaries.

A term which is widely found nowadays is **Estuary English**, and many learners of English have been given the impression that this is a new accent of English. In reality there is no such accent, and the term should be used with care. The idea originates from the sociolinguistic observation that some people in public life who would previously have been expected to speak with a BBC (or RP) accent now find it acceptable to speak with some characteristics of the accents of the London area (the estuary referred to is the Thames estuary), such as glottal stops, which would in earlier times have caused comment or disapproval.

If you are a native speaker of English and your accent is different from BBC you should try, as you work through the course, to note what your main differences are for purposes of comparison. I am not, of course, suggesting that you should try to change your pronunciation! If you are a learner of English you are recommended to concentrate on BBC initially, though when you have worked through the course and become familiar with this you will probably find it an interesting exercise to listen analytically to other accents of English, to see if you can identify the ways in which they differ from BBC and even to learn to pronounce some examples of different accents yourself.

Notes on problems and further reading

The recommendation to use the name *BBC pronunciation* rather than *RP* is new to this edition of the book, and is not universally accepted. It is used in the *Daniel Jones English Pronouncing Dictionary* (15th edition; edited and revised by P. Roach and J. Hartman, 1997), in Trudgill (1999) and in Ladefoged (2000); for discussion, see the Introductions to the *Longman Pronunciation Dictionary* (Wells, 2000; pp. xiii, and the 15th Edition of the *Daniel Jones English Pronouncing Dictionary* (p. v). In the original *English Pronouncing Dictionary* of 1917, by the way, the term used was *Public School Pronunciation* (*PSP*). Where other writers have used the term *RP* in discussion of standard accents, I have left the term unchanged. Other writers have suggested the name *GB* (*General British*) as a term preferable to RP;

I do not feel this is satisfactory, since the accent being described belongs to England, and citizens of other parts of Britain are understandably reluctant to accept that this accent is the standard for countries such as Scotland and Wales. The BBC has an excellent Pronunciation Unit, but most people are not aware that it has no power to persuade broadcasters to use particular pronunciations: BBC broadcasters only use it on an optional basis, and the Corporation obliges the Pronunciation Unit to charge a fee for their advice.

I feel that if we had a completely free choice of model accent it would be possible to find more suitable ones: Scottish and Irish accents, for example, have a much more straightforward relationship between spelling and sounds than does BBC, and have simpler vowel systems, and would therefore be easier for most foreign learners to acquire. However, the majority of English teachers would be reluctant to learn to speak in the classroom with a different accent, so it seems this is not a practical possibility.

For introductory reading on the choice of English accent, see O'Connor (1980: 5–6); Brown (1990: 12–13); Cruttenden (1994: Chapter 7). For a discussion of the status of RP, see Abercrombie (1965). For those who want to know more about British accents, a simple introduction is Hughes and Trudgill (1996); more advanced works are Trudgill (1999) and Foulkes and Docherty (1999). Undoubtedly the major work on accents of English is Wells (1982), which is a very valuable source of information (see especially pp. 117–18 and 279–301 on RP).

Much of what has been written on the subject of "Estuary English" has been in minor or ephemeral publications. A valuable collection of such works has been made available by J. C. Wells on the internet. See http://www.phon.ucl.ac.uk/home/estuary

A problem area that has received a lot of attention is the choice of symbols for representing English phonemes. In the past, many different conventions have been proposed and students have often been confused by finding that the symbols used in one book are different from the ones they have learned in another. The symbols used in this book are in most respects those devised by A. C. Gimson for his *Introduction to the Pronunciation of English* (the latest version of which is the revision by Cruttenden; see Cruttenden, 1994). These symbols are now used in almost all modern works on

English pronunciation published in Britain, and can therefore be looked on as a *de facto* standard. Although good arguments can be made for some alternative symbols, the advantages of having a common set of symbols for pronunciation teaching materials and pronunciation entries in dictionaries are so great that it would be very regrettable to go back to the confusing diversity of earlier years. The subject of symbolisation is returned to in Section 5.2 of Chapter 5.

Notes for teachers
Pronunciation teaching has not always been popular with teachers and language-teaching theorists, and in the 1970s and 1980s it was fashionable to treat it as a rather outdated activity. It was claimed, for example, that it attempted to make learners try to sound like native speakers of Received Pronunciation, that it discouraged them through difficult and repetitive exercises and that it failed to give importance to communication. A good example of this attitude is to be found in Brown and Yule (1983: 26–7). The criticism was misguided, I believe, and it is encouraging to see that in recent years there has been a significant growth of interest in pronunciation teaching and many new publications on the subject. No pronunciation course that I know has ever said that learners must try to speak with a perfect RP accent. To claim this mixes up **models** with **goals**: the *model* chosen is BBC (RP), but the *goal* is normally to develop the learner's pronunciation sufficiently to permit effective communication with native speakers.

Pronunciation exercises can be difficult, of course, but if we eliminate everything difficult from language teaching, we may end up doing very little beyond getting students to play little communication games. It is, incidentally, quite incorrect to suggest that the classic works on pronunciation and phonetics teaching concentrated on mechanically perfecting vowels and consonants: Jones (1956, first published 1909), for example, writes "'Good' speech may be defined as a way of speaking which is clearly intelligible to all ordinary people. 'Bad' speech is a way of talking which is difficult for most people to understand . . . A person may speak with sounds very different from those of his hearers and yet be clearly intelligible to all of them, as for instance when a Scotsman or an American addresses an English audience with clear articulation. Their speech cannot be described as other than 'good'" (pp. 4–5).

Much has been written recently about **International English**, with a view to defining what is used in common by the millions of people around the world who use English as a foreign language (Crystal, 1997; Jenkins, 2000). This is a different goal from that of this book, which is describing a specific accent. The discussion of the subject in Cruttenden (1994: Chapter 13) is recommended as a survey of the main issues, and the concept discussed there of **Minimum General Intelligibility** is a useful contribution to the International English debate.

There are many different and well-tried methods of teaching and testing pronunciation, some of which are used in this book. I do not feel that it is suitable in this book to go into a detailed analysis of classroom methods, but there are several excellent treatments of the subject; see, for example, Kenworthy (1987); Dalton and Seidlhofer (1994); Celce-Murcia *et al.* (1996). At a more advanced level, Ioup and Weinberger (1987) is a collection of papers on **Interlanguage Phonology** that is relevant to the study of learners' problems.

2   The production of speech sounds

2.1 Articulators above the larynx

All the sounds we make when we speak are the result of muscles contracting. The muscles in the chest that we use for breathing produce the flow of air that is needed for almost all speech sounds; muscles in the larynx produce many different modifications in the flow of air from the chest to the mouth. After passing through the larynx, the air goes through what we call the **vocal tract,** which ends at the mouth and nostrils. Here the air from the lungs escapes into the atmosphere. We have a large and complex set of muscles that can produce changes in the shape of the vocal tract, and in order to learn how the sounds of speech are produced it is necessary to become familiar with the different parts of the vocal tract. These different parts are called **articulators**, and the study of them is called **articulatory phonetics**.

Fig. 1 is a diagram that is used frequently in the study of phonetics. It represents the human head, seen from the side, displayed as though

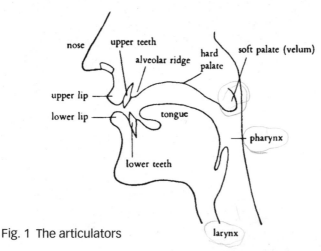

Fig. 1 The articulators

it had been cut in half. You will need to look at it carefully as the articulators are described, and you will often find it useful to have a mirror and a good light placed so that you can look at the inside of your mouth.

i) The **pharynx** is a tube which begins just above the larynx. It is about 7 cm long in women and about 8 cm in men, and at its top end it is divided into two, one part being the back of the mouth and the other being the beginning of the way through the nasal cavity. If you look in your mirror with your mouth open, you can see the back of the pharynx.

ii) The **velum** or **soft palate** is seen in the diagram in a position that allows air to pass through the nose and through the mouth. Yours is probably in that position now, but often in speech it is raised so that air cannot escape through the nose. The other important thing about the velum is that it is one of the articulators that can be touched by the tongue. When we make the sounds **k** and **g** the tongue is in contact with the lower side of the velum, and we call these **velar** consonants.

iii) The **hard palate** is often called the "roof of the mouth". You can feel its smooth curved surface with your tongue.

iv) The **alveolar ridge** is between the top front teeth and the hard palate. You can feel its shape with your tongue. Its surface is really much rougher than it feels, and is covered with little ridges. You can only see these if you have a mirror small enough to go inside your mouth (such as those used by dentists). Sounds made with the tongue touching here (such as **t** and **d**) are called **alveolar**.

v) The **tongue** is, of course, a very important articulator and it can be moved into many different places and different shapes. It is usual to divide the tongue into different parts, though there are no clear dividing lines within the tongue. Fig. 2 shows the tongue on a larger scale with these parts shown: **tip**, **blade**, **front**, **back** and **root**. (This use of the word "front" often seems rather strange at first.)

vi) The **teeth** (upper and lower) are usually shown in diagrams like Fig. 1 only at the front of the mouth, immediately behind the lips. This is for the sake of a simple diagram, and you should remember that most speakers have teeth to the sides of their

9

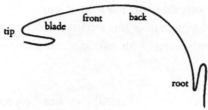

Fig. 2 Sub-divisions of the tongue

mouths, back almost to the soft palate. The tongue is in contact with the upper side teeth for many speech sounds. Sounds made with the tongue touching the front teeth are called **dental**.

vii) The **lips** are important in speech. They can be pressed together (when we produce the sounds **p, b**), brought into contact with the teeth (as in **f, v**), or rounded to produce the lip-shape for vowels like **uː**. Sounds in which the lips are in contact with each other are called **bilabial**, while those with lip-to-teeth contact are called **labiodental**.

The seven articulators described above are the main ones used in speech, but there are three other things to remember. Firstly, the larynx (which will be studied in Chapter 4) could also be described as an articulator – a very complex and independent one. Secondly, the **jaws** are sometimes called articulators; certainly we move the lower jaw a lot in speaking. But the jaws are not articulators in the same way as the others, because they cannot themselves make contact with other articulators. Finally, although there is practically nothing that we can do with the **nose** and the **nasal cavity**, they are a very important part of our equipment for making sounds (which is sometimes called our **vocal apparatus**), particularly nasal consonants such as **m, n**. Again, we cannot really describe the nose and the nasal cavity as articulators in the same sense as (i) to (vii) above.

2.2 Vowel and consonant

The words **vowel** and **consonant** are very familiar ones, but when we study the sounds of speech scientifically we find that it is not easy to define exactly what they mean. The most common view is that vowels are sounds in which there is no obstruction to the flow of air as it passes from the larynx to the lips. A doctor who wants to look at the back of a patient's mouth often asks them to say "ah"; making this vowel sound is the best way of presenting an unobstructed view. But if we make a sound like **s** or **d** it can be clearly felt that we are making it difficult or impossible for the air to pass through the mouth. Most people would have no doubt that sounds like **s** and **d** should be called consonants. However, there are many cases where the decision is not so easy to make. One problem is that some English sounds that we think of as consonants, such as the sounds at the beginning of the words 'hay' and 'way', do not really obstruct the flow of air more than some vowels do. Another problem is that different languages have different ways of dividing their sounds into vowels and consonants; for example, the usual sound produced at the beginning of the word 'red' is felt to be a consonant by most English speakers, but in some other languages (some dialects of Chinese, for example) the same sound is treated as one of the vowels.

If we say that the difference between vowels and consonants is a difference in the way that they are produced, there will inevitably be some cases of uncertainty or disagreement; this is a problem that cannot be avoided. It is possible to establish two distinct groups of sounds (vowels and consonants) in another way. Consider English words beginning with the sound **h**; what sounds can come next after this **h**? We find that most of the sounds we normally think of as vowels can follow (for example **e** in the word 'hen'), but practically none of the sounds we class as consonants. Now think of English words beginning with the two sounds **bɪ**; we find many cases where a consonant can follow (for example **d** in the word 'bid', or l in the word 'bill'), but hardly any cases where a vowel may follow. What we are doing here is looking at the different contexts and positions in which particular sounds can occur; this is the study of the **distribution** of the sounds, and is of great importance in phonology. Study of the sounds found at the beginning and end of English words has shown that two groups of sounds with quite different patterns of distribution can be identified, and these two groups are those of vowel and consonant. If we look at the vowel–consonant distinction in this way, we must say that the most important difference between vowel and consonant is not the way that they are made, but their different distributions. Of course, the distribution of vowels and consonants is different for each language.

There are many interesting theoretical problems connected with the vowel–consonant distinction, but we will not return to this question. For the rest of this course it will be assumed that the sounds are clearly divided into vowels and consonants.

We begin the study of English sounds in this course by looking at vowels, and it is necessary to say something about vowels in general before turning to the vowels of English. We need to know in what ways vowels differ from each other. The first matter to consider is the shape and position of the tongue. It is usual to simplify the very complex possibilities by describing just two things: firstly, the vertical distance between the upper surface of the tongue and the palate and, secondly, the part of the tongue, between front and back, which is raised highest. Let us look at some examples:

i) Make a vowel like the **iː** in the English word 'see' and look in a mirror; if you tilt your head back slightly you will be able to see that the tongue is held up close to the roof of the mouth. Now make an **æ** vowel (as in the word 'cat') and notice how the distance between the surface of the tongue and the roof of the mouth is now much greater. The difference between **iː** and **æ** is a difference of tongue height, and we would describe **iː** as a relatively **close** vowel and **æ** as a relatively **open** vowel. Tongue height can be changed by moving the tongue up or down, or moving the lower jaw up or down. Usually we use some combination of the two sorts of movement, but when drawing side-of-the-head diagrams such as Fig. 1 and Fig. 2 it is usually found simpler to illustrate tongue shapes for vowels as if tongue height were altered by tongue movement alone, without any accompanying jaw movement. So we would illustrate the tongue height difference between **iː** and **æ** as in Fig. 3.

ii) In making the two vowels described above, it is the front part of the tongue that is raised. We could therefore describe **iː** and **æ** as comparatively **front** vowels. By changing the shape of the tongue we can produce vowels in which a different part of the tongue is the highest point. A vowel in which the back of the tongue is the highest point is called a **back** vowel. If you make the vowel in the word 'calm', which we write phonetically as **ɑː**, you can see that the back of the tongue is raised. Compare this with **æ** in front of

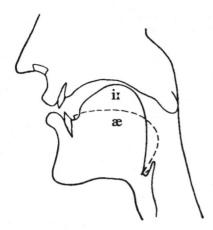

Fig. 3 Tongue positions for iː and æ

a mirror; **æ** is a front vowel and **aː** is a back vowel. The vowel in 'too' (**uː**) is also a comparatively back vowel, but compared with **aː** it is close.

So now we have seen how four vowels differ from each other; we can show this in a simple diagram (Fig. 4).

	Front	Back
Close	**iː**	**uː**
Open	**æ**	**aː**

Fig. 4 Extreme vowel positions for English

However, this diagram is rather inaccurate. Phoneticians need a very accurate way of classifying vowels, and have developed a set of vowels, arranged in a close–open, front–back diagram similar to Fig. 4 but which are not the vowels of any particular language. These **cardinal vowels** are a standard reference system, and people being trained in phonetics at an advanced level have to learn to make them accurately and recognise them correctly. If you learn the cardinal vowels, you are not learning to make English sounds, but you are learning about the range of vowels that the human vocal apparatus can make, and also learning a useful way of describing, classifying

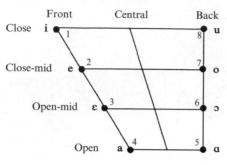

Fig. 5 Primary cardinal vowels

and comparing vowels. They are recorded on Track 21 of CD 2 and at the end of cassette 2.

It has become traditional to locate cardinal vowels on a four-sided figure (a quadrilateral) of the shape seen in Fig. 5 (the design used here is the one recommended by the International Phonetic Association). The exact shape is not really important – a square would do quite well – but we will use the traditional shape. The vowels on Fig. 5 are the so-called **primary** cardinal vowels; these are the vowels that are most familiar to the speakers of most European languages, and there are other cardinal vowels (**secondary** cardinal vowels) that sound less familiar. Cardinal vowel no. 1 has the symbol [i], and is defined as the vowel which is as close and as front as it is possible to make a vowel without obstructing the flow of air enough to produce friction noise; friction noise is the sort of hissing sound that one hears in consonants like **s** or **f**. Cardinal vowel no. 5 has the symbol [ɑ] and is defined as the most open and back vowel that it is possible to make. Cardinal vowel no. 8 [u], is fully close and back and no. 4 [a], is fully open and front. After establishing these extreme points, it is possible to put in intermediate points (vowels no. 2, 3, 6 and 7). Many students when they hear these vowels find that they sound strange and exaggerated; you must remember that they are extremes of vowel quality. It is useful to think of the cardinal vowel framework like a map of an area of country that you are interested in. Obviously, if the map is to be useful to you it must cover all the area; but if it covers the whole area of interest it must inevitably go a little way beyond that and include some places that you might never want to go to. However, it is still important to know where the edges of the map are drawn. When you are familiar with these extreme vowels, you have (as mentioned above) learned a way of describing, classifying and comparing vowels. For example, we can say that the English vowel æ (the vowel in 'cat') is not as open as cardinal vowel no. 4 [a]. (In this course cardinal vowels will always be printed within square brackets to distinguish them clearly from English vowel sounds.)

We have now looked at how we can classify vowels according to their tongue height and their frontness or backness. There is another important variable of vowel quality, and that is lip-rounding. Although the lips can have many different shapes and positions, we will at this stage consider only three possibilities. These are:

i) **Rounded**, where the corners of the lips are brought towards each other and the lips pushed forwards. This is most clearly seen in cardinal vowel no. 8 [u].

ii) **Spread**, with the corners of the lips moved away from each other, as for a smile. This is most clearly seen in cardinal vowel no. 1 [i].

iii) **Neutral**, where the lips are not noticeably rounded or spread. The noise most English people make when they are hesitating (written 'er') has neutral lip position.

Now, using the principles that have just been explained, we will examine some of the English vowels.

2.3 English short vowels
○ AU2, Exs 1–4

English has a large number of vowel sounds; the first ones to be examined are short vowels. The symbols for these short vowels are: ɪ, e, æ, ʌ, ɒ, ʊ. Short vowels are only *relatively* short; as we shall see later, vowels can have quite different lengths in different contexts.

Each vowel is described in relation to the cardinal vowels.

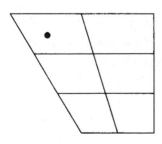

ɪ (example words: 'bit', 'pin', 'fish') The diagram shows that, though this vowel is in the close front area, compared with cardinal vowel no. 1 [i] it is more open, and nearer in to the centre. The lips are slightly spread.

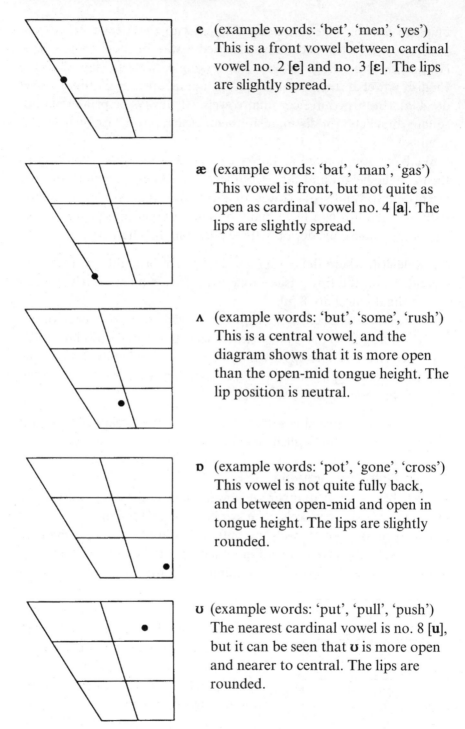

e (example words: 'bet', 'men', 'yes')
This is a front vowel between cardinal vowel no. 2 [e] and no. 3 [ɛ]. The lips are slightly spread.

æ (example words: 'bat', 'man', 'gas')
This vowel is front, but not quite as open as cardinal vowel no. 4 [a]. The lips are slightly spread.

ʌ (example words: 'but', 'some', 'rush')
This is a central vowel, and the diagram shows that it is more open than the open-mid tongue height. The lip position is neutral.

ɒ (example words: 'pot', 'gone', 'cross')
This vowel is not quite fully back, and between open-mid and open in tongue height. The lips are slightly rounded.

ʊ (example words: 'put', 'pull', 'push')
The nearest cardinal vowel is no. 8 [u], but it can be seen that **ʊ** is more open and nearer to central. The lips are rounded.

There is one other short vowel, for which the symbol is ə. This central vowel – which is called **schwa** – is a very familiar sound in English; it is heard in the first syllable of the words 'about', 'oppose', 'perhaps', for example. Since it is different from the other vowels in several important ways, we will study it separately in Chapter 9.

Notes on problems and further reading

One of the most difficult aspects of phonetics at this stage is the large number of technical terms that have to be learned. Every phonetics textbook gives a description of the articulators, and I will not attempt to list all of them. Two useful introductions are Ladefoged (1993: Chapter l), and O'Connor (1991: Chapter 2).

The best-known discussion of the vowel–consonant distinction is by Pike (1943: 66–79). He suggests that since the two approaches to the distinction produce such different results we should use new terms: sounds which do not obstruct the airflow (traditionally called "vowels") should be called vocoids, and sounds which do obstruct the airflow (traditionally called "consonants") should be called contoids. This leaves the terms "vowel" and "consonant" for use in labelling phonological elements according to their distribution and their role in syllable structure; see Section 5.8 of Laver (1994). While vowels are usually vocoids and consonants are usually contoids, this is not always the case; for example, **j** in 'yet' and **w** in 'wet' are (phonetically) vocoids but function (phonologically) as consonants. A study of the distributional differences between vowels and con-sonants in English is described in O'Connor and Trim (1953); a briefer treatment is in Cruttenden (1994: Sections 4.2 and 5.6). The classification of vowels has a large literature; I would recommend Jones (1975: Chapter 8); Ladefoged (1993) gives a brief introduction on pp. 12–14, and much more detail in Chapter 9; see also Aber-crombie (1967: 55–60 and Chapter 10). The *Handbook of the International Phonetic Association* (1999: Section 2.6) explains the IPA's principles of vowel classification. The distinction between *primary* and *secondary* Cardinal Vowels is a rather dubious one which appears to be based to some extent on a division between those vowels which are familiar and those which are unfamiliar to speakers of most European languages. It is possible to classify vowels quite unambiguously without resorting to this notion by specifying their front/back, close/open and lip positions.

Written exercises

1   On the diagram provided, various articulators are indicated by numbered arrows (a – e). Give the names for the articulators.

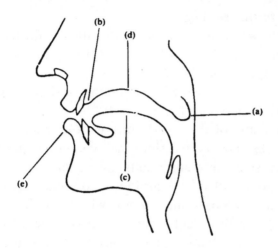

2   Using the descriptive labels introduced for vowel classification, say what the following Cardinal Vowels are:

   a) **u**   *b)* **e**   *c)* **a**   *d)* **i**   *e)* **o**

3   Draw a vowel quadrilateral and indicate on it the correct places for the following English vowels:

   a) **æ**   *b)* **ʌ**   *c)* **ɪ**   *d)* **e**

4   Write the symbols for the vowels in the following words:
   a) bread   *b)* rough   *c)* foot   *d)* hymn
   e) pull   *f)* cough   *g)* mat   *h)* friend

3 Long vowels, diphthongs and triphthongs

3.1 Long and short vowels

In Chapter 2 the short vowels were introduced. In this chapter we look at other types of English vowel sound. The first to be introduced here are the five long vowels; these are the vowels which tend to be longer than the short vowels in similar contexts. It is necessary to say "in similar contexts" because, as we shall see later, the length of all English vowel sounds varies very much according to their context (such as the type of sound that follows them) and the presence or absence of stress. To remind you that these vowels tend to be long, the symbols consist of one vowel symbol plus a length mark made of two dots ɪ. Thus we have: iː, ɜː, ɑː, ɔː, uː. We will now look at each of these long vowels individually.

You may have noticed that these five long vowels are different from the six short vowels described in Chapter 2, not only in length but also in quality. If we compare some similar pairs of long and short vowels, for example ɪ with iː, or ʊ with uː, or æ with ɑː, we can see distinct differences in quality (resulting from differences in tongue

 AU3, Exs 1–5

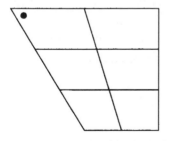

iː (example words: 'beat', 'mean', 'peace') This vowel is nearer to cardinal vowel no. 1 [i] (that is, it is more close and front) than the short vowel of 'bid', 'pin', 'fish' described in Chapter 2. Although the tongue shape is not much different from cardinal vowel no. 1, the lips are only slightly spread and this results in a rather different vowel quality.

19

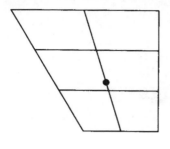

ɜː (example words: 'bird', 'fern', 'purse')
This is a central vowel which is well-known in most English accents as a hesitation sound (spelt 'er'), but which many foreigners find difficult to copy. The lip position is neutral.

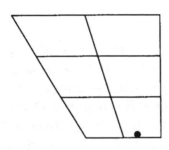

ɑː (example words: 'card', 'half', 'pass')
This is an open vowel in the region of cardinal vowel no. 5 [ɑː], but not as back as this. The lip position is neutral.

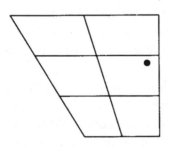

ɔː (example words: 'board', 'torn', 'horse') The tongue height for this vowel is between cardinal vowel no. 6 [ɔ] and no. 7 [o], and closer to the latter. This vowel is almost fully back and has quite strong lip-rounding.

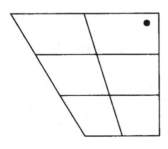

uː (example words: 'food', 'soon', 'loose') The nearest cardinal vowel to this is no. 8 [u], but it is much less back and less close, while the lips are only moderately rounded.

shape and position, and lip position) as well as in length. For this reason, all the long vowels have symbols which are different from those of short vowels; you can perhaps see that the long and short vowel symbols would still all be different from each other even if we omitted the length mark, so it is important to remember that the length mark is used not because it is essential but because it helps learners to remember the length difference. Perhaps the only case where a long and short vowel are closely similar in quality is that of ə and ɜː; but ə is a special case, as we shall see later.

3.2 Diphthongs

AU3, Exs 6 & 7

BBC pronunciation has a large number of **diphthongs**, sounds which consist of a movement or **glide** from one vowel to another. A vowel which remains constant and does not glide is called a **pure vowel**, and one of the most common pronunciation mistakes that result in a learner of English having a "foreign" accent is the production of pure vowels where a diphthong should be pronounced.

In terms of length, diphthongs are like the long vowels described above. Perhaps the most important thing to remember about all the diphthongs is that the first part is much longer and stronger than the second part; for example, most of the diphthong **aɪ** (as in the words 'eye', 'I') consists of the **a** vowel, and only in about the last quarter of the diphthong does the glide to ɪ become noticeable. As the glide to ɪ happens, the loudness of the sound decreases. As a result, the ɪ part is shorter and quieter. Foreign learners must, therefore, always remember that the last part of English diphthongs must not be made too strongly.

The total number of diphthongs is eight (though ʊə is increasingly rare). The easiest way to remember them is in terms of three groups divided as in this diagram:

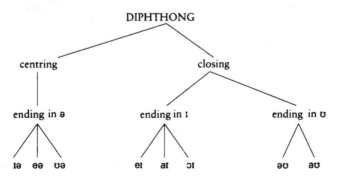

The centring diphthongs glide towards the ə (schwa) vowel, as the symbols indicate.

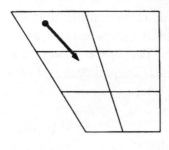

ɪə (example words: 'beard', 'Ian', 'fierce') The starting point is a little closer than ɪ in 'bit', 'bin'.

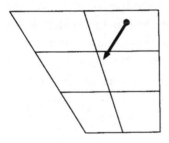

eə (example words: 'aired', 'cairn', 'scarce') This diphthong begins with the same vowel sound as the e of 'get', 'men'.

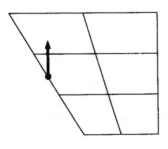

ʊə (example words: 'moored', 'tour') For speakers who have this diphthong, this has a starting point slightly closer than ʊ in 'put', 'pull'. Many speakers pronounce ɔː instead.

The closing diphthongs have the characteristic that they all end with a glide towards a closer vowel. Because the second part of the diphthong is weak, they often do not reach a position that could be called close. The important thing is that a glide from a relatively more open towards a relatively more close vowel is produced.

Three of the diphthongs glide towards ɪ, as described below:

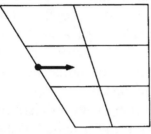

eɪ (example words: 'paid', 'pain', 'face') The starting point is the same as the e of 'get', 'men'.

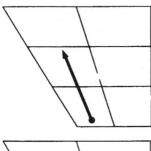

aɪ (example words: 'tide', 'time', 'nice')
This diphthong begins with an open vowel which is between front and back; it is quite similar to the ʌ of the words 'cut', 'bun'.

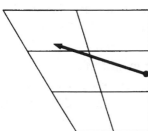

ɔɪ (example words: 'void', 'loin', 'voice')
The first part of this diphthong has the same quality as ɔː in 'ought', 'born'.

Two diphthongs glide towards ʊ, so that as the tongue moves closer to the roof of the mouth there is at the same time a rounding movement of the lips. This movement is not a large one, again because the second part of the diphthong is weak.

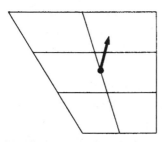

əʊ (example words: 'load', 'home', 'most')
The vowel position for the beginning of this is the same as for the "schwa" vowel ə, as found in the first syllable of the word 'about'. The lips may be slightly rounded in anticipation of the glide towards ʊ, for which there is quite noticeable lip-rounding.

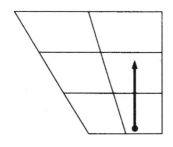

aʊ (example words: 'loud', 'gown', 'house') This diphthong begins with a vowel similar to ɑː. Since this is an open vowel, a glide to ʊ would necessitate a large movement. Usually in English the glide towards ʊ begins but is not completed, the end of the diphthong being somewhere between close-mid and open-mid in tongue height. There is only slight lip-rounding.

3.3 Triphthongs

The most complex English sounds of the vowel type are the **triphthongs**. They can be rather difficult to pronounce, and very difficult to recognise. A triphthong is a glide from one vowel to another and then to a third, all produced rapidly and without interruption. For example, a careful pronunciation of the word 'hour' begins with a vowel quality similar to ɑː, goes on to a glide towards the back close rounded area (for which we use the symbol ʊ), then ends with a mid-central vowel (schwa, ə). We use the symbols aʊə to represent the way we pronounce 'hour', but this is not always an accurate representation of the pronunciation.

The triphthongs can be looked on as being composed of the five closing diphthongs described in the last section, with ə added on the end. Thus we get:

eɪ + ə = eɪə   əʊ + ə = əʊə
aɪ + ə = aɪə   aʊ + ə = aʊə
ɔɪ + ə = ɔɪə

The principal cause of difficulty for the foreign learner is that in present-day English the extent of the vowel movement is very small, except in very careful pronunciation. Because of this, the middle of the three vowel qualities of the triphthong (that is, the ɪ or ʊ part) can hardly be heard and the resulting sound is difficult to distinguish from some of the diphthongs and long vowels. To add to the difficulty, there is also the problem of whether a triphthong is felt to contain one, or two syllables. Words such as 'fire' **faɪə** or 'hour' **aʊə** are probably felt by most English speakers (with BBC pronunciation) to consist of only one syllable, whereas 'player' **pleɪə** or 'slower' **sləʊə** are more likely to be heard as two syllables.

We will not go through a detailed description of each triphthong. This is partly because there is so much variation in the amount of vowel movement according to how slow and careful the pronunciation is, and also because the "careful" pronunciation can be found by looking at the description of the corresponding diphthong and adding ə to the end. However, to help identify these triphthongs, some example words are given here:

eɪə 'layer', 'player'   əʊə 'lower', 'mower'
aɪə 'liar', 'fire'   aʊə 'power', 'hour'
ɔɪə 'loyal', 'royal'

Notes on problems and further reading

Long vowels and diphthongs can be seen as a group of vowel sounds that are consistently longer *in a given context* than the short vowels described in the previous chapter. Some writers give the label **tense** to long vowels and diphthongs and **lax** to the short vowels. This is done (and explained) in Jakobson and Halle (1964) and in Chomsky and Halle (1968).

As mentioned in the notes on Chapter 1, the choice of symbols has in the past tended to vary from book to book, and this is particularly noticeable in the case of length marks for long vowels (this issue comes up again in Section 5.2 of Chapter 5); you could read Cruttenden (1994: Section 8.5).

The phonemes **iː** and **uː** are usually classed as long vowels; it is worth noting that most English speakers pronounce them with something of a diphthongal glide, so that a possible alternative transcription could be **ɪi** and **ʊu** respectively. This is not normally proposed, however.

It seems that triphthongs in BBC pronunciation are in a rather unstable state, resulting in the loss of some distinctions: in the case of some speakers, for example, it is not easy to distinguish between 'tyre' **taɪə**, 'tower' **taʊə** and 'tar' **tɑː**. BBC newsreaders often pronounce 'Ireland' as **ɑːlənd**, particularly in the context 'Northern Ireland'. Gimson (1964) suggested that a change in the phonemic system of RP is in progress in this area.

Notes for teachers

I mention above that **iː** and **uː** are often pronounced as slightly diphthongal: although this glide is often noticeable, I have never found it helpful to try to teach foreign learners to pronounce **iː** and **uː** in this way. Foreign learners who wish to get close to the BBC model should be careful not to pronounce the "r" that is often found in the spelling corresponding to **ɑː, ɔː** and **ɜː** ('ar', 'or', 'er').

Most of the essential pronunciation features of the diphthongs are described in Chapter 3. Two additional points are worth making. The diphthong **ʊə** is included, but this is not used as much as the others – many English speakers use **ɔː** in words like 'moor', 'mourn', 'tour'. However, I feel that it is important for foreign learners to be aware of this diphthong because of the distinctiveness of words in pairs like 'moor' and 'more', 'poor' and 'paw' for many speakers. The other diphthong that requires comment is əʊ. English speakers seem to be especially sensitive to the quality of this diphthong, particularly to the first part. It often happens that foreign learners, having understood that the first part of the diphthong is not a back vowel, exaggerate this by using a vowel that is too front, producing a diphthong like [eʊ]; unfortunately, this gives the impression of a "posh" accent – it sounds like someone trying to copy an upper-class pronunciation, since [eʊ] for əʊ is very noticeable in the speech of the Royal Family.

Written exercises

1   On the vowel diagram given below, indicate the glides for the diphthongs in the following words:

   a) fright   *c)* clear
   b) home   *d)* cow

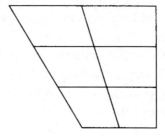

2   Write the symbols for the long vowels in the following words:

   a) broad   *d)* learn   *g)* err
   b) ward   *e)* cool   *h)* seal
   c) calf   *f)* team   *i)* curl

3   Write the symbols for the diphthongs in the following words:

   a) tone   *d)* way   *g)* hair
   b) style   *e)* beer   *h)* why
   c) out   *f)* coil   *i)* they

4 Voicing and consonants

4.1 The larynx

We begin this chapter by studying the **larynx**. The larynx has several very important functions in speech, but before we can look at these functions we must examine its anatomy and physiology, that is, how it is constructed and how it works.

The larynx is in the neck; it has several parts, shown in Fig. 6. Its main structure is made of **cartilage**, a material that is similar to bone but less hard. If you press down on your nose, the hard part that you can feel is cartilage. The larynx's structure is made of two large cartilages. These are hollow and are attached to the top of the **trachea**; when we breathe, the air passes through the trachea and the larynx. The front of the larynx comes to a point and you can feel this point at the front of your neck – particularly if you are a man and/or slim. This point is commonly called the **Adam's Apple**.

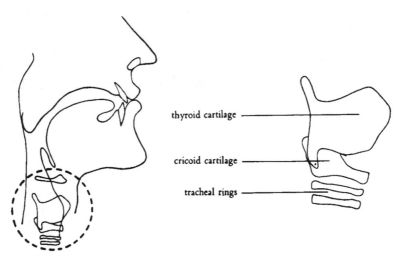

thyroid cartilage

cricoid cartilage

tracheal rings

Fig. 6 The larynx

Inside the "box" made by these two cartilages are the **vocal folds**, which are two thick flaps of muscle rather like a pair of lips; an older name for these is **vocal cords**. Looking down the throat is difficult to do, and requires special optical equipment, but Fig. 7 shows in diagram form the most important parts. At the front the vocal folds are joined together and fixed to the inside of the thyroid cartilage. At the back they are attached to a pair of small cartilages called the **arytenoid cartilages** so that if the arytenoid cartilages move, the vocal folds move too.

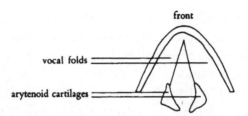

Fig. 7 The inside of the larynx seen from above

The arytenoid cartilages are attached to the top of the cricoid cartilage, but they can move so as to move the vocal folds apart or together (Fig. 8). We use the word **glottis** to refer to the opening between the vocal folds. If the vocal folds are apart we say that the glottis is open; if they are pressed together we say that the glottis is closed. This seems quite simple, but in fact we can produce a very complex range of changes in the vocal folds and their positions. These changes are often important in speech. Let us first look at four easily recognisable states of the vocal folds; it would be useful to practise moving your vocal folds into these different positions.

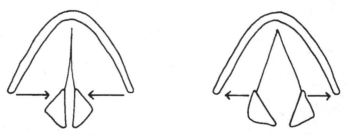

Fig. 8 Arytenoid cartilages causing closing and opening of the glottis

i) Wide apart: The vocal folds are wide apart for normal breathing and usually during voiceless consonants like **p**, **f**, **s** (Fig. 9a). Your vocal folds are probably apart now.

ii) Narrow glottis: If air is passed through the glottis when it is narrowed as in Fig. 9b, the result is a fricative sound for which the symbol is **h**. The sound is not very different from a whispered vowel. It is called a **voiceless glottal fricative**. (Fricatives are discussed in more detail in Chapter 6.) Practise saying **ahahaha-haha** – alternating between this state of the vocal folds and that described in (iii) below.

iii) Position for vocal fold vibration: When the edges of the vocal folds are touching each other, or nearly touching, air passing through the glottis will usually cause vibration (Fig. 9c). Air is pressed up from the lungs and this air pushes the vocal folds apart so that a little air escapes. As the air flows quickly past the edges of the vocal folds, the folds are brought together again. This opening and closing happens very rapidly and is repeated regularly, averaging roughly between two and three hundred times per second in a woman's voice and about half that rate in an adult man's voice.

iv) Vocal folds tightly closed: The vocal folds can be firmly pressed together so that air cannot pass between them (Fig. 9d). When this happens in speech we call it a **glottal stop** or **glottal plosive**, for which we use the symbol **ʔ**. You can practise this by coughing gently; then practise the sequence **aʔaʔaʔaʔaʔa**.

4.2 Respiration and voicing

Section 4.1 referred several times to air passing between the vocal folds. The normal way for this airflow to be produced is for some of the air in the lungs to be pushed out; when air is made to move out of the lungs we say that there is an **egressive pulmonic airstream**. All speech sounds are made with some movement of air, and the egressive pulmonic is by far the most commonly found air movement in the languages of the world. There are other ways of making air move in the vocal tract, but they are not usually relevant in the study of English pronunciation, so we will not discuss them here.

How is air moved into and out of the lungs? It is important to know something about this, since it will make it easier to understand

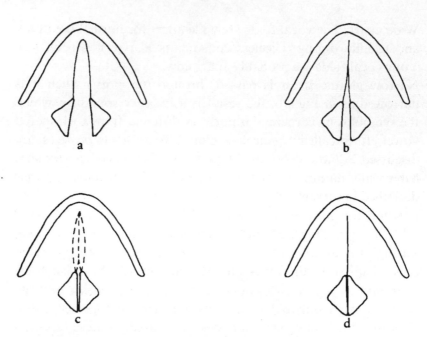

Fig. 9 Four different states of the glottis

many aspects of speech, particularly the nature of stress and intonation. The lungs are like sponges that can fill with air, and they are contained within the rib cage (Fig. 10). If the rib cage is lifted upwards and outwards there is more space in the chest for the lungs and they expand, with the result that they take in more air. If we allow the rib cage to return to its rest position quite slowly, some of the air is expelled and can be used for producing speech sounds. If we wish to make the egressive pulmonic airstream continue without

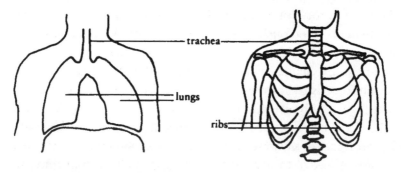

Fig.10 The lungs and the rib cage

breathing in again (for example when saying a long sentence and not wanting to be interrupted) we can make the rib cage press down on the lungs so that more air is expelled.

In talking about making airflow into and out of the lungs, the process has been described as though the air were free to pass with no obstruction. But, as we saw in Chapter 2, to make speech sounds we must obstruct the airflow in some way – breathing by itself makes very little sound. We obstruct the airflow by making one or more obstructions or **strictures** in the vocal tract, and one place where we can make a stricture is in the larynx, by bringing the vocal folds close to each other as described in the previous section. Remember that there will be no vocal fold vibration unless the vocal folds are in the correct position and the air below the vocal folds is under enough pressure to be forced through the glottis.

If the vocal folds vibrate we will hear the sound that we call **voicing** or **phonation**. There are many different sorts of voicing that we can produce – think of the differences in the quality of your voice between singing, shouting and speaking quietly, or think of the different voices you might use reading a story to young children in which you have to read out what is said by characters such as giants, fairies, mice or ducks; many of the differences are made with the larynx. We can make changes in the vocal folds themselves – they can, for example, be made longer or shorter, more tense or more relaxed or be more or less strongly pressed together. The pressure of the air below the vocal folds (the **subglottal pressure**) can also be varied. Three main differences are found:

i) Variations in **intensity** – we produce voicing with high intensity for shouting, for example, and with low intensity for speaking quietly.
ii) Variations in **frequency** – if the vocal folds vibrate rapidly, the voicing is at high frequency; if there are fewer vibrations per second the frequency is lower.
iii) Variations in **quality** – we can produce different-sounding voice qualities, such as those we might call harsh, breathy, murmured or creaky. We will consider the ways in which we make use of these variables in later chapters.

4.3 Plosives

A **plosive** is a consonant articulation with the following character-istics:

- One articulator is moved against another, or two articulators are moved against each other, so as to form a stricture that allows no air to escape from the vocal tract. The stricture is, then, total.
- After this stricture has been formed and air has been compressed behind it, it is **released**; that is, air is allowed to escape.
- If the air behind the stricture is still under pressure when the plosive is released, it is probable that the escape of air will produce noise loud enough to be heard. This noise is called **plosion**.
- There may be voicing during part or all of the plosive articulation.

To give a complete description of a plosive consonant we must describe what happens at each of the following four phases in its production:

i) The first phase is when the articulator or articulators move to form the stricture for the plosive. We call this the **closing phase**.
ii) The second phase is when the compressed air is stopped from escaping. We call this the **compression phase**.
iii) The third phase is when the articulators used to form the stricture are moved so as to allow air to escape. This is the **release phase**.
iv) The fourth phase is what happens immediately after (iii), so we will call it the **post-release phase**.

4.4 English plosives

English has six plosive consonants: **p**, **t**, **k**, **b**, **d**, **g**. The glottal plosive **?** occurs frequently but it is of less importance, since it is usually just an alternative pronunciation of **p**, **t** or **k** in certain contexts. The plosives have different places of articulation. The plosives **p** and **b** are bilabial since the lips are pressed together (Fig. 11); **t** and **d** are alveolar since the tongue blade is pressed against the alveolar ridge (Fig. 12). Normally the tongue does not touch the front teeth as it does in the dental plosives found in many languages. The plosives **k** and **g** are velar; the back of the tongue is pressed against the area where the hard palate ends and the soft palate begins (Fig. 13).

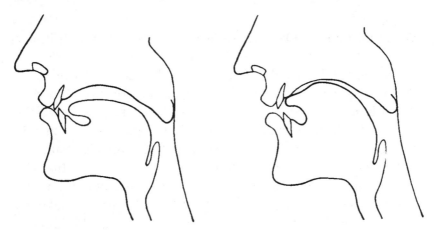

Fig.11 Bilabial articulation   Fig. 12 Alveolar articulation

The plosives **p**, **t** and **k** are always voiceless; **b**, **d** and **g** are sometimes fully voiced, sometimes partly voiced and sometimes voiceless. We will consider what **b**, **d** and **g** should be called in Section 4.5 below.

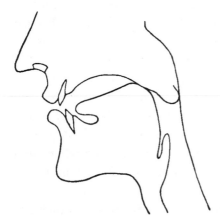

Fig. 13 Velar articulation

All six plosives can occur at the beginning of a word (**initial position**), between other sounds (**medial position**) and at the end of a word (**final position**). To begin with we will look at plosives preceding vowels (which can be abbreviated as CV, where C stands for a consonant and V stands for a vowel), between vowels (VCV) and following vowels (VC). We will look at more complex environments in later chapters.

i) Initial position (CV): The closing phase for **p, t, k** and **b, d, g** takes place silently. During the compression phase there is no voicing in **p, t, k**; in **b, d, g** there is normally very little voicing – it begins only just before the release. If the speaker pronounces an initial **b, d** or **g** very slowly and carefully there may be voicing during the entire compression phase (the plosive is then fully voiced), while in rapid speech there may be no voicing at all.

  The release of **p, t, k** is followed by audible plosion, that is, a burst of noise. There is then, in the post-release phase, a period during which air escapes through the vocal folds, making a sound like **h**. This is called **aspiration**. Then the vocal folds come together and voicing begins. The release of **b, d, g** is followed by weak plosion, and this happens at about the same time as, or shortly after, the beginning of voicing. The most noticeable and important difference, then, between initial **p, t, k** and **b, d, g** is the aspiration of the voiceless plosives **p, t, k**. The different phases of the plosive all happen very rapidly, of course, but the ear distinguishes clearly between **p, t, k** and **b, d, g**. If English speakers hear a fully voiced initial plosive, they will hear it as one of **b, d, g** but will notice that it does not sound quite natural. If they hear a voiceless unaspirated plosive they will also hear that as one of **b, d, g**, because it is aspiration, not voicing which distinguishes initial **p, t, k** from **b, d, g**. Only when they hear a voiceless aspirated plosive will they hear it as one of **p, t, k**; experiments have shown that we perceive aspiration when there is a delay between the sound of plosion and the beginning (or **onset**) of voicing.

  In initial position **b, d, g** cannot be preceded by any consonant, but **p, t, k** may be preceded by **s**. When one of **p, t, k** is preceded by **s** it is unaspirated. From what was said above it should be clear that the unaspirated **p, t, k** of the initial combinations **sp, st, sk** have the sound quality that makes English speakers perceive a plosive as one of **b, d, g**; and if a recording of a word beginning with one of **sp, st, sk** is heard with the **s** removed, an initial **b, d** or **g** is heard by English speakers.

ii) Medial position (VCV): The pronunciation of **p, t, k** and **b, d, g** in medial position depends to some extent on whether the syllables preceding and following the plosive are stressed. In general we can say that a medial plosive may have the characteristics either of final or of initial plosives.

◯ AU4, Exs 2 & 3

iii) Final position (VC) Final **b**, **d**, **g** normally have little voicing; if there is voicing, it is at the beginning of the compression phase; **p**, **t**, **k** are, of course, voiceless. The plosion following the release of **p**, **t**, **k** and **b**, **d**, **g** is very weak and often not audible. The difference between **p**, **t**, **k** and **b**, **d**, **g** is primarily the fact that vowels preceding **p**, **t**, **k** are much shorter. The shortening effect of **p**, **t**, **k** is most noticeable when the vowel is one of the long vowels or diphthongs.

4.5 Fortis and lenis

Are **b**, **d**, **g** voiced plosives? The description of them makes it clear that it is not very accurate to call them "voiced"; in initial and final position they are scarcely voiced at all, and any voicing they may have seems to have no perceptual importance. Some phoneticians say that **p**, **t**, **k** are produced with more force than **b**, **d**, **g**, and that it would therefore be better to give the two sets of plosives (and some other consonants) names that indicate that fact; so the voiceless plosives **p**, **t**, **k** are sometimes called **fortis** (meaning 'strong') and **b**, **d**, **g** are then called **lenis** (meaning 'weak'). It is probably true that **p**, **t**, **k** are produced with more force (though nobody has really proved it – force of articulation is very difficult to define and measure). On the other hand, the terms fortis and lenis are difficult to remember. Despite this, we shall follow the practice of many books and use these terms.

The plosive phonemes of English can be presented in the form of a table as shown here:

	Place of articulation		
	Bilabial	Alveolar	Velar
Fortis ("voiceless")	**p**	**t**	**k**
Lenis ("voiced")	**b**	**d**	**g**

Tables like this can be produced for all the different consonants. Each major type of consonant (such as plosives like **p, t** and **k**, fricatives like **s** and **z** and nasals like **m** and **n**) obstructs the airflow in a different way, and these are classed as different **manners of articulation**.

Notes on problems and further reading

4.1, 4.2 If you need to know more about the larynx and about respiration in relation to speech, see Borden and Harris (1994: 58–9); Laver (1994).

4.3 The outline of the stages in the production of plosives is based on Cruttenden (1994), and is slightly different from the earlier editions of this book. In classifying consonants it is possible to go to a very high level of complexity if one wishes to account for all the possibilities; see, for example, Pike (1943: 85–156).

4.4 It has been pointed out that the transcription **sb, sd, sg** could be used quite appropriately instead of **sp, st, sk**; see Davidsen-Nielsen (1969). The vowel length difference before final voiceless consonants is apparently found in many (possibly all) languages, but in English this difference – which is very slight in most languages – has become exaggerated so that it has become the most important factor in distinguishing between final **p, t, k** and **b, d, g**; see Chen (1970). Some phonetics books wrongly state that **b, d, g** lengthen preceding vowels, rather than that **p, t, k** shorten them. The conclusive evidence on this point is that if we take the pair 'right' **raɪt** and 'ride' **raɪd**, and then compare 'rye' **raɪ**, the length of the **aɪ** diphthong when no consonant follows is practically the same as in 'ride'; the **aɪ** in 'right' is much shorter than the **aɪ** in 'ride' and 'rye'.

4.5 The "fortis/lenis" distinction is a very complicated question. It is necessary to consider how one could measure "force of articulation"; many different laboratory techniques have been tried to see if the articulators are moved more energetically for fortis consonants, but all have proved inconclusive. The only difference that seems reasonably reliable is that fortis consonants have higher air pressure in the vocal tract, but Lisker (1970) has argued convincingly that this is not conclusive evidence for "force of articulation". It is possible to ask phonetically untrained speakers whether they feel more energy is used in pronouncing **p, t, k** than in **b, d, g**, but there are many difficulties in doing this. A useful review of the "force of articulation" question is in Catford (1977: 199–208). I feel the best conclusion is that any term one uses to deal with this distinction (whether "fortis"/"lenis" or "voiceless"/"voiced") is to be looked on as a **cover term** – a term which has no simple physical meaning but which may stand for a large and complex set of phonetic characteristics.

Written exercises

1   Try to write brief descriptions of the actions of the articulators and the respiratory system in the words given below. Here as an example is a description of the pronunciation of the word 'be' **biː**

> Starting from the position for normal breathing, the lips are closed and the lungs are compressed to create air pressure in the vocal tract. The tongue moves to the position for a close front vowel, with the front of the tongue raised close to the palate. The vocal folds are brought close together and voicing begins; the lips then open, releasing the compressed air. Voicing continues for the duration of an **iː** vowel. Then the lung pressure is lowered, voicing ceases and the articulators return to the normal breathing position.

Words to describe: (a) goat; (b) ape.

2   Transcribe the following words:

a) bake	*d*) bought	*g*) bored
b) goat	*e*) tick	*h*) guard
c) doubt	*f*) bough	*i*) pea

37

5 The phoneme

5.1 The phoneme

In Chapters 2–4 we have been studying some of the sounds of English. It is now necessary to consider some fundamental theoretical questions. What do we *mean* when we use the word "sound"? How do we establish what are the sounds of English, and how do we decide how many there are of them?

When we speak, we produce a continuous stream of sounds. In studying speech we divide this stream into small pieces that we call **segments**. The word 'man' is pronounced with a first segment **m**, a second segment **æ** and a third segment **n**. It is not always easy to decide on the number of segments. To give a simple example, in the word 'mine' the first segment is **m** and the last is **n**, as in the word 'man' discussed above. But should we regard the **aɪ** in the middle as one segment or two? We will return to this question.

As well as the question of how we divide speech up into segments, there is the question of how many different sounds (or segment types) there are in English. Chapters 2 and 3 introduced the set of vowels found in English. Each of these can be pronounced in many slightly different ways, so that the total range of sounds actually produced by speakers is practically infinite. Yet we feel quite confident in saying that the number of English vowels is not more than twenty. Why is this? The answer is that if we put one of those twenty in the place of one of the others, we can change the meaning of a word. For example, if we substitute **æ** for **e** in the word 'bed' we get a different word: 'bad'. But in the case of two slightly different ways of pronouncing what we regard as "the same sound", we usually find that, if we substitute one for the other, a change in the meaning of a word does not result. For example, if we substitute a more open vowel (for example, cardinal vowel no. 4 [a]) for the æ in the word 'bad', the word is still heard as 'bad'.

The principles involved here may be easier to understand if we look at a similar situation related to the letters of the alphabet that we use in writing English. The letter of the alphabet in writing is a unit which corresponds fairly well to the unit of speech we have been talking about earlier in this chapter – the segment. In the alphabet we have five letters that are called vowels: 'a', 'e', 'i', 'o', 'u'. If we choose the right context we can show how substituting one letter for another will change meaning. Thus with a letter 'p' before and a letter 't' after the vowel letter, we get the five words spelt 'pat', 'pet', 'pit', 'pot', 'put', each of which has a different meaning. We can do the same with *sounds*. If we look at the short vowels ɪ, e, æ, ʌ, ɒ, ʊ, for example, we can see how substituting one for another in between the plosives **p** and **t** gives us six different words as follows (given in spelling on the left):

'pit' **pɪt**
'pet' **pet**
'pat' **pæt**
'putt' **pʌt**[*]
'pot' **pɒt**
'put' **pʊt**

Let us return to the example of letters of the alphabet. If people who knew nothing about the alphabet saw these four characters:

A   a   ɑ   u

they would not know that to users of the alphabet three of these characters all represent the same letter, while the fourth is a different letter. Of course, they would quickly discover, through noticing differences in meaning, that 'u' is a different letter from the first three. What would our illiterate observers discover about these three? They would eventually come to the conclusion about the written characters 'a' and 'ɑ' that the former occurs most often in printed and typed writing while the latter is more common in handwriting, but that if you substitute one for the other it will not cause a difference in meaning. If our observers then examined a lot of typed

[*] This is a rare word, used only in the game of golf.

and printed material they would eventually establish that a word that began with 'a' when it occurred in the middle of a sentence would begin with 'A', and *never* with 'a', at the beginning of a sentence. They would also find that names could begin with 'A' but *never* with 'a'; they would conclude that 'A' and 'a' were different ways of writing the same letter and that a context in which one of them could occur was always a context in which the other could not. As will be explained below, we find similar situations in speech sounds.

If you have not thought about such things before, you may find some difficulty in understanding the ideas that you have just read about. The principal difficulty lies in the fact that what is being talked about in our example of letters is at the same time something *abstract* (the alphabet, which you cannot see or touch) and something *real* and *concrete* (marks on paper). The alphabet is something that its users know; they also know that it has twenty-six letters. But when the alphabet is used to write with, these letters appear on the page in a practically infinite number of different shapes and sizes.

Now we will leave the discussion of letters and the alphabet; these have only been introduced in this chapter in order to help explain some important general principles. Let us go back to the sounds of speech and see how these principles can be explained. As was said earlier in this chapter, we can divide speech up into segments, and we can find great variety in the way these segments are made. But just as there is an abstract alphabet as the basis of our writing, so there is an abstract set of units as the basis of our speech. These units are called **phonemes**, and the complete set of these units is called the **phonemic system** of the language. The phonemes themselves are abstract, but there are many slightly different ways in which we make the sounds that represent these phonemes, just as there are many ways in which we may make a mark on a piece of paper to represent a particular (abstract) letter of the alphabet.

We find cases where it makes little difference which of two possible ways we choose to pronounce a sound. For example, the **b** at the beginning of a word such as 'bad' will usually be pronounced with practically no voicing. Sometimes, though, a speaker may produce the **b** with full voicing, perhaps in speaking very emphatically. If this is done, the sound is still identified as the phoneme **b**, even though we can hear that it is different in some way. We have in this example two different ways of making **b** – two different **realisations** of the phoneme. One can be substituted for the other without changing the meaning.

We also find cases in speech similar to the writing example of capital 'A' and little 'a' (where one can only occur where the other cannot). For example, we find that the realisation of **t** in the word 'tea' is aspirated (as are all voiceless plosives when they occur before stressed vowels at the beginning of syllables). In the word 'eat', the realisation of **t** is unaspirated (as are all voiceless plosives when they occur at the end of a syllable and are not followed by a vowel). The aspirated and unaspirated realisations are both recognised as **t** by English speakers despite their differences. But the aspirated realisation will never be found in the place where the unaspirated realisation is appropriate, and vice versa. When we find this strict separation of places where particular realisations can occur, we say that the realisations are in **complementary distribution**. One more technical term needs to be introduced: when we talk about different realisations of phonemes, we sometimes call these realisations **allophones**. In the last example, we were studying the aspirated and unaspirated allophones of the phoneme **t**. Usually we do not indicate different allophones when we write symbols to represent sounds.

5.2 Symbols and transcription

You have now seen a number of symbols of several different sorts. Basically the symbols are for one of two purposes: either they are symbols for phonemes (**phonemic** or **phoneme** symbols) or they are **phonetic symbols** (which is what the symbols were first introduced as).

We will look first at phonemic symbols. The most important point to remember is the rather obvious-seeming fact that the number of phonemic symbols must be exactly the same as the number of phonemes we decide exist in the language. It is rather like typing on a keyboard – there is a fixed number of keys that you can press. However, some of our phoneme symbols consist of two characters; for example, we usually treat **tʃ** (as in 'chip' **tʃɪp**) as one phoneme, so **tʃ** is a phoneme *symbol* consisting of two *characters* (**t** and **ʃ**).

One of the traditional exercises in pronunciation teaching by phonetic methods is that of **phonemic transcription**, where every speech sound must be identified as one of the phonemes and written with the appropriate symbol. There are two different kinds of transcription exercise: in one, **transcription from dictation**, the student must listen to a person – or a tape-recording – and write down what they hear; in the other, **transcription from a written text**, the student is given a passage of dialogue written in orthography and must use phonemic symbols to represent how she or he thinks it would be pronounced by a speaker of a particular accent. In a phonemic transcription, then, only the phonemic symbols may be used; this has the advantage that it is comparatively quick and easy to learn to use it. The disadvantage is that as you continue to learn more about phonetics you become able to hear a lot of sound differences that you were not aware of before, and students at this stage find it frustrating not to be able to write down more detailed information.

The phonemic system described here for the BBC accent contains forty-four phonemes. We can display the complete set of these phonemes by the usual classificatory methods used by most phoneticians; the vowels and diphthongs can be located in the vowel quadrilateral – as was done in Chapters 2 and 3 – and the consonants can be placed in a chart or table according to place of articulation, manner of articulation and voicing. Obviously, human beings can make many more sounds than these, and phoneticians use a much larger set of symbols when they are trying to represent sounds more accurately. The best-known set of symbols is that of the International Phonetic Association's alphabet (the letters IPA are used to refer to the Association and also to its alphabet). The vowel symbols of the cardinal vowel system (plus a few others) are usually included on the chart of this alphabet, which is reproduced at the beginning of the book (p. xi). It is important to note that in addition to the many symbols on the chart there are a lot of **diacritics**, marks which modify the symbol in some way; for example, the symbol for cardinal vowel no. 4 [a] may be modified by putting two dots above it. This **centralisation** diacritic then gives us the symbol [ä] for a vowel which is nearer to central than [a]. It would not be possible in this course to teach you to use all these symbols and diacritics, but someone who did know them all could write a transcription that was much more accurate in phonetic detail – and contained much more information – than a phonemic transcription. Such a transcription would be called a **phonetic transcription**; a phonetic transcription containing a lot of information about the exact quality of the sounds would be called a **narrow** phonetic transcription, while one which only included a little more information than a phonemic transcription would be called a **broad** phonetic transcription. In this course, phonetic symbols are used occasionally when it is necessary to give an accurate label to an allophone of some English phoneme, but we do not do any phonetic transcription of continuous speech. That is a rather specialised exercise. When symbols are used to represent precise phonetic values, not just to represent phonemes, we enclose them in square brackets [ ], as we have done already with cardinal vowels. In many phonetics books, phoneme symbols are enclosed within slant brackets / /, but this seems unnecessary for our purposes.

It should now be clear that there is a difference between phonemic symbols and phonetic symbols. Since the phonemic symbols do not have to indicate precise phonetic quality, it is possible to choose among several possible symbols to represent a particular phoneme; this has had the unfortunate result that different books on English pronunciation have used different symbols, causing quite a lot of confusion to students. In this course we are using the symbols now most frequently used in English publishing. It would be too long a task to examine other writers' symbols in detail, but it is worth considering some of the reasons for the differences. One factor is the complication and expense of using special symbols which create problems in typing and printing; it could, for example, be argued that **a** is a symbol that is found in practically all type-faces whereas **æ** is unusual, and that the **a** symbol should be used for the vowel in 'cat' instead of **æ**. Some writers have concentrated on producing a set of phoneme symbols that need the minimum number of special or non-standard symbols. Other writers have thought it important that the symbols should be as close as possible to the symbols that a phonetician would choose to give a precise indication of sound quality. To use the same example again, referring to the vowel in 'cat', it would be argued that if the vowel is noticeably closer than cardinal vowel no. 4 [a], it is more suitable to use the symbol **æ**, which is usually used to represent a vowel between open-mid and open. There can be disagreements about the most important characteristics of a sound that a symbol should indicate; one example is the vowels of the words 'bit' and 'beat'. Some writers have claimed that the most important difference between them is that the former is short and the latter long, and transcribed the former with **i** and the latter with **iː** (the difference being entirely in the length mark); other writers have said that the length (or quantity) difference is less important than the quality difference, and transcribe the vowel of 'bit' with the symbol ɪ and that of 'beat' with **i**. Yet another point of view is that quality and quantity are both important and should both be indicated; this point of view results in a transcription using ɪ for 'bit' and **iː**, a symbol different from ɪ both in shape of symbol (suggesting quality difference) and in length mark (indicating quantity difference), for 'beat'. This is the approach taken in this course.

5.3 Phonology

Chapters 2–4 were mainly concerned with matters of **phonetics** – the comparatively straightforward business of describing the sounds that we use in speaking. When we talk about how phonemes function in language, and the relationships among the different phonemes – when, in other words, we study the *abstract* side of the sounds of language we are studying a related but different subject that we call **phonology**. Only by studying both the phonetics and the phonology of English is it possible to acquire a full understanding of the use of sounds in English speech. Let us look briefly at some areas that come within the subject of phonology; these areas of study will be covered in more detail later in the course.

Study of the phonemic system

It is sometimes helpful to think of the phonemic system as similar to the set of cards used in a card game, or the set of pieces used in a game of chess. In chess, for example, the exact shape and colour of the pieces are not important to the game as long as they can be reliably distinguished. But the number of pieces, the moves they can make and their relationship to all the other pieces are very important; we would say that if any of these were to be changed, the game would no longer be what we call chess. Similarly, playing-cards can be printed in many different styles and sizes; but while changing these things do not affect the game played with them, if we were to remove one card from the pack or add one card to it before the start of a game, nobody would accept that we were playing the game correctly.

In a similar way, we have a more or less fixed set of "pieces" (phonemes) with which to play the game of speaking English. There may be many slightly different realisations of the various phonemes, but the most important thing for communication is that we should be able to make use of the full set of phonemes.

Phoneme sequences and syllable structure

In every language we find that there are restrictions on the sequences of phonemes that are used. For example, no English word begins with the consonant sequence **zbf** and no words end with the sequence **æh**. In phonology we try to analyse what the restrictions and regularities are in a particular language, and it is usually found helpful to do this by studying the **syllables** of the language.

Suprasegmental phonology

Many significant sound contrasts are not the result of differences between phonemes. For example, **stress** is important: when the word 'import' is pronounced with the first syllable sounding stronger than the second, English speakers hear it as a noun, whereas when the second syllable is stronger the word is heard as a verb. **Intonation** is also important: if the word 'right' is said with the pitch of the voice rising, it is likely to be heard as a question or as an invitation to a speaker to continue, while falling pitch is more likely to be heard as confirmation or agreement. These examples show sound contrasts that extend over several segments (phonemes), and such contrasts are called **suprasegmental**. We will look at a number of other aspects of suprasegmental phonology later in the course.

Notes on problems and further reading

This chapter is theoretical rather than practical. There is no shortage of material to read on the subject of the phoneme, but much of it is rather difficult and assumes a lot of background knowledge. For basic reading I would suggest Katamba (1989: Chapter 2), Cruttenden (1994: Chapter 5, Section 3) or Giegerich (1992: 29–33). There are many classic works: Jones (1976; first published 1950) is widely regarded as such, although it is often criticised nowadays for being superficial or even naive. Another classic is Pike's *Phonemics* (1947), subtitled "A Technique for Reducing Languages to Writing":

this is essentially a practical handbook for people who need to analyse the phonemes of unknown languages, and contains many examples and exercises.

The subject of symbols is a large one: there is a good survey in Abercrombie (1967: Chapter 7). The IPA has tried as far as possible to keep to Roman-style symbols, although it is inevitable that these symbols have to be supplemented with **diacritics**. The IPA's present practice on symbolisation is set out in the *Handbook of the IPA* (IPA, 1999).There is a lot of information about symbol design and choice in Pullum and Ladusaw (1996). Those interested in the history of the IPA's way of classifying sounds should read Albright (1958). Some phoneticians working at the end of the nineteenth century tried to develop non-alphabetic sets of symbols whose shape would indicate all essential phonetic characteristics; these are described in Abercrombie (1967: Chapter 7).

It is obvious that one must choose between, on the one hand, symbols that are very informative but slow to write and, on the other, symbols that are not very precise but are quick and convenient to use. Pike (1943) presents at the end of his book an "analphabetic notation" designed to permit the coding of sounds with great precision on the basis of their articulation; an indication of the complexity of the system is the fact that the full specification of the vowel [o] requires eighty-eight characters! On the opposite side, many American writers have avoided the IPA symbols as being too complex and have tried to use as far as possible symbols and diacritics which are already in existence for various special alphabetic requirements of European languages and which are available on standard keyboards. For example where the IPA has ʃ and ʒ, symbols not usually found outside phonetics, Americans use č and ž, the mark above the symbols being widely used for Slavonic languages that do not use the Cyrillic alphabet. The widespread use of computer printers and word- processing has revolutionised the use of symbols, and sets of phonetic fonts are widely available via the internet. We are still some way, however, from having a universally agreed set of IPA symbol codes, and for much computer-based phonetic research it is necessary to make do with conventions which use existing keyboard characters. Most European researchers have adopted the SAMPA alphabet; details can be seen on the SAMPA website at http://www.phon.ucl.ac.uk/home/sampa/home.htm

Note for teachers
It should be made clear to students that the treatment of the phoneme in this chapter is only an introduction. It is difficult to go into detailed examples since not many symbols have been introduced at this stage, so further consideration of phonological issues is left until later chapters.

Written exercises
The words in the following list should be transcribed first phonemically, then (in square brackets) phonetically. In your phonetic transcription you can use the following diacritics:

- **b, d, g** pronounced without voicing are transcribed [b̥, d̥, g̥]
- **p, t, k** pronounced with aspiration are transcribed [pʰ, tʰ, kʰ]
- **iː, ɑː, ɔː, ɜː, uː** when shortened by a following fortis consonant should be transcribed **iˑ, ɑˑ, ɔˑ, ɜˑ, uˑ**
- **ɪ, e, æ, ʌ, ɒ, ʊ, ə** when shortened by a following fortis consonant should be transcribed **ɪ̆, ĕ, æ̆, ʌ̆, ɒ̆, ŭ, ə̆**. Use the same mark for diphthongs.

Example spelling: 'peat'; phonemic: **piːt** phonetic: [pʰiˑt]

Words for transcription

a) speed	*c)* book	*e)* car	*g)* appeared	*i)* stalk
b) partake	*d)* goat	*f)* bad	*h)* toast	

6 Fricatives and affricates

6.1 Production of fricatives and affricates

Fricatives are consonants with the characteristic that, when they are produced, air escapes through a small passage and makes a hissing sound. Most languages have fricatives, the most commonly found being something like **s**. Fricatives are continuant consonants, which means that you can continue making them without interruption as long as you have enough air in your lungs. Plosives, which were described in Chapter 4, are not continuants. You can demonstrate the importance of the narrow passage for the air in the following ways:

i)   Make a long, hissing **s** sound and gradually lower your tongue so that it is no longer close to the roof of the mouth. The hissing sound will stop as the air passage gets larger.
ii) Make a long **f** sound and, while you are producing this sound, use your fingers to pull the lower lip away from the upper teeth. Notice how the hissing sound of the air escaping between teeth and lip suddenly stops.

Affricates are rather complex consonants. They begin as plosives and end as fricatives. A familiar example is the affricate heard at the beginning and end of the word 'church'. It begins with an articulation practically the same as that for **t**, but instead of a rapid release with plosion and aspiration, as we would find in the word 'tip', the tongue moves to the position for the fricative ʃ that we find at the beginning of the word 'ship'. So the plosive is followed immediately by fricative noise. Since phonetically this affricate is composed of **t** and ʃ we represent it as **tʃ**, so that the word 'church' is transcribed as tʃɜːtʃ.

However, the definition of an affricate must be a little more restricted than what has been said so far. We would not class all

48

sequences of plosive plus fricative as affricates; for example, we find in the middle of the word 'breakfast' the plosive **k** followed by the fricative **f**. English speakers would generally not accept that **kf** forms a consonantal unit in the way that **tʃ** seems to. It is usually said that the plosive and the following fricative must be made with the same articulators – to use a technical term, the plosive and fricative must be **homorganic**. The sounds **k** and **f** are not homorganic, but **t** and **ʃ**, both being made with the tongue blade against the alveolar ridge, *are* homorganic. This still leaves the possibility of quite a large number of affricates, since, for example, **t** is homorganic not only with **ʃ** but also with **s**, so **ts** would also count as an **affricate**. Although the affricates can be said to be composed of a plosive and a fricative, it is usual to regard them as being single, independent phonemes of English. In this way, **t** is one phoneme, **ʃ** is another and **tʃ** yet another. We would say that the pronunciation of the word 'church' **tʃɜːtʃ** is composed of three phonemes, **tʃ**, **ɜː** and **tʃ**. We will look at this question of "two sounds = one phoneme" from the theoretical point of view in a later chapter.

6.2 The fricatives of English

English has quite a complex system of fricative phonemes. They can be seen in the table below:

	PLACE OF ARTICULATION				
	Labiodental	Dental	Alveolar	Post-alveolar	Glottal
Fortis ("voiceless")	f	θ	s	ʃ	h
Lenis ("voiced")	v	ð	z	ʒ	

With the exception of glottal, each place of articulation has a pair of phonemes, one fortis and one lenis. This is similar to what was seen with the plosives. The fortis fricatives are said to be articulated with greater force than the lenis, and their friction noise is louder. The lenis fricatives have very little or no voicing in initial and final positions, but may be voiced when they occur between voiced

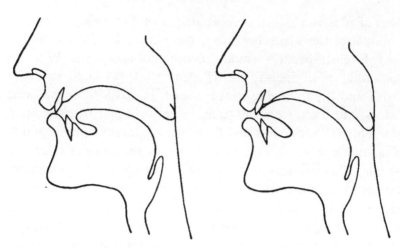

Fig. 14   a Labiodental fricative   b Dental fricative

sounds. The fortis fricatives have the effect of shortening a preceding vowel, as do fortis plosives. Thus in a pair of words like 'ice' **aɪs** and 'eyes' **aɪz**, the **aɪ** diphthong in the first word is considerably shorter than in the second. Since there is only one fricative with glottal place of articulation, it would be rather misleading to call it fortis or lenis (which is why there is a line on the chart above dividing **h** from the other fricatives).

AU6, Exs 1–3

We will now look at the fricatives separately, according to their place of articulation.

f, v (example words: 'fan', 'van'; 'safer', 'saver'; 'half, 'halve')

These are **labiodental**, that is, the lower lip is in contact with the upper teeth as shown in Fig. 14a. The fricative noise is never very strong and is scarcely audible in the case of **v**.

θ, ð (example words: 'thumb', 'thus'; 'ether', 'father'; 'breath', 'breathe')

The dental fricatives are sometimes described as if the tongue were placed between the teeth, and it is common for teachers to make their students do this when they are trying to teach them to make this sound. In fact, however, the tongue is normally placed *behind* the

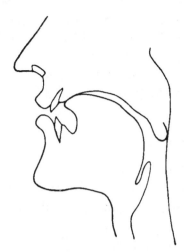

Fig. 14c Post-alveolar fricative

teeth, as shown in Fig. 14b, with the tip touching the inside of the lower front teeth and the blade touching the inside of the upper teeth. The air escapes through the gaps between the tongue and the teeth. As with **f** and **v**, the fricative noise is weak.

s, z (example words: 'sip', 'zip'; 'facing', 'phasing'; 'rice', 'rise')

These are alveolar fricatives, with the same place of articulation as **t** and **d**. The air escapes through a narrow passage along the centre of the tongue, and the sound produced is comparatively intense. The tongue position is shown in Fig. 12 in Chapter 4.

ʃ, ʒ (example words: 'ship' (initial ʒ is very rare in English); 'Russia', 'measure'; Irish', 'garage')

These fricatives are called post-alveolar, which can be taken to mean that the tongue is in contact with an area slightly further back than that for **s, z** (see Fig. 14c). If you make **s**, then **ʃ**, you should be able to feel your tongue move backwards.

The air escapes through a passage along the centre of the tongue, as in **s** and **ʃ**, but the passage is a little wider. Most BBC speakers have rounded lips for **ʃ** and **ʒ**, and this is an important difference between these consonants and **s** and **z**. **ʃ** is a common and widely-distributed phoneme, but **ʒ** is not. All the fricatives described so far (**f, v, θ, ð, s, z, ʃ**) can be found in initial, medial and final positions, as shown in the example words. In the case of **ʒ**, however, the distribution is much more limited. Very few English words begin with **ʒ** (most of them have come into the language comparatively recently from French) and not many end with this consonant. Only medially, in words such as 'measure', 'usual' (**meʒə, juːʒuəl**) is it found at all commonly.

h (example words: 'head', 'ahead', 'playhouse')

The place of articulation of this consonant is glottal. This means that the narrowing that produces the friction noise is between the vocal folds, as described in Chapter 4. If you breathe out silently, then produce **h**, you are moving your vocal folds from wide apart to close together. However, this is not producing speech. When we produce **h** in speaking English, many different things happen in different contexts. In the word 'hat', the **h** is followed by an **æ** vowel. The tongue, jaw and lip positions for the vowel are all produced simultaneously with the **h** consonant, so that the glottal fricative has an **æ** quality. The same is found for all vowels following **h**; it always has the quality of the vowel it precedes, so that in theory if you could listen to a tape-recording of **h**-sounds cut off from the beginnings of different vowels in words like 'hit', 'hat', 'hot', 'hut', etc., you should be able to identify which vowel would have followed the **h**. One way of stating the above facts is to say that *phonetically* **h** is a voiceless vowel with the quality of the voiced vowel that follows it.

Phonologically, **h** is a consonant. It is usually found before vowels. As well as being found in initial position it is found medially in words such as: 'ahead' **əhed**, 'greenhouse' **griːnhaʊs**, 'boathook' **bəʊthʊk**. It is noticeable that when **h** occurs between voiced sounds (as in the words 'ahead' and 'greenhouse'), it is pronounced with voicing – not the normal voicing of vowels but a weak, slightly fricative sound called **breathy voice**. It is not necessary for foreign learners to attempt to copy this voicing, although it *is* important to pronounce **h** where it should occur in BBC pronunciation. Many English speakers are surprisingly sensitive about this consonant; they tend to judge as sub-standard a pronunciation in which **h** is missing. In reality, however, practically all English speakers, however carefully they speak, omit the **h** in unstressed pronunciations of the words 'her', 'he', 'him', 'his' and the auxiliary 'have', 'has', 'had', although few are aware that they do this.

There are two rather uncommon sounds that need to be introduced; since they are said to have some association with **h**, they will be mentioned here. The first is the sound produced by some speakers in words which begin orthographically (that is, in their spelling form) with 'wh'; most BBC speakers pronounce the initial sound in such words (e.g. 'which', 'why', 'whip', 'whale') as **w**, but there are some (particularly when they are speaking clearly or emphatically) who pronounce the sound used by most American and Scottish speakers, a *voiceless* fricative with the same lip, tongue and jaw position as **w**. The phonetic symbol for this voiceless fricative is ʍ. We can find pairs of words showing the difference between this sound and the voiced sound **w** (which is introduced in Chapter 7):

'witch' **wɪtʃ**	'which' ʍɪtʃ
'wail' **weɪl**	'whale' ʍeɪl
'Wye' **waɪ**	'why' ʍaɪ
'wear' **weə**	'where' ʍeə

The obvious conclusion to draw from this is that, since substituting one sound for the other causes a difference in meaning, the two sounds are two different phonemes. It is therefore rather surprising to find that practically all writers on the subject of the phonemes of English decide that this answer is not correct, and that the sound ʍ in 'which', 'why', etc., is *not* a phoneme of English but is a realisation of a sequence of two phonemes, **h** and **w**. Fortunately we do not need to worry much about this problem in describing the BBC accent. However, it should be noted that in the analysis of the many accents of English that do have a "voiceless w" there is not much more theoretical justification in treating the sound as **h** plus **w** than there is for treating **p** as **h** plus **b**. Whether the question of this sound is approached phonetically or phonologically, there is no **h** sound in the "voiceless w".

A very similar case is the sound found at the beginning of words such as 'huge', 'human', 'hue'. Phonetically this sound is a voiceless palatal fricative (for which the phonetic symbol is ç); there is no glottal fricative at the beginning of 'huge', etc. However, it is usual to treat this sound as **h** plus **j** (the latter is another consonant that is introduced in Chapter 7 – it is the sound at the beginning of 'yes', 'yet'). Again we can see that a phonemic analysis does not necessarily have to be exactly in line with phonetic facts. If we were to say that these two sounds ʍ and ç were phonemes of English, we would have two extra phonemes that do not occur very frequently. We will follow the usual practice of transcribing the sound at the beginning of 'huge', etc., as **hj** just because it is convenient and common practice.

6.3 The affricates ⌒ AU6, Exs 4 & 5

tʃ, **dʒ** are the only two affricate phonemes in English. As with the plosives and most of the fricatives, we have a fortis/lenis pair, and the voicing characteristics are the same as for these other consonants. **tʃ** is slightly aspirated in the positions where **p**, **t**, **k** are aspirated, but not strongly enough for it to be necessary for foreign learners to give much attention to it. The place of articulation is the same as for **ʃ**, **ʒ**; that is, it is post-alveolar. This means that the **t** component of **tʃ** has a place of articulation rather further back in the mouth than the **t** plosive usually has. When **tʃ** is final in the syllable it has the effect of shortening a preceding vowel, as do other fortis consonants. **tʃ** and **dʒ** often have rounded lips.

6.4 Fortis consonants

All the consonants described so far, with the exception of **h**, belong to pairs distinguished by the difference between fortis and lenis. Since the remaining consonants to be described are not paired in this way, a few points that still have to be made about fortis consonants are included in this chapter.

The first point concerns the shortening of a preceding vowel by a syllable-final fortis consonant. As was said in Chapter 4, the effect is most noticeable in the case of long vowels and diphthongs, although it does also affect short vowels.

What happens if something other than a vowel precedes a fortis consonant? This arises in syllables ending with **l**, **m**, **n**, **ŋ**, followed by a fortis consonant such as **p**, **t**, **k** as in 'belt' **belt**, 'bump' **bʌmp**, 'bent' **bent**, 'bank' **bæŋk**. The effect on those continuant consonants is the same as on a vowel: they are considerably shortened.

A similar question arises with initial fortis consonants. When **p**, **t**, **k** come at the beginning of a syllable and are followed by a vowel, they are aspirated, as was explained in Chapter 4. This means that the beginning of a vowel is voiceless in this context. However, **p**, **t**, **k** may be followed not by a vowel but by one of **l**, **r**, **j**, **w**. These voiced continuant consonants undergo a similar process: they lose their voicing. So words like 'play' **pleɪ**, 'tray' **treɪ**, 'quick' **kwɪk** contain devoiced **l**, **r**, **w**, whereas 'lay', 'ray', 'wick' contain voiced **l**, **r**, **w**. Consequently, if for example 'tray' were to be pronounced without devoicing of the **r** (i.e. with fully voiced **r**) English speakers would be likely to hear the word 'dray'.

Voiceless consonants are usually articulated with open glottis, i.e. with the vocal folds separated. This is always the case with fricatives, where airflow is essential for successful production. However, with plosives an alternative possibility is to produce the consonant with completely closed glottis. This type of articulation is found quite widely in English pronunciation, especially that of younger speakers. This **glottalised** pronunciation, in which a glottal stop occurs just before **p**, **t**, **k** or **tʃ**, is only found in certain contexts, and foreign learners usually find the rules too difficult to learn, from the practical point of view; it is therefore simpler to keep to the more conservative pronunciation and not try to use glottalisation. However, it is worth pointing out the fact that this occurs, since many learners notice the glottal stops and want to know what it is that they are hearing. A few examples are given below.

The most widespread glottalisation is that of **tʃ** at the end of a stressed syllable (I leave defining what "stressed syllable" means until Chapter 8). If we use the symbol **ʔ** to represent a glottal closure, the phonetic transcription for various words containing **tʃ** can be given as follows:

	With glottalisation	*Without glottalisation*
'nature'	**neɪʔtʃə**	**neɪtʃə**
'catching'	**kæʔtʃɪŋ**	**kætʃɪŋ**
'riches'	**rɪʔtʃɪz**	**rɪtʃɪz**

There is similar glottalisation of **p**, **t**, **k**, although this is not found so regularly. It normally happens when the plosive is followed by another consonant or a pause; for example:

	With glottalisation	Without glottalisation
'actor'	æʔktə	æktə
'petrol'	peʔtrəl	petrəl
'mat'	mæʔt	mæt
'football'	fʊʔtbɔːl	fʊtbɔːl

Foreign learners do not need to learn this type of pronunciation, but many seem to acquire it unintentionally through speaking to English people. It is undoubtedly becoming more widely used in BBC pronunciation.

Notes on problems and further reading
The description of fricatives is in general quite straightforward. However, something that is mentioned only briefly in Section 6.2 is the difference between fricatives in terms of the width and depth of the air passage. The terms **slit** and **groove** are sometimes used: the air passage in **s** and **z** is said to be grooved and that in ʃ and ʒ slit. Laver (1994: Section 9.5) uses the terms "grooved" and "flat".

The dental fricative ð is something of a problem: although there are not many English words in which this sound appears, those words are ones which occur very frequently – words like 'the', 'this', 'there', 'that', and so on. This consonant often shows so little friction noise that on purely phonetic grounds it seems incorrect to class it as a fricative. It is more like a weak (lenis) dental plosive. This matter is discussed again in Chapter 14, Section 14.2.

On the phonological side, I have brought in a discussion of the phonemic analysis of two "marginal" fricatives which present a problem (though not a particularly important or fundamental one): I feel that this is worth discussing in that it gives a good idea of the sort of problem that can arise in analysing the phonemic system of a language. The other problem area is the glottalisation described at the end of the chapter. There is, I think, now a growing awareness of how frequently this is to be found in the speech of younger speakers; however, it not at all easy to formulate rules stating the contexts in which this occurs. There is discussion in Brown (1990: 28–30), in Cruttenden (1994: Section 9.2.8) and in Wells (1982: Section 3.4.5).

Notes for teachers

Although it is important to be aware of the ways in which fricatives differ from each other, I have never found it helpful to teach learners to aim consciously at slit and groove articulations – it is not something that most people feel they have control over, so simple imitation works better. Although I do not recommend explicitly teaching learners to produce glottalisation of **p**, **t**, **k**, **tʃ**, I have sometimes found advanced learners have been able to pick up this pronunciation, and I find the increase in naturalness in their accent very striking.

Written exercises

1   Transcribe the following words phonemically:

   a) fishes   *e)* achieves
   b) shaver   *f)* others
   c) sixth   *g)* measure
   d) these   *h)* ahead

2   Following the style introduced in Exercise 1 for Chapter 4, describe the movements of the articulators in the first word of the above list.

7 Nasals and other consonants

So far we have studied two major groups of consonants – the plosives and fricatives – and also the affricates – **tʃ** and **dʒ**; this is a total of seventeen. There remain the nasals – **m, n, ŋ** – and four others – **l, r, j** and **w**; these four are not easy to fit into groups. All of these seven consonants are continuants and usually have no friction noise, but in other ways they are very different from each other.

7.1 Nasals

The basic characteristic of a nasal consonant is that the air escapes through the nose. For this to happen, the soft palate must be lowered; in the case of all the other consonants and vowels, the soft palate is raised and air cannot pass through the nose. In nasal consonants, however, air does not pass through the mouth; it is prevented by a complete closure in the mouth at some point. If you produce a long sequence **dndndndndndndn** without moving your tongue from the position for alveolar closure, you will feel your soft palate moving up and down. The three types of closure are: bilabial (lips), alveolar (tongue blade against alveolar ridge) and velar (back of tongue against the palate). This set of places produces three nasal consonants – **m, n, ŋ** – which correspond to the three places of articulation for the pairs of plosives **p b, t d, k g**.

The consonants **m** and **n** are simple and straightforward with distributions like those of the plosives. There is in fact little to describe. However, **ŋ** is a different matter. It is a sound that gives considerable problems to foreign learners, and one that is so unusual in its phonological aspect that some people argue that it is not one of the phonemes of English at all. The place of articulation of **ŋ** is the same as that of **k, g**; it is a useful exercise to practise making a continuous **ŋ** sound. If you do this, it is very important not to produce a **k** or **g** at the end – pronounce the ŋ like **m** or **n**.

◯ AU7, Exs 1 & 2

We will now look at some ways in which the distribution of ŋ is unusual.

i) In initial position we find **m** and **n** occurring freely, but ŋ never occurs in this position. With the possible exception of ʒ, this makes ŋ the only English consonant that cannot occur initially.

ii) Medially, ŋ occurs quite frequently, but there is in the BBC accent a rather complex and quite interesting rule concerning the question of when ŋ may be pronounced without a following plosive. When we find the letters 'nk' in the middle of a word in its orthographic form, a **k** will always be pronounced; however, some words with orthographic 'ng' in the middle will have a pronunciation containing ŋg and others will have ŋ without **g**. For example, in BBC pronunciation we find the following:

A	B
'finger' fɪŋgə	'singer' sɪŋə
'anger' æŋgə	'hanger' hæŋə

In the words of column A the ŋ is followed by **g**, while the words of column B have no **g**. What is the difference between A and B? The important difference is in the way the words are constructed – their **morphology**. The words of column B can be divided into two grammatical pieces: 'sing' + '-er', 'hang' + '-er'. These pieces are called **morphemes**, and we say that column B words are morphologically different from column A words, since these can *not* be divided into two morphemes. 'Finger' and 'anger' consist of just one morpheme each.

We can summarise the position so far by saying that (within a word containing the letters 'ng' in the spelling) ŋ occurs without a following **g** if it occurs at the end of a morpheme; if it occurs in the middle of a morpheme it has a following **g**.

Let us now look at the ends of words *ending* orthographically with 'ng'. We find that these always end with ŋ; this ŋ is never followed by a **g**. Thus we find that the words 'sing' and 'hang' are pronounced as **sɪŋ** and **hæŋ**; to give a few more examples, 'song' is **sɒŋ**, 'bang' is **bæŋ** and 'long' is **lɒŋ**. We do not need a separate explanation for this: the rule given above, that **g** is not pronounced after ŋ at the end of a morpheme, works in these cases too, since the end of a word must also be the end of a morpheme. (If this point seems difficult, think of the comparable case of words and sentences: a sound that comes at the end of a sentence must necessarily also come at the end of a word, so that the final **k** of 'This is a book' is also the final **k** of the word 'book'.)

Unfortunately, rules tend to have exceptions. The main exception to the above morpheme-based rule concerns the comparative and superlative suffixes '-er' and '-est'. According to the rule given above, the adjective 'long' will be pronounced **lɒŋ**, which is correct. It would also predict correctly that if we add another morpheme to 'long', such as the suffix '-ish', the pronunciation of ŋ would again be without a following **g**. However, it would additionally predict that the comparative and superlative forms 'longer' and 'longest' would be pronounced with no **g** following the ŋ, while in fact the correct pronunciation of the words is:

'longer' **lɒŋgə**   'longest' **lɒŋgəst**

As a result of this, the rule must be modified; it must state that comparative and superlative forms of adjectives are to be treated as single-morpheme words for the purposes of this rule. The resulting rule is, of course, difficult to understand. It is important to remember that English speakers in general (apart from those trained in phonetics) are quite ignorant of this rule, and yet if a foreigner uses the wrong pronunciation (that is, pronounces ŋg where ŋ should occur, or ŋ where ŋg should be used), they notice that a mispronunciation has occurred.

iii) A third way in which the distribution of ŋ is unusual is the small number of vowels it is found to follow. It never occurs after a diphthong or long vowel, and in fact there are only five vowels ever found preceding this consonant: ɪ, e, æ, ʌ and ɒ.

The velar nasal consonant ŋ is, in summary, phonetically simple (it is no more difficult to produce than **m** or **n**) but phonologically complex (it is, as we have shown, not easy to describe the contexts in which it occurs).

7.2 The consonant l

◯ AU7, Ex 3

A **lateral** consonant is one in which the passage of air through the mouth does not go in the usual way along the centre of the tongue; instead, there is complete closure between the centre of the tongue and the part of the roof of the mouth where contact is to be made (the alveolar ridge in the case of **l**). Because of this complete closure along the centre, the only way for the air to escape is along the sides of the tongue. If you make a long **l** sound you may be able to feel that the sides of your tongue are pulled in and down while the centre is raised, but it is not easy to become consciously aware of this; what is more revealing (if you can do it) is to produce a long sequence of alternations between **d** and **l** without any intervening vowel. If you produce **dldldldldldl** without moving the middle of the tongue, you will be able to feel the movement of the sides of the tongue that is necessary for the production of a lateral. It is also possible to see this movement in a mirror if you open your lips wide as you produce it. Finally, it is also helpful to see if you can feel the movement of air past the sides of the tongue; this is not really possible in a voiced sound (the obstruction caused by the vibrating vocal folds reduces the airflow), but if you try to make a very loud whispered **l**, you should be able to feel the air rushing along the sides of your tongue.

We find **l** initially, medially and finally, and its distribution is therefore not particularly limited. In BBC pronunciation, the consonant has one unusual characteristic: the realisation of **l** found before vowels sounds quite different from that found in other contexts. For example, the realisation of **l** in the word 'lea' **liː** is quite different from that in 'eel' **iːl** .The sound in **iːl** is what we call a "dark **l**"; it has a quality rather similar to a [**u**] vowel, with the back of the tongue raised. The sound in **liː** is what is called a "clear **l**"; it resembles an [**i**] vowel, with the front of the tongue raised. The "dark **l**" is also found when it precedes a consonant, as in 'eels' **iːlz**. We can therefore predict which realisation of **l** (clear or dark) will occur in a particular context: clear **l** will never occur before consonants or before a pause, but only before vowels; dark **l** never occurs before vowels. We can say, using terminology introduced in Chapter 5, that clear l and dark l are allophones of the phoneme l in complementary distribution. Most English speakers do not consciously know about the difference between clear and dark l, yet they are quick to detect the difference when they hear English speakers with different accents, or when they hear foreign learners who have not learned the correct pronunciation.

Another allophone of l is found when it follows **p** or **k** at the beginning of a stressed syllable. The l is then devoiced, i.e. produced without the voicing found in most realisations of this phoneme. The situation is (as explained in Chapter 4) similar to aspiration when a vowel follows **p, t** or **k** in a stressed syllable; the first part of the vowel is devoiced.

7.3 The consonant r   ◠ AU7, Ex 4

This consonant is important in that considerable differences in its articulation and its distribution are found in different accents of English. As far as the articulation of the sound is concerned, there is really only one pronunciation that can be recommended to the foreign learner, and that is what is called a post-alveolar approximant. An **approximant**, as a type of consonant, is rather difficult to describe; informally, we can say that it is an articulation in which the articulators approach each other but do not get sufficiently close to each other to produce a "complete" consonant such as a plosive, nasal or fricative. The difficulty with this is that articulators are always in some positional relationship with each other, and any vowel articulation could also be classed as an approximant – but the term "approximant" is usually used only for consonants.

The important thing about the articulation of **r** is that the tip of the tongue approaches the alveolar area in approximately the way it would for a **t** or **d**, but never actually makes contact with any part of the roof of the mouth. You should be able to make a long **r** sound and feel that no part of the tongue is in contact with the roof of the mouth at any time. This is, of course, very different from the "r-sounds" of many other languages where some kind of tongue–palate contact is made. The tongue is in fact usually slightly curled backwards with the tip raised; consonants with this tongue shape are usually called **retroflex**. If you pronounce an alternating sequence of **d** and **r** (**drdrdrdrdrdr**) while looking in a mirror you should be able to see more of the underside of the tongue in the **r** than in the **d**, where the tongue tip is not raised and the tongue is not curled back. The "curling-back" process usually carries the tip of the tongue to a position slightly further back in the mouth than that for alveolar consonants such as **t** and **d**, which is why this approximant is called "post-alveolar". A rather different **r** sound is found at the beginning of a syllable if it is preceded by **p, t** or **k**; it is then voiceless and slightly fricative. This pronunciation is found in words such as 'press', 'tress', 'cress'.

One final characteristic of the articulation of **r** is that it is usual for the lips to be slightly rounded; foreign learners should do this but should be careful not to exaggerate it. If the lip-rounding is too strong the consonant will sound too much like **w**, which is the sound that most English children produce until they have learned to pronounce **r** in the adult way.

The distributional peculiarity of **r** in the BBC accent is very easy to state: this phoneme only occurs before vowels. No one has any difficulty in remembering this rule, but foreign learners (most of whom, quite reasonably, expect that if there is a letter 'r' in the spelling then an **r** should be pronounced) find it difficult to apply the rule to their own pronunciation. There is no problem with words like the following:

i)   'red' **red**   'arrive' **əraɪv**   'hearing' **hɪərɪŋ**

In these words **r** is followed by a vowel. But in the following words there is no **r** in the pronunciation:

ii)   'car' **kɑː**   'ever' **evə**   'here' **hɪə**
iii)   'hard' **hɑːd**   'verse' **vɜːs**   'cares' **keəz**

Many accents of English do pronounce **r** in words like those of (ii) and (iii) (for example, most American, Scots and West of England accents); accents which have **r** in final position (before a pause) and before a consonant are called **rhotic** accents, while accents in which **r** only occurs before vowels (such as BBC) are called **non-rhotic**.

7.4 The consonants j and w

⌒ AU7, Ex 5

These are the consonants found at the beginning of words such as 'yet' and 'wet'. They are known as approximants (introduced in

Section 7.3 above). The most important thing to remember about these phonemes is that they are phonetically like vowels but phonologically like consonants (in earlier works on phonology they were known as "semivowels"). From the phonetic point of view the articulation of **j** is practically the same as that of a front close vowel such as **iː**, but is very short. In the same way **w** is closely similar to **uː**. If you make the initial sound of 'wet' or 'yet' very long, you will be able to hear this. But despite this vowel-like character, we use them like consonants. For example, they only occur before vowel phonemes; this is a typically consonantal distribution. We can show that a word beginning with **w** or **j** is regarded as beginning with a consonant in the following way: the indefinite article is 'a' before a consonant (as in 'a cat', 'a dog'), and 'an' before a vowel (as in 'an apple', 'an orange'). If a word beginning with **w** or **j** is preceded by the indefinite article, it is the 'a' form that is found (as in 'a way', 'a year'). Another example is that of the definite article. Here the rule is that 'the' is pronounced as **ðə** before consonants (as in 'the dog' **ðə dɒg**, 'the cat' **ðə kæt**) and as **ði** before vowels (as in 'the apple' **ði æpl**, 'the orange' **ði ɒrɪndʒ**). This evidence illustrates why it is said that **j** and **w** are phonologically consonants. However, it is important to remember that to pronounce them as fricatives (as many foreign learners do), or even affricates, is a mispronunciation. Only in special contexts do we hear friction noise in **j** or **w**; this is when they are preceded by **p**, **t** or **k** at the beginning of a syllable, as in these words:

'pure' **pjʊə**   (no words begin with **pw**)
'tune' **tjuːn**   'twin' **twɪn**
'queue' **kjuː**   'quit' **kwɪt**

The **j** and **w** sounds are devoiced (that is, become voiceless) and are slightly fricative in these contexts. For place of articulation, we regard **j** as palatal and **w** as bilabial.

This completes our examination of the consonant phonemes of English. It is useful to place them on a consonant chart, and this is done in Table 1. On this chart, the different places of articulation are arranged from left to right and the manners of articulation are arranged from top to bottom. When there is a pair of phonemes with the same place and manner of articulation but differing in whether they are fortis or lenis (voiceless or voiced), the symbol for the fortis consonant is placed to the left of the symbol for the lenis consonant.

Table 1 *Chart of English consonant phonemes*

Place of articulation

Manner of articulation		Bilabial	Labiodental	Dental	Alveolar	Palato-alveolar (Post-alveolar)	Palatal	Velar	Glottal
	Plosive	p b			t d			k g	
	Fricative		f v	θ ð	s z	ʃ ʒ			h
	Affricate					tʃ dʒ			
	Nasal	m			n			ŋ	
	Lateral				l				
	Approximant	w			r		j		

Notes on problems and further reading

The notes for this chapter are devoted to giving further detail on a particularly difficult theoretical problem. The argument that ŋ is an allophone of **n**, not a phoneme in its own right, is so widely accepted by contemporary phonological theorists that few seem to feel it worthwhile to explain it fully. Since the velar nasal is introduced in this chapter, I have chosen to attempt this here. However, it is a rather complex theoretical matter, and you may prefer to leave consideration of it until after the discussion of problems of phonemic analysis in Chapter 13.

There are brief discussions of the phonemic status of ŋ in Chomsky and Halle (1968: 85), Hyman (1975: 74–6) and Ladefoged (1993: 64); for a fuller treatment see Wells (1982: 60–4) or Giegerich (1992: 297–301). Everyone agrees that English has at least two contrasting nasal phonemes, **m** and **n**. However, there is disagreement about whether there is a third nasal phoneme. In favour of accepting ŋ as a phoneme is the fact that traditional phoneme theory more or less demands its acceptance despite the general tendency to make phoneme inventories as small as possible. Consider **minimal pairs** (pairs of words in which a difference in meaning depends on the difference of one phoneme) like these: 'sin' **sɪn** – 'sing' **sɪŋ**; 'sinner' **sɪnə** – 'singer' **sɪŋə**.

There are three main arguments against accepting ŋ as a phoneme:

i) In some English accents it can easily be shown that ŋ is an allophone of **n**, which suggests that something similar might be true of BBC pronunciation too.

ii) If ŋ is a phoneme, its distribution is very different from that of **m** and **n**, being restricted to syllable-final position (phonologically) and to morpheme-final position (morphologically) unless it is followed by **k** or **g**.

iii) English speakers with no phonetic training are said to feel that ŋ is not a 'single sound' like **m** and **n**. Sapir (1925) said that "no native speaker of English could be made to feel in his bones" that ŋ formed part of a series with **m** and **n**. This is, of course, very hard to establish, although that does not mean that Sapir was wrong.

We need to look at point (i) in more detail and go on to see how this leads to the argument against having **ŋ** as a phoneme. Please note that I am not trying to argue that this proposal must be correct; my aim is just to explain the argument. The whole question may seem of little or no practical consequence, but we ought to be interested in any phonological problem if it appears that conventional phoneme theory is not able to deal satisfactorily with it.

In some English accents, particularly those of the Midlands, **ŋ** is only found in front of **k** and **g**. For example:

'sink' **sɪŋk**	'singer' **sɪŋgə**
'sing' **sɪŋg**	'singing' **sɪŋgɪŋg**

(This was my own pronunciation as a boy, living in the West Midlands, but I now usually have the BBC pronunciation **sɪŋk**, **sɪŋ**, **sɪŋə**, **sɪŋɪŋ**.) In the case of an accent like this, it can be shown that within the morpheme the only nasal that occurs before **k** and **g** is **ŋ**. Neither **m** nor **n** can occur in this environment. Thus within the morpheme **ŋ** is in complementary distribution with **m** and **n**. Since **m** and **n** are already established as distinct English phonemes in other contexts (**mæp**, **næp**, etc.), it is clear that for such non-BBC accents **ŋ** must be an allophone of one of the other nasal consonant phonemes. We choose **n** because when a morpheme-final **n** is followed by a morpheme-initial **k** or **g** it is usual for that **n** to change to **ŋ**; however, a morpheme-final **m** followed by a morpheme-initial **k** or **g** usually doesn't change to **ŋ**. Thus:

'rain-coat' **reɪŋkəʊt** *but* 'tram-car' **træmkɑː**

So in an analysis which contains no **ŋ** phoneme, we would transcribe 'rain-coat' phonemically as **reɪnkəʊt** and 'sing', 'singer', 'singing' as **sɪng**, **sɪngə**, **sɪngɪng**. The phonetic realisation of the **n** phoneme as a velar nasal will be accounted for by a general rule that we will call Rule 1:

Rule 1: **n** is realised as **ŋ** when it occurs in an environment in which it precedes either **k** or **g**.

Let us now look at BBC pronunciation. As explained in Section 7.1 above, the crucial difference between 'singer' **sɪŋə** and 'finger' **fɪŋgə** is that 'finger' is a single, indivisible morpheme whereas 'singer' is composed of two morphemes 'sing' and '-er'. When **ŋ** occurs without a following **k** or **g** it is always immediately before a morpheme boundary. Consequently, the sound **ŋ** and the sequence **ŋg** are in complementary distribution. But within the morpheme there is no contrast between the sequence **ŋg** and the sequence **ng**, which makes it possible to say that **ŋ** is also in complementary distribution with the sequence **ng**.

After establishing these 'background facts', we can go on to state the argument as follows:

i) English has only **m** and **n** as nasal phonemes.
ii) The sound **ŋ** is an allophone of the phoneme **n**.
iii) The words 'finger', 'sing', 'singer', 'singing' should be represented phonemically as **fɪngə, sɪng, sɪngə, sɪngɪng**.
iv) Rule 1 (above) applies to all these phonemic representations to give these phonetic forms: [**fɪŋgə, sɪŋg, sɪŋgə, sɪŋgɪŋg**]
v) A further rule (Rule 2) must now be introduced:

> *Rule 2*: **g** is deleted when it occurs after **ŋ** and before a morpheme boundary.

It should be clear that Rule 2 will not apply to 'finger' because the **ŋ** is not immediately followed by a morpheme boundary. However, the rule does apply to all the others, hence the final phonetic forms: **fɪŋgə, sɪŋ, sɪŋə, sɪŋɪŋ**.

vi) Finally, it is necessary to remember the exception we have seen in the case of comparatives and superlatives.

The argument against treating **ŋ** as a phoneme may not appeal to you very much. The important point, however, is that if one is prepared to use the kind of complexity and abstractness illustrated above, one can produce quite far-reaching changes in the phonemic analysis of a language.

The other consonants – **l**, **r**, **w** and **j** – do not, I think, need further explanation, except to mention that the question of whether **j**, **w** are consonants or vowels is examined on distributional grounds in O'Connor and Trim (1953).

Written exercises

1 List all the consonant phonemes of the BBC accent, grouped according to manner of articulation.
2 Transcribe the following words phonemically:

a) sofa *e)* square
b) verse *f)* anger
c) steering *g)* bought
d) breadcrumb *h)* nineteen

3 When the vocal tract is in its resting position for normal breathing, the soft palate is usually lowered. Describe what movements are carried out by the soft palate in the pronunciation of the following words:

a) banner *b)* mid *c)* angle

8 The syllable

The syllable is a very important unit. Most people seem to believe that, even if they cannot define what a syllable is, they can count how many syllables there are in a given word or sentence. If they are asked to do this they often tap their finger as they count, which illustrates the syllable's importance in the rhythm of speech. As a matter of fact, if one tries the experiment of asking English speakers to count the syllables in, say, a recorded sentence, there is often a considerable amount of disagreement.

8.1 The nature of the syllable

When we looked at the nature of vowels and consonants in Chapter 1 it was shown that one could decide whether a particular sound was a vowel or a consonant on phonetic grounds (in relation to how much they obstructed the airflow) or on phonological grounds (vowels and consonants having different distributions). We find a similar situation with the syllable, in that it may be defined both phonetically and phonologically. Phonetically (that is, in relation to the way we produce them and the way they sound), syllables are usually described as consisting of a centre which has little or no obstruction to airflow and which sounds comparatively loud; before and after this centre (that is, at the beginning and end of the syllable), there will be greater obstruction to airflow and/or less loud sound. We will now look at some examples:

i) What we might call a **minimum syllable** would be a single vowel in isolation, e.g. the words 'are' ɑː, 'or' ɔː, 'err' ɜː. These are preceded and followed by silence. Isolated sounds such as **m**, which we sometimes produce to indicate agreement, or ʃ, to ask for silence, must also be regarded as syllables.

ii) Some syllables have an **onset** (that is, they have more than just silence preceding the centre of the syllable):

'bar' **bɑː**   'key' **kiː**   'more' **mɔː**

iii) Syllables may have no onset but have a **coda**:

'am' **æm**   'ought' **ɔːt**   'ease' **iːz**

iv) Some syllables have onset and coda:

'run' **rʌn**   'sat' **sæt**   'fill' **fɪl**

This is one way of looking at syllables. Looking at them from the phonological point of view is quite different. What this involves is looking at the possible combinations of English phonemes; the study of the possible phoneme combinations of a language is called **phonotactics**. It is simplest to start by looking at what can occur in initial position – in other words, what can occur at the beginning of the first word when we begin to speak after a pause. We find that the word can begin with a vowel, or with one, two or three consonants. No word begins with more than three consonants. In the same way, we can look at how a word ends when it is the last word spoken before a pause; it can end with a vowel, or with one, two, three or (in a small number of cases) four consonants. No word ends with more than four consonants.

8.2 The structure of the English syllable

Let us now look in more detail at syllable onsets. If the first syllable of the word in question begins with a vowel (any vowel may occur, though ʊ is rare) we say that this initial syllable has a **zero onset**. If the syllable begins with one consonant, that initial consonant may be any consonant phoneme except ŋ; ʒ is rare. We now look at syllables beginning with two consonants. When we have two or more consonants together we call them a **consonant cluster**.

Initial two-consonant clusters are of two sorts in English. One sort is composed of **s** followed by one of a small set of consonants; examples of such clusters are found in words such as 'sting' **stɪŋ**, 'sway' **sweɪ**, 'smoke' **sməʊk**. The **s** in these clusters is called the **pre-initial** consonant and the other consonant (**t**, **w**, **m** in the above examples) the **initial** consonant. These clusters are shown in Table 2.

Table 2 *Two-consonant clusters with pre-initial* **s**

Pre-initial	Initial																	
	p	t	k	b	d	g	f	θ	s	ʃ	h	v	ð	z	ʒ	m	n	ŋ
s plus **p**	spɪn	stɪk	skɪn	–	–	–	sfɪə	–	–	–	–	–	–	–	–	smel	snəʊ	–

Note: Two-consonant clusters of **s** plus **l**, **w**, **j** are also possible (e.g. **slɪp**, **swɪŋ**, **sjuː**), and even perhaps **sr** in 'syringe' **srɪndʒ** for some speakers. These clusters can be analysed *either* as pre-initial **s** plus initial **l**, **w**, **j**, **r** *or* initial **s** plus post-initial **l**, **w**, **j**, **r**. There is no clear answer to the question of which analysis is better; here they are treated in the latter way, and appear in Table 3.

The other sort begins with one of a set of about fifteen consonants, followed by one of the set **l**, **r**, **w**, **j** as in, for example, 'play' **pleɪ**, 'try' **traɪ**, 'quick' **kwɪk**, 'few' **fjuː**. We call the first consonant of these clusters the **initial consonant** and the second the **post-initial**. There are some restrictions on which consonants can occur together. This can best be shown in table form, as shown in Table 3. When we look at three-consonant clusters we can recognise a clear relationship between them and the two sorts of two-consonant cluster described above; examples of three-consonant initial clusters are: 'split' **splɪt**, 'stream' **striːm**, 'square' **skweə**. The **s** is the pre-initial consonant, the **p**, **t** and **k** that follow **s** in the three example words are the initial consonant and the **l**, **r** and **w** are post-initial. In fact, the number of possible initial three-consonant clusters is quite small and they can be set out in full (words given in spelling form):　　◯　AU8, Ex 2

		Post-initial			
		l	r	w	j
s plus initial	p	'splay'	'spray'	–	'spew'
	t	–	'string'	–	'stew'
	k	'sclerosis'	'screen'	'squeak'	'skewer'

◯　AU8, Exs 3 & 4

We now have a similar task to do in studying final consonant clusters. Here we find the possibility of up to four consonants at the end of a word. If there is no final consonant we say that there is a **zero coda**. When there is one consonant only, this is called the **final consonant**. Any consonant may be a final consonant except **h**, **r**, **w**, **j**. There are two sorts of two-consonant final cluster, one being a final consonant preceded by a **pre-final** consonant and the other a final consonant followed by a **post-final** consonant. The pre-final consonants form a small set: **m**, **n**, **ŋ**, **l**, **s**. We can see these in 'bump' **bʌmp**, 'bent' **bent**, 'bank' **bæŋk**, 'belt' **belt**, 'ask' **ɑːsk**. The post-final consonants also form a small set: **s**, **z**, **t**, **d**, **θ**; example words are: 'bets' **bets**, 'beds' **bedz**, 'backed' **bækt**, 'bagged' **bægd**, 'eighth' **eɪtθ**. These post-final consonants can often be identified as separate morphemes (although not always, e.g. 'axe' **æks** is a single

Table 3 *Two-consonant clusters with post-initial* l, r, w, j

	p	t	k	b	d	g	f	θ	s	ʃ	h	v	ð	z	ʒ	m	n	ŋ	l	r	w	j
l	pleɪ	–	kleɪ	blæk	–	gluː	flaɪ	–	slɪp	–	–	–	–	–	–	–	–	–	–	–	–	–
r	preɪ	treɪ	kraɪ	brɪŋ	drɪp	grɪm	fraɪ	θrəʊ	?[1]	ʃruː	–	–	–	–	–	–	–	–	–	–	–	–
w	–	twɪn	kwɪk	–	dwel	?[2]	–	θwɔːt	swɪm	?[3]	–	–	–	–	–	–	–	–	–	–	–	–
j	pjɔː	tjuːn	kjuː	bjuːti	djuː	?[4]	fjuː	?[5]	sjuː	–	hjuːdʒ	vjuː	–	–	–	mjuːz	njuːz	–	ljuːd	–	–	–

Post-initial

Notes on doubtful cases:

1 Some people pronounce the word 'syringe' as **srɪndʒ**; there are no other cases of **sr**, unless one counts foreign place names (e.g. Sri Lanka).

2 Many Welsh names (including some well-known outside Wales) – such as girls' names like Gwen and place names like the county of Gwent – have initial **gw** and English speakers seem to find them perfectly easy to pronounce.

3 Two cases make **ʃw** seem familiar: the vowel name 'schwa', and the name of the soft drinks brand Schweppes. This is, however, a very infrequent consonant cluster for English.

4 The only possible occurrence of **gj** would be in the archaic (heraldic) word 'gules', which is in very few people's vocabulary.

5 **θj** occurs in the archaic word 'thew' only.

morpheme and its final **s** has no separate meaning). A point of pronunciation can be pointed out here: the release of the first plosive of a plosive-plus-plosive cluster such as the **g** (of **gd**) in **bægd** or the **k** (of **kt**) in **bækt** is usually without plosion and is therefore practically inaudible.

⌒ AU8, Ex 5

There are two types of final three-consonant cluster; the first is pre-final plus final plus post-final, as set out in the following table:

		Pre-final	Final	Post-final
'helped'	he	l	p	t
'banks'	bæ	ŋ	k	s
'bonds'	bɒ	n	d	z
'twelfth'	twe	l	f	θ

The second type shows that more than one post-final consonant can occur in a final cluster: final plus post-final 1 plus post-final 2. Post-final 2 is again one of **s, z, t, d, θ**.

		Pre-final	Final	Post-final 1	Post-final 2
'fifths'	fɪ	–	f	θ	s
'next'	ne	–	k	s	t
'lapsed'	læ	–	p	s	t

Most four-consonant clusters can be analysed as consisting of a final consonant preceded by a pre-final and followed by post-final 1 and post-final 2, as shown below:

		Pre-final	Final	Post-final 1	Post-final 2
'twelfths'	twe	l	f	θ	s
'prompts'	prɒ	m	p	t	s

A small number of cases seem to require different analysis, as consisting of a final consonant with no pre-final but three post-finals:

		Pre-final	Final	Post-final 1	Post-final 2	Post-final 3
'sixths'	sɪ	–	k	s	θ	s
'texts'	te	–	k	s	t	s

To sum up, we may describe the English syllable as having the following maximum phonological structure:

pre-initial	initial	post-initial	VOWEL	pre-final	final	post-final 1	post-final 2	post-final 3

|_____| |_____|

          Onset   Coda

It will be noticed that there must be a vowel in the centre of the syllable. There is a special case, that of **syllabic consonants** (which are introduced in Chapter 9); we do not, for example, analyse the word 'students' **stjuːdnts** as consisting of one syllable with the three-consonant cluster **stj** for its onset and ending with a four-consonant cluster **dnts**. To fit in with what English speakers feel, we say that the word contains two syllables, with the consonant **d** dividing them and the second syllable ending with the cluster **nts**; in other words, we treat the word as though there was a vowel between **d** and **n**, although a vowel only occurs here in very slow, careful pronunciation. This phonological problem will be discussed in Chapter 13.

Recent work in phonology makes use of a rather more refined analysis of the syllable in which the vowel and the coda (if there is one) are known as the **rhyme**; if you think of rhyming English verse you will see that this works by matching just that part of the last syllable of a line. The rhyme is divided into the **peak** (normally the vowel) and the **coda** (but note that this is optional: the rhyme may have no coda, as in a word like 'me'). As we have seen, the syllable may also have an onset, but this is not obligatory. The structure is thus the following:

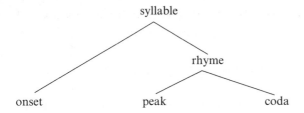

8.3 Syllable division

There are still problems with this phonetic description of the syllable: an unanswered question is how we decide on the division between syllables when we find a connected sequence of them as we usually do in normal speech. We will look at two words that are good examples of this difficulty. Most English speakers feel that the word 'going' **gəʊɪŋ** consists of two syllables; we could decide on phonetic grounds that the **ʊ** in the middle is the dividing point between the two syllables, since the articulation is slightly closer to obstructing airflow than the vowels next to it. This would not answer the question of whether the **ʊ** belongs to the first or to the second syllable; of course, we know that the **ʊ** is part of the **əʊ** diphthong phoneme, but this is a fact of phonology, not of the phonetic structure of the syllable. Another difficult case is the word 'extra' **ekstrə**. One problem is that by some definitions the **s** in the middle, between **k** and **t**, would be counted as a syllable, which most English speakers would reject. They feel that the word has two syllables. However, the most controversial issue relates to where the two syllables are to be divided; the possibilities are (using the symbol . to signify a syllable boundary):

  i) **e.kstrə**
 ii) **ek.strə**
iii) **eks.trə**
 iv) **ekst.rə**
  v) **ekstr.ə**

How can we decide on the division? No single rule will tell us what to do without bringing up problems.

One of the most widely accepted guidelines is what is known as the **maximum onsets principle**. This principle states that where two syllables are to be divided, any consonants between them should be attached to the right-hand syllable, not the left, as far as possible. If we just followed this rule, we would have to divide 'extra' as (i) **e.kstrə**, but we know that an English syllable cannot begin **kstr**. Our rule must therefore state that consonants are assigned to the right-hand syllable as far as possible *within the restrictions governing syllable onsets and codas*. This means that we must reject (i) **e.kstrə** because of its impossible onset, and (v) **ekstr.ə** because of its impossible coda. We then have to choose between (ii), (iii) and (iv). The maximum onsets rule makes us choose (ii). However, there are many problems still remaining. For example, in looking at isolated syllables, we never find one ending with one of the vowels **ɪ, e, æ, ʌ, ɒ** or **ʊ**, so we must conclude that syllables with a short vowel and no coda do not occur in English (unless the vowel is **ə**, as will be explained in Chapter 9).

How, then, should we divide words like 'better' **betə**? The maximal onsets principle tells us to put the **t** on the right-hand syllable, giving **be.tə**, but that means that the first syllable is analysed as **be**, which we have just seen is not allowed. The maximal onsets principle must therefore also be modified to allow a consonant to be assigned to the left syllable if that prevents a short vowel from occurring at the end of a syllable. We can then analyse the word as **bet.ə**, which seems more satisfactory.

There are words like 'carry' **kæri**, however, which still give us problems: if we divide the word **kæ.ri**, we get a syllable-final **æ**, but if we divide it **kær.i** we have a syllable-final **r**, and both of these are non-occurring in BBC English. We have to decide on the lesser of two evils here, and the preferable solution is to divide the word as **kær.i** on the grounds that in the many rhotic accents of English (see Section 7.3) this division would be the natural one to make.

One further possibility should be mentioned: when one consonant stands between vowels and it is difficult to assign the consonant to one syllable or the other – as in 'better' and 'carry' – we could say that the consonant belongs to *both* syllables. The term used by phonologists for a consonant in this situation is **ambisyllabic**.

8.4 Practical conclusions

Analysing syllable structure, as we have been doing in this chapter, can be useful to foreign learners of English. Obviously there are many more limitations on possible combinations of vowels and consonants, but an understanding of the basic structures described above will help learners to become aware of precisely what type of consonant cluster presents pronunciation problems – most learners find some English clusters difficult, but few find *all* of them difficult.

Notes on problems and further reading

The study of syllable structure is a subject of considerable interest to phonologists. If you want to read further in this area, I would recommend Giegerich (1992: Chapter 6), Katamba (1989: Chapter 9), Hogg and McCully (1987: Chapter 2) and Goldsmith (1990: Chapter 3). Some writers believe that it is possible to describe the possible combinations of phonemes with little reference to the syllable as an independent unit in theoretical phonology; see, for example, Harris (1994: Section 2.3). Cruttenden (1994: Chapter 10), Section 9, and Kreidler (1989: 117–38) describe the phonotactics of English in more detail.

A paper that has had a lot of influence on more recent work is Fudge (1969). This paper brings up two ideas first discussed by earlier writers: The first is that **sp, st, sk** could be treated as individual phonemes, removing the pre-initial position from the syllable onset altogether and removing **s** from the pre-final set of consonants; the second is that since post-initial **j** only occurs before **ʊ, uː** and **ʊə** (which in his analysis all begin with the same vowel), one could postulate a diphthong **ju** and remove **j** from post-initial position. These are interesting proposals, but there is not enough space here to examine the arguments in full.

There are many different ways of deciding how to divide syllables. To see two different approaches, see the Introductions to the *Longman Pronunciation Dictionary* (Wells, 2000) and the *English Pronouncing Dictionary* (15th edition, eds. Jones, Roach and Hartman, 1997: xiii).

Note for teachers

The last paragraph of Chapter 8 explains why the study of syllable structure is relevant to the learner of English. English has a more complex syllable structure than most languages, and it follows from what is said in this chapter that it is advisable to discover exactly which types of consonant cluster are difficult for learners of a particular native-language background and construct exercises to give practice in them. There is discussion of this problem in Celce-Murcia *et al.* (1996: 80–9) and Dalton and Seidlhofer (1994: 34–8).

Written exercises
Using the analysis of the word 'cramped' given below as a model, analyse the structure of the following one-syllable English words:

	Initial	Post-initial		Pre-final	Final	Post-final
'cramped'	k	r	æ	m	p	t
	Onset		Peak		Coda	

a) squealed
b) eighths
c) splash
d) texts

9 Strong and weak syllables

9.1 Strong and weak

One of the most noticeable features of English is that some of its syllables are **strong** while many others are **weak**; this is also true of many other languages, but it is necessary to study how these weak syllables are pronounced and where they occur in English. The distribution of strong and weak syllables is a subject that will be met in several later chapters. For example, we will look later at **stress**, which is very important in deciding whether a syllable is strong or weak. **Elision** is a closely related subject, and in considering **intonation** the difference between strong and weak syllables is also important. Finally, words with "strong" and "weak" forms are clearly a related matter. In this chapter we look at the general nature of weak syllables.

What do we mean by "strong" and "weak"? To begin with, we can look at how we use these terms to refer to phonetic characteristics of syllables. When we compare weak syllables with strong syllables, we find the vowel in a weak syllable tends to be shorter, of lower intensity and different in quality. For example, in the word 'father' **fɑːðə** the second syllable, which is weak, is shorter than the first, is less loud and has a vowel that cannot occur in strong syllables. In a word like 'bottle' **bɒtl̩** the weak second syllable contains no vowel at all, but consists entirely of the consonant l̩. We call this a **syllabic consonant**.

There are other ways of characterising strong and weak syllables. We could describe them partly in terms of stress (by saying, for example, that strong syllables are stressed and weak syllables un-stressed) but, until we describe what "stress" *means*, such a description would not be very useful. The most important thing to note at present is that any strong syllable will have as its peak one of the vowel phonemes (or possibly a triphthong) listed in Chapter 3, but not ə, i or u. If the vowel is short, then the strong syllable will always have a coda as well. Weak syllables, on the other hand, as they are defined here, can only have one of a very small number of possible peaks. At the end of a word, we may have a weak syllable ending with a vowel (i.e. with no coda):

i) the vowel ə ("schwa");

ii) a close front unrounded vowel in the general area of iː and ɪ (symbolised i);

iii) a close back rounded vowel in the general area of uː and ʊ (symbolised u).

Examples would be:

i) 'better' **betə**   ii) 'happy' **hæpi**   iii) 'thank you' **θæŋk ju**

We also find weak syllables in word-final position with a coda if the vowel is ə. For example:

i) 'open' **əʊpən**   ii) 'sharpen' **ʃɑːpən**

Inside a word, we can find the above vowels acting as peaks without codas in weak syllables; for example, look at the second syllable in each of these words:

i) 'photograph' **fəʊtəgrɑːf**   ii) 'radio' **reɪdiəʊ**
iii) 'influence' **ɪnfluəns**

In addition, the vowel ɪ can act as a peak without coda if the following syllable begins with a consonant:

iv) 'architect' **ɑːkɪtekt**

In the rest of this chapter we will look at the different types of weak syllable in more detail.

9.2 The ə vowel ("schwa")   ◠ AU9, Ex 1

The most frequently occurring vowel in English is ə, which is always associated with weak syllables. In quality it is mid (that is, half-way between close and open) and central (that is, half-way between front and back). It is generally described as lax, that is, not articulated with much energy. Of course, the quality of this vowel is not always the same, but the variation is not important.

Not all weak syllables contain ə, though many do. Learners of English need to learn where ə is appropriate and where it is not. To do this we often have to use information that traditional phonemic theory would not accept as relevant – we must consider spelling. The question to ask is: if the speaker were to pronounce a particular weak syllable as strong instead, which vowel would it be most likely to have, according to the usual rules of English spelling? Knowing this will not tell us which syllables in a word or utterance should be weak – that is something we look at in later chapters – but it will give us a rough guide to the correct pronunciation of weak syllables. Let us look at some examples:

i) Spelt with 'a'; strong pronunciation would have æ
    '*a*ttend' **ətend**   'char*a*cter' **kærəktə**
    'barr*a*cks' **bærəks**

ii) Spelt with 'ar'; strong pronunciation would have ɑː
    'p*ar*ticular' **pətɪkjələ**   'mol*ar*' **məʊlə**
    'mon*ar*chy' **mɒnəki**

iii) Adjectival endings spelt 'ate'; strong pronunciation would have eɪ
    'intim*ate*' **ɪntɪmət**   'accur*ate*' **ækjərət**
    'desol*ate*' **desələt** (although there are exceptions to this: 'private' is usually **praɪvɪt**)

iv) Spelt with 'o'; strong pronunciation would have ɒ or əʊ
    't*o*morrow' **təmɒrəʊ**   'potato' **pəteɪtəʊ**
    'carr*o*t' **kærət**

v) Spelt with 'or'; strong pronunciation would have ɔː
    'f*or*get' **fəget**   'ambassad*or*' **æmbæsədə**
    'opp*or*tunity' **ɒpətjuːnəti**

vi) Spelt with 'e'; strong pronunciation would have e
    'settlem*ent*' **setl̩mənt**   'viol*et*' **vaɪələt**
    'postm*en*' **pəʊstmən**

vii) Spelt with 'er'; strong pronunciation would have ɜː
    'p*er*haps' **pəhæps**   'strong*er*' **strɒŋgə**
    'sup*er*man' **suːpəmæn**

viii) Spelt with 'u'; strong pronunciation would have ʌ
    'Aut*u*mn' **ɔːtəm**   's*u*pport' **səpɔːt**
    'halib*u*t' **hælɪbət**

ix) Spelt with 'ough' (there are many pronunciations for the letter-sequence 'ough')

'thor*ough*' θʌrə   'bor*ough*' bʌrə

ix) Spelt with 'ou'; strong pronunciation might have aʊ

'graci*ous*' greɪʃəs   'call*ous*' kæləs

9.3 Close front and close back vowels

Two other vowels are commonly found in weak syllables, one close front (in the general region of iː and ɪ) and the other close back rounded (in the general region of uː and ʊ). In strong syllables it is comparatively easy to distinguish iː from ɪ, uː from ʊ, but in weak syllables the difference is not so clear. For example, although it is easy enough to decide which vowel one hears in 'beat' or 'bit', it is much less easy to decide which vowel one hears in the second syllable of words such as, for example, 'easy' or 'busy'. There are accents of English (for example Welsh accents) in which the second syllable sounds most like the iː in the first syllable of 'easy', and others (for example Yorkshire accents) in which it sounds more like the ɪ in the first syllable of 'busy'. In present-day BBC pronunciation, however, the matter is not so clear. There is uncertainty, too, about the corresponding close back rounded vowels. If we look at the words 'good to eat' and 'food to eat', we must ask if the word 'to' is pronounced with the ʊ vowel phoneme of 'good' or the uː phoneme of 'food'. Again, which vowel comes in 'to' in 'I want to'?

One common feature is that the vowels in question are more like iː or uː when they precede another vowel, less so when they precede a consonant or pause. You should notice one further thing: with the exception of one or two very artificial examples, there is really no possibility in these contexts of a phonemic contrast between iː and ɪ, or between uː and ʊ. Effectively, then, the two distinctions, which undoubtedly exist within strong syllables, are **neutralised** in weak syllables of BBC pronunciation. How should we transcribe the words 'easy' and 'busy'? We will use the close front unrounded case as an example, since it is more straightforward. The possibilities, using our phoneme symbols, are the following:

	'easy'	'busy'
i)	iːziː	bɪziː
ii)	iːzɪ	bɪzɪ

Few speakers with a BBC accent seem to feel satisfied with any of these transcriptions. There is a possible solution to this problem, but it goes against standard phoneme theory. We can symbolise this weak vowel as **i**, that is, using the symbol for the vowel in 'beat' but without the length mark. Thus:

iːzi   bɪzi

The **i** vowel is neither the **iː** of 'beat' nor the **ɪ** of 'bit', and is not in contrast with them. We can set up a corresponding vowel **u** that is neither the **uː** of 'shoe' nor the **ʊ** of 'book' but a weak vowel that shares the characteristics of both. If we use **i** and **u** in our transcription as well as **iː**, **ɪ**, **uː** and **ʊ**, it is no longer a true phonemic transcription in the traditional sense. However, this need not be too serious an objection, and the fact that native speakers seem to think that this transcription fits better with their feelings about the language is a good argument in its favour.

⏺ AU9, Ex 2

Let us now look at where these vowels are found, beginning with close front unrounded ones. We find **i** occurring:

i) In word-final position in words spelt with final 'y' or 'ey' (after one or more consonant letters), e.g. 'happy' **hæpi**, 'valley' **væli**, and in morpheme-final position when such words have suffixes beginning with vowels, e.g. 'happier' **hæpiə**, 'easiest' **iːziəst**, 'hurrying' **hʌriiŋ**.

ii) In a prefix such as those spelt 're', 'pre', 'de' if it precedes a vowel and is unstressed, for example in 'react' **riækt**, 'preoccupied' **priɒkjəpaɪd**, 'deactivate' **diæktɪveɪt**.

iii) In the suffixes spelt 'iate', 'ious' when they have two syllables, for example in 'appreciate' **əpriːʃieɪt**, 'hilarious' **hɪleəriəs**.

iv) In the following words when unstressed: 'he', 'she', 'we', 'me', 'be' and the word 'the' when it precedes a vowel.

In most other cases of syllables containing a short close front unrounded vowel we can assign the vowel to the **ɪ** phoneme, as in the first syllable of 'resist' rɪzɪst, 'inane' ɪneɪn, 'enough' ɪnʌf, the middle syllable of 'incident' ɪnsɪdənt, 'orchestra' ɔːkɪstrə, 'artichoke' aːtɪtʃəʊk, and the final syllable of 'swimming' swɪmɪŋ, 'liquid' lɪkwɪd, 'optic' ɒptɪk. It can be seen that this vowel is most often represented in spelling by the letters 'i' and 'e'.

Weak syllables with close back rounded vowels are not so commonly found. We find **u** most frequently in the words 'you', 'to', 'into', 'do', when they are unstressed and are not immediately preceding a consonant, and 'through' and 'who' in all positions when they are unstressed. This vowel is also found before another vowel within a word, as in 'evacuation' ɪvækjueɪʃn̩, 'influenza' ɪnfluenzə.

9.4 Syllabic consonants

In the above sections we have looked at vowels in weak syllables. We must also consider syllables in which no vowel is found. In this case, a consonant, either **l**, **r** or a nasal, stands as the peak of the syllable instead of the vowel, and we count these as weak syllables like the vowel examples given earlier in this chapter. It is usual to indicate that a consonant is syllabic by means of a small vertical mark (ˌ) for example 'cattle' kætl̩.

Syllabic l   ⌒ AU9, Ex 3

Syllabic **l** is perhaps the most noticeable example of the English syllabic consonants, although it would be wrong to expect to find it in all accents. It occurs after another consonant, and the way it is produced depends to some extent on the nature of that consonant. If the preceding consonant is alveolar, as in 'bottle' bɒtl̩, 'muddle' mʌdl̩, 'tunnel' tʌnl̩, the articulatory movement from the preceding consonant to the syllabic **l** is quite simple. The sides of the tongue, which are raised for the preceding consonant, are lowered to allow air to escape over them (this is called **lateral release**). The tip and blade of the tongue do not move until the articulatory contact for the **l** is released. The **l** is a "dark l" (as explained in Chapter 7). In some accents – particularly London ones, and "Estuary English" – we often find a close back rounded vowel instead (for example 'bottle' bɒtu). Where do we find syllabic **l** in the BBC accent? It is useful to look at the spelling as a guide. The most obvious case is where we have a word ending with one or more consonant letters followed by 'le' (or, in the case of noun plurals or third person singular verb forms, 'les'). Examples are:

i) with alveolar consonant preceding
    'cattle' **kætl̩**   'bottle' **bɒtl̩**
    'wrestle' **resl̩**   'muddle' **mʌdl̩**
ii) with non-alveolar consonant preceding
    'couple' **kʌpl̩**   'trouble' **trʌbl̩**
    'struggle' **strʌgl̩**   'knuckle' **nʌkl̩**

Such words usually lose their final letter 'e' when a suffix beginning with a vowel is attached, but the l usually remains syllabic. Thus:

    'bottle' – 'bottling'   **bɒtl̩ – bɒtl̩ɪŋ**
    'muddle' – 'muddling'   **mʌdl̩ – mʌdl̩ɪŋ**
    'struggle' – 'struggling'   **strʌgl̩ – strʌgl̩ɪŋ**

Similar words not derived in this way do not have the syllabic l̩ – it has been pointed out that the two words 'coddling' (derived from the verb 'coddle') and 'codling' (meaning "small cod", derived by adding the diminutive suffix '-ling' to 'cod') show a contrast between syllabic and non-syllabic l: 'coddling' **kɒdl̩ɪŋ** and 'codling' **kɒdlɪŋ**. In the case of words such as 'bottle', 'muddle', 'struggle', which are quite common, it would be a mispronunciation to insert a vowel between the l and the preceding consonant in the accent described here. There are many accents of English which may do this, so that, for example, 'cattle' is pronounced **kætəl**, but this is not the case in BBC pronunciation.

    We also find syllabic l in words spelt, at the end, with one or more consonant letters followed by 'al' or 'el', for example:

    'panel' **pænl̩**   'papal' **peɪpl̩**
    'petal' **petl̩**   'parcel' **pɑːsl̩**
    'kernel' **kɜːnl̩**   'Babel' **beɪbl̩**
    'pedal' **pedl̩**   'ducal' **djuːkl̩**

In some less common or more technical words, it is not obligatory to pronounce syllabic l and the sequence əl may be used instead, although it is less likely: 'missal' **mɪsl̩** or **mɪsəl**; 'acquittal' **əkwɪtl̩** or **əkwɪtəl**.

Syllabic n

Of the syllabic nasals, the most frequently found and the most important is n̩. When should it be pronounced? A general rule could be made that weak syllables which are phonologically composed of a plosive or fricative consonant plus ən are uncommon except in initial position in the words. So we can find words like 'tonight' tənaɪt, 'canary' kəneəri with an ə before n, but medially and finally – as in words like 'threaten', 'threatening' – we find much more commonly a syllabic n: θretn̩, θretn̩ɪŋ. To pronounce a vowel before the nasal consonant would sound strange (or at best overcareful) in BBC. Syllabic n is most common after alveolar plosives and fricatives; in the case of t and d followed by n the plosive is nasally released by lowering the soft palate, so that in the word 'eaten' iːtn̩, for example, the tongue does not move in the tn̩ sequence but the soft palate is lowered at the end of t so that compressed air escapes through the nose. We do not find n̩ after l or tʃ, dʒ, so that for example 'sullen' must be pronounced sʌlən, 'Christian' as krɪstʃən (though this word may be pronounced with t plus i or j instead of tʃ) and 'pigeon' as pɪdʒən.

Syllabic n̩ after non-alveolar consonants is not so widespread. In words where the syllable following a velar consonant is spelt 'an' or 'on' (for example, 'toboggan', 'wagon') it is rarely heard, the more usual pronunciation being təbɒgən, wægən. After bilabial consonants, in words like 'happen', 'happening', 'ribbon' we can consider it equally acceptable to pronounce them with syllabic n̩ (hæpn̩, hæpn̩ɪŋ, rɪbn̩) or with ən (hæpən, hæpənɪŋ, rɪbən). As we will see, syllabic m̩ is also possible in this context. In a similar way, after velar consonants in words like 'thicken', 'waken', syllabic n̩ is possible but ən is also acceptable. Syllabic velar nasal ŋ̩ is also possible in this context.

After f or v, syllabic n̩ is more common than ən (except, as with the other cases described, in word-initial syllables). Thus 'seven', 'heaven', 'often' are more usually sevn̩, hevn̩, ɒfn̩ than sevən, hevən, ɒfən.

In all the examples given so far the syllabic n̩ has been following another consonant; sometimes it is possible for another consonant to precede that consonant, but in this case a syllabic consonant is less likely to occur. If n is preceded by l and a plosive, as in 'Wilton', the pronunciation **wɪltn̩** is possible, but **wɪltən** is also found regularly. If s precedes, as in 'Boston', a final syllabic nasal is less frequent, while clusters formed by nasal + plosive + syllabic nasal are very unusual: thus 'Minton', 'lantern', 'London', 'abandon' will normally have ə in the last syllable and be pronounced **mɪntən**, **læntən**, **lʌndən**, **əbændən**. Other nasals also discourage a following plosive plus syllabic nasal, so that for example 'Camden' is normally pronounced **kæmdən**.

Syllabics **m**, **ŋ**

We will not spend much time on the syllabic pronunciation of these consonants. Both can occur as syllabic, but only as a result of processes such as assimilation and elision that I have not yet described. We find them sometimes in words like 'happen', which can be pronounced **hæpm̩**, though **hæpn̩** and **hæpən** are equally acceptable, and 'uppermost', which could be pronounced as **ʌpm̩əʊst** though **ʌpəməʊst** would be more usual. Examples of possible syllabic velar nasals would be 'thicken' **θɪkŋ̩** (where **θɪkən** and **θɪkn̩** are also possible), and 'broken key' **brəʊkŋ̩ kiː**, where the nasal consonant occurs between velar consonants (again, **n̩** or **ən** could be substituted for **ŋ̩**).

A note about symbols: the usual convention for the syllabic mark is that it should be placed below symbols that do not come below the line, for example **m̩**, **n̩** but above a symbol that does come below the line, for example **ŋ̍**. In this course, however, it is felt preferable to put the mark underneath the symbol in all cases of syllabic consonants.

Syllabic **r**

In many accents of the type called "rhotic" (as explained in Chapter 7), such as most American accents, syllabic **r̩** is very common. The word 'particular', for example, would probably be pronounced **pr̩tɪkəlr̩** in careful speech by most Americans, while BBC speakers would pronounce this word **pətɪkjələ**. Syllabic **r̩** is less common in BBC, and in most cases where it occurs there are perfectly acceptable alternative pronunciations without the syllabic consonant.

There are a few pairs of words (minimal pairs) in which a difference in meaning appears to depend on whether a particular **r** is syllabic or not, for example:

'Hungary' **hʌŋgri̩**   'hungry' **hʌŋgri**

But we find no case of syllabic **r̩** where it would not be possible to substitute either non-syllabic **r** or **ər**; in the example above, 'Hungary' could equally well be pronounced **hʌŋgəri**.

Combinations of syllabic consonants

It is not unusual to find two syllabic consonants together. Examples are: 'national' **næʃn̩l̩**, 'literal' **lɪtr̩l̩**, 'visionary' **vɪʒn̩ri̩**, 'veteran' **vetr̩n̩**. It is important to remember that it is often not possible to say with certainty whether a speaker has pronounced a syllabic consonant, a non-syllabic consonant or a non-syllabic consonant plus **ə**. For example, the word 'veteran' given above could be pronounced in other ways than **vetr̩n̩**. A BBC speaker might instead say **vetrən**, **vetərn̩** or **vetərən**. The transcription makes it look as if the difference between these words is clear; it is not. In examining colloquial English it is often more or less a matter of arbitrary choice how one transcribes such a word. Transcription has the unfortunate tendency to make things seem simpler and more clear-cut than they really are.

Notes on problems and further reading

9.1 I have at this point tried to bring in some preliminary notions of stress and prominence without giving a full explanation. By this stage in the course it is important to be getting familiar with the difference between stressed and unstressed syllables, and the nature of "schwa". However, the subject of stress is such a large one that I have felt it best to leave its main treatment until later. On the subject of schwa, see Jones (1975: Sections 355–72); Cruttenden (1994: Section 8.9.12).

9.2 The introduction of **i** and **u** is a relatively recent idea, but it is now widely accepted as a convention in influential dictionaries such as the *Longman Dictionary of Contemporary English* (Summers, 1987), the *Longman Pronunciation Dictionary* (Wells, 2000), the *Cambridge International Dictionary of English* (Procter, 1995) and the *Daniel Jones English Pronouncing Dictionary* (15th edition; eds.

Roach and Hartman, 1997; see p. xiv of the Introduction to that dictionary). Since I mention native speakers' feelings in this connection, and since I am elsewhere rather sceptical about appeals to native speakers' feelings, I had better explain that in this case my evidence comes from the native speakers of English I have taught in practical classes on transcription over many years. A substantial number of these students have either been speakers with BBC pronunciation or had accents only slightly different from it, and their usual reaction to being told to use ɪ for the vowel at the end of 'easy', 'busy' has been one of puzzlement and frustration; like them, I cannot equate this vowel with the vowel of 'bit'. I am, however, reluctant to use iː, which suggests a stronger vowel than should be pronounced (like the final vowel in 'evacuee', 'Tennessee'). I must emphasise that the vowels **i** and **u** are not included in the set of English phonemes but are simply additional symbols to make the writing and reading of transcription easier. The Introduction to the *Daniel Jones English Pronouncing Dictionary* (eds. Roach and Hartman, 1997) discusses some of the issues involved in syllabic consonants and weak syllables: see pp. xiv–xv.

Notes for teachers
Introduction of the "schwa" vowel has been deliberately delayed until this chapter, since I wanted it to be presented in the context of weak syllables in general. Since students should by now be comparatively well informed about basic segmental phonetics, it is very important that their production and recognition of this vowel should be good before moving on to the following chapters.

This chapter is in a sense a crucial point in the course: although the segmental material of the preceding chapters is important as a foundation, the relationship between strong and weak syllables and the overall prosodic characteristics of words and sentences are essential to intelligibility, and most of the remaining chapters of the course are concerned with such matters.

Written exercises
The following sentences have been partially transcribed, but the vowels have been left blank. Fill in the vowels, taking care to identify which vowels are weak; put no vowel at all if you think a syllabic

consonant is appropriate, but put a syllabic mark beneath the syllabic consonant.

1   A particular problem of the boat was a leak
    p t kj l   pr bl m v ð b   t w z   l   k

2   Opening the bottle presented no difficulty
    p n ŋ   ð b t l   pr z nt d n   d f k lt

3   There is no alternative to the Government's proposal
    ð   r z n   lt n tv t ð   g v   nm nt spr   p zl

4   We ought to make a collection to cover the expenses
    w   tt   m k   k l k ʃ nt   k v   ð   ksp ns z

5   Finally they arrived at a harbour at the edge of the mountains
    f n l   ð   r v d t   h b r t ð   dʒ v ð   m   nt nz

10 Stress in simple words

10.1 The nature of stress

◯ AU10, Ex 1

Stress has been mentioned several times already in this course without any attempt to define what the word means. The nature of stress is simple enough: practically everyone would agree that the first syllable of words like 'father', 'open', 'camera' is stressed, that the middle syllable is stressed in 'potato', 'apartment', 'relation' and that the final syllable is stressed in 'about', 'receive', 'perhaps'. Also, most people feel they have some sort of idea of what the difference is between stressed and unstressed syllables, although they might explain it in many different ways.

We will mark a stressed syllable in transcription by placing a small vertical line (') high up, just before the syllable it relates to; the words quoted above will thus be transcribed as follows:

'fɑːðə	pə'teɪtəʊ	ə'baʊt
'əʊpən	ə'pɑːtmənt	rɪ'siːv
'kæmr̩ə	rɪ'leɪʃn̩	pə'hæps

What are the characteristics of stressed syllables that enable us to identify them? It is important to understand that there are two different ways of approaching this question. One is to consider what the speaker does in producing stressed syllables and the other is to consider what characteristics of sound make a syllable seem to a listener to be stressed. In other words we can study stress from the point of view of **production** and of **perception**; the two are obviously closely related, but are not identical. The production of stress is generally believed to depend on the speaker using more muscular energy than is used for unstressed syllables. Measuring muscular effort is difficult, but it seems possible, according to experimental studies, that when we produce stressed syllables, the muscles that we use to expel air from the lungs are often more active, producing higher subglottal pressure. It seems probable that similar things happen with muscles in other parts of our speech apparatus.

Many experiments have been carried out on the perception of stress, and it is clear that many different sound characteristics are important in making a syllable recognisably stressed. From the perceptual point of view, all stressed syllables have one characteristic in common, and that is **prominence**. Stressed syllables are recognised as stressed because they are more prominent than unstressed syllables. What makes a syllable prominent? At least four different factors are important.

i) Most people seem to feel that stressed syllables are **louder** than unstressed; in other words, loudness is a component of prominence. In a sequence of identical syllables (e.g. **bɑːbɑːbɑːbɑː**), if one syllable is made louder than the others, it will be heard as stressed. However, it is important to realise that it is very difficult for a speaker to make a syllable louder without changing other characteristics of the syllable such as those explained below (ii–iv); if one literally changes *only* the loudness, the perceptual effect is not very strong.

ii) The **length** of syllables has an important part to play in prominence. If one of the syllables in our "nonsense word" **bɑːbɑːbɑːbɑː** is made longer than the others, there is quite a strong tendency for that syllable to be heard as stressed.

iii) Every voiced syllable is said on some **pitch**; pitch in speech is closely related to the frequency of vibration of the vocal folds and to the musical notion of low- and high-pitched notes. It is essentially a *perceptual* characteristic of speech. If one syllable of our "nonsense word" is said with a pitch that is noticeably different from that of the others, this will have a strong tendency to produce the effect of prominence. For example, if all syllables are said with low pitch except for one said with high pitch, then the high-pitched syllable will be heard as stressed and the others as unstressed. To place some **movement** of pitch (e.g. rising or falling) on a syllable is even more effective.

iv) A syllable will tend to be prominent if it contains a vowel that is different in **quality** from neighbouring vowels. If we change one of the vowels in our "nonsense word" (e.g. **bɑːbiːbɑːbɑː**) the "odd" syllable **biː** will tend to be heard as stressed. This effect is not very powerful nor very important, but there is one particular way in which it is relevant in English: the previous chapter explained how the most frequently encountered vowels in weak syllables are **i, u, ɪ** and **ə** (syllabic consonants are also quite common). We can look on stressed syllables as occurring against a "background" of these weak syllables, so that their prominence is increased by contrast with these background qualities.

Prominence, then, is produced by four main factors: (i) loudness, (ii) length, (iii) pitch and (iv) quality. Generally these four factors work together in combination, although syllables may sometimes be made prominent by means of only one or two of them. Experimental work has shown that these factors are not equally important; the strongest effect is produced by pitch, and length is also a powerful factor. Loudness and quality have much less effect.

10.2 Levels of stress

Up to this point we have talked about stress as though there were a simple distinction between "stressed" and "unstressed" syllables with no intermediate levels; such a treatment would be a **two-level** analysis of stress. Usually, however, we have to recognise one or more intermediate levels. It should be remembered that in this chapter we are dealing only with stress *within the word*; this means that we are looking at words as they are said in isolation, which is a rather artificial situation: we do not often say words in isolation, except for a few such as 'yes', 'no', 'possibly', 'please' and interrogative words such as 'what', 'who', etc. However, looking at words in isolation does help us to see stress placement and stress levels more clearly than studying them in the context of continuous speech.

Let us begin by looking at the word 'around' **ə'raʊnd**, where the stress always falls clearly on the last syllable and the first syllable is weak. From the point of view of stress, the most important fact about the way we pronounce this word is that on the second syllable the pitch of the voice does not remain level, but usually falls from a higher to a lower pitch. We might diagram the pitch movement as shown below, where the two parallel lines represent the speaker's high and low pitch level:

The prominence that results from this pitch movement, or tone, gives the strongest type of stress; this is called **primary stress**.

In some words, we can observe a type of stress that is weaker than primary stress but stronger than that of the first syllable of 'around'; for example, in the first syllables of the words 'photographic' **fəʊtəgræfɪk**, 'anthropology' **ænθrəpɒlədʒi**. The stress in these words is called **secondary stress**. It is sometimes represented in transcription with a low mark (ˌ) so that the examples could be transcribed as ˌfəʊtə'græfɪk, ˌænθrə'pɒlədʒi. This convention will only be used where necessary in this course.

We have now identified two levels of stress: primary and secondary; this also implies a third level which can be called **unstressed** and is regarded as being the absence of any recognisable amount of prominence. These are the three levels that we will use in describing English stress. However, it is worth noting that unstressed syllables containing ə, ɪ, i or u, or a syllabic consonant will sound less prominent than an unstressed syllable containing some other vowel. For example, the first syllable of 'poetic' **pəʊ'etɪk** is more prominent than the first syllable of 'pathetic' **pə'θetɪk**. This *could* be used as a basis for a further division of stress levels, giving us a third ("tertiary") and fourth level. It is also possible to suggest a tertiary level of stress in some polysyllabic words. To take an example, it has been suggested that the word 'indivisibility' shows four different levels: the syllable **bɪl** is strongest (carrying primary stress), the initial syllable **ɪn** has secondary stress, while the third syllable **vɪz** has a level of stress which is weaker than those two but stronger than the second, fourth, sixth and seventh (which are all unstressed). Using the symbol ˳ to mark this tertiary stress, the word could be represented like this: ˌɪndɪˌvɪzɪ'bɪləti. While this may be a phonetically correct account of some pronunciations, the introduction of tertiary stress seems to introduce an unnecessary degree of complexity.

10.3 Placement of stress within the word
We now come to a question that causes a great deal of difficulty, particularly to foreign learners (who cannot simply dismiss it as an

academic question): how can one select the correct syllable or syllables to stress in an English word? As is well known, English is not one of those languages where word stress can be decided simply in relation to the syllables of the word, as can be done in French (where the last syllable is usually stressed), Polish (where the syllable before the last – the penultimate syllable – is usually stressed) or Czech (where the first syllable is usually stressed). Many writers have said that English word stress is so difficult to predict that it is best to treat stress placement as a property of the individual word, to be learned when the word itself is learned. Certainly anyone who tries to analyse English stress placement has to recognise that it is a highly complex matter. However, it must also be recognised that in most cases (though certainly not all), when English speakers come across an unfamiliar word, they can pronounce it with the correct stress; in principle, it should be possible to discover what it is that the English speaker knows and to write it in the form of rules. The following summary of ideas on stress placement in nouns, verbs and adjectives is an attempt to present a few rules in the simplest possible form. Nevertheless, practically all the rules have exceptions and readers may feel that the rules are so complex that it would be easier to go back to the idea of learning the stress for each word individually.

In order to decide on stress placement, it is necessary to make use of some or all of the following information:

i) Whether the word is morphologically **simple**, or whether it is **complex** as a result either of containing one or more affixes (that is, prefixes or suffixes) or of being a compound word.

ii) What the grammatical category of the word is (noun, verb, adjective, etc.).

iii) How many syllables the word has.

iv) What the phonological structure of those syllables is.

It is sometimes difficult to make the decision referred to in (i). The rules for complex words are different from those for simple words and these will be dealt with in Chapter 11. Obviously, single-syllable words present no problems: if they are pronounced in isolation they are said with primary stress.

Point (iv) above is something that should be dealt with right away, since it affects many of the other rules that we will look at later. It is possible to divide syllables into two basic categories: **strong** and **weak**. We saw in Chapter 8 that one component of a syllable is the **rhyme**, which contains the syllable peak and the coda. A strong syllable has a rhyme which *either* has a syllable peak which is a long vowel or diphthong, *or* a vowel followed by a coda (that is, one or more consonants). Weak syllables have a syllable peak which is a short vowel, and no coda unless the syllable peak is the schwa vowel ə or (in some circumstances) ɪ. Examples of strong syllables are:

> 'die' **daɪ** 'heart' **hɑːt** 'bat' **bæt**

Examples of weak syllables (with syllable divisions shown) are:

> 're' in 'reduce' **rɪ.djuːs** 'bi' in 'herbicide' **hɜː.bɪ.saɪd** 'pen' in 'open' **əʊ.pən**

The important point to remember is that, although we do find unstressed strong syllables (as in the last syllable of 'dialect' **'daɪəlekt**), *only* strong syllables can be stressed. Weak syllables are always unstressed. This piece of knowledge does not by any means solve all the problems of how to place English stress, but it does help in some cases.

Two-syllable words

AU10, Ex 3

Here the choice is still simple: either the first or the second syllable will be stressed – not both. We will look first at verbs. The basic rule is that if the second syllable of the verb is a strong syllable, then that second syllable is stressed. Thus:

> 'apply' **ə'plaɪ**   'attract' **ə'trækt**
> 'arrive' **ə'raɪv**   'assist' **ə'sɪst**

If the final syllable is weak, then the first syllable is stressed. Thus:

> 'enter' **'entə**   'open' **'əʊpən**
> 'envy' **'envi**   'equal' **'iːkwəl**

A final syllable is also unstressed if it contains əʊ (e.g. 'follow' **'fɒləʊ**, 'borrow' **'bɒrəʊ**).

Two-syllable simple adjectives are stressed according to the same rule, giving:

> 'lovely' **'lʌvli**   'divine' **dɪ'vaɪn**
> 'even' **'iːvn̩**   'correct' **kə'rekt**
> 'hollow' **'hɒləʊ**   'alive' **ə'laɪv**

As with most stress rules, there are exceptions; for example, 'honest' **'ɒnɪst**, 'perfect' **'pɜːfɪkt** (or **'pɜːfekt**), both of which end with strong syllables but are stressed on the first syllable.

Nouns require a different rule: if the second syllable contains a short vowel, then the stress will usually come on the first syllable. Otherwise it will be on the second syllable.

'money' **'mʌni**	'estate' **ɪ'steɪt**
'product' **'prɒdʌkt**	'balloon' **bə'luːn**
'larynx' **'lærɪŋks**	'design' **dɪ'zaɪn**

Other two-syllable words such as adverbs and prepositions seem to behave like verbs and adjectives.

Three-syllable words

Here we find a more complicated picture. In verbs, if the final syllable is strong, then it will be stressed. Thus:

'entertain' **entə'teɪn**   'resurrect' **rezə'rekt**

If the last syllable is weak, then it will be unstressed, and stress will be placed on the preceding (penultimate) syllable if that syllable is strong. Thus:

'encounter' **ɪŋ'kaʊntə**   'determine' **dɪ'tɜːmɪn**

If both the second and third syllable are weak, then the stress falls on the initial syllable:

'parody' **'pærədi**

Nouns require a slightly different rule. Here, if the final syllable is weak, or ends with əʊ, then it is unstressed; if the syllable preceding this final syllable is strong, then that middle syllable will be stressed. Thus:

'mimosa' **mɪ'məʊzə**	'disaster' **dɪ'zɑːstə**
'potato' **pə'teɪtəʊ**	'synopsis' **sɪ'nɒpsɪs**

If the second and third syllables are both weak, then the first syllable is stressed:

'quantity' **'kwɒntəti**	'emperor' **'empərə**
'cinema' **'sɪnəmə**	'custody' **'kʌstədi**

Most of the above rules show stress tending to go on strong syllables. However, three-syllable simple nouns are different. Even if the final syllable is strong, the stress will usually be placed on the first syllable. The last syllable is usually quite prominent, so that in some cases it could be said to have secondary stress.

'intellect'	**ˈɪntəlekt**	'marigold'	**ˈmærɪɡəʊld**
'alkali'	**ˈælkəlaɪ**	'stalactite'	**ˈstæləktaɪt**

Adjectives seem to need the same rule, to produce stress patterns such as:

'opportune'	**ˈɒpətjuːn**	'insolent'	**ˈɪnsələnt**
'derelict'	**ˈderəlɪkt**	'anthropoid'	**ˈænθrəpɔɪd**

The above rules do not, of course, cover all English words. They apply only to major categories of lexical words (nouns, verbs and adjectives in this chapter), not to function words such as articles and prepositions. There is not enough space in this course to deal with simple words of more than three syllables, nor with special cases of loan words (words brought into the language from other languages comparatively recently). Complex and compound words are dealt with in Chapter 11. One problem that we must also leave until Chapter 11 is the fact that there are many cases of English words with alternative possible stress patterns (e.g. 'controversy' as either **ˈkɒntrəvɜːsi** or **kənˈtrɒvəsi**). Other words – which we will look at in studying connected speech – change their stress pattern according to the context they occur in. Above all, there is not space to discuss the many exceptions to the above rules. Despite the exceptions, it seems better in many ways to attempt to produce some stress rules (even if they are rather crude and inaccurate) than to claim that there is no rule or regularity in English word stress.

Notes on problems and further reading
The subject of English stress has received a large amount of attention, and the references given here are only a small selection from an enormous number. As I implied in the notes on the previous chapter, incorrect stress placement is a major cause of intelligibility problems for foreign learners, and is therefore a subject that needs to be treated very seriously.

10.1 I have deliberately avoided using the term *accent*, which is found widely in the literature on stress. This is for three main reasons:

i) It increases the complexity of the description without, in my view, contributing much to its value.

ii) Different writers do not agree with each other about the way the term should be used.

iii) The word 'accent' is used elsewhere to refer to different varieties of pronunciation (e.g. "a foreign accent"); it is confusing to use it for a quite different purpose – to a lesser extent we also have this problem with the word 'stress', which can be used to refer to psychological tension.

There is a good discussion of the confusing nature of the terms 'stress' and 'accent' in Clark and Yallop (1995: 41–2). Their Section 9.6 on stress in English (pp. 348–57) is a useful summary. For a review of the production and perception of stress, see Laver (1994: 512–17).

10.2 On the question of the number of levels of stress, in addition to Laver (1994: 516), see also Wells (2000).

10.3 It is said in this chapter that one may take one of two positions. One is that stress is not predictable by rule and must be learned word by word (see, for example, Jones 1975: Sections 920–1). The second (which I prefer) is to say that, difficult though the task is, one must try to find a way of writing rules that express what native speakers naturally tend to do in placing stress (while acknowledging that there will always be a substantial residue of cases which appear to follow no regular rules). A very thorough treatment is given by Fudge (1984). More recently, Giegerich (1992) has presented a clear analysis of English word stress (including a useful explanation of strong and weak syllables) that is well worth reading; see p. 146 and Chapter 7.

There is another approach to English stress rules which is radically different. This is based on **generative phonology**, an analysis which was first presented in Chomsky and Halle (1968) and has been followed by a large number of works exploring the same field. To anyone not familiar with this type of treatment, the presentation will seem difficult or even unintelligible; within the generative approach, many different theories, all with different names, tend to come and go with changes in fashion. The following paragraph is an attempt to summarise the main characteristics of basic generative phonology, and recommends some further reading for those interested in learning about it in detail.

The level of phonology is very abstract in this theory. An old-fashioned view of speech communication would be that what the speaker intends to say is coded – or *represented* – as a string of phonemes just like a phonemic transcription, and what a hearer hears is also converted by the brain from sound waves into a similar string of phonemes. A generative phonologist, however, would say that this phonemic representation is not accurate; the representation in the brain of the speaker or hearer is much more abstract and is often quite different from the 'real' sounds recognisable in the sound wave. You may hear the word 'football' pronounced as **fʊpbɔːl**, but your brain recognises the word as made up of 'foot' and 'ball' and interprets it phonologically as **fʊtbɔːl**. You may hear ə in the first syllable of 'photography', in the second syllable of 'photograph' and in the third syllable of 'photographer', but the brain recognises links between these ə vowels and əʊ, ɒ and æ respectively, and supplies the *underlying* vowels. In speaking, underlying segments may be realised as different sounds as the stress pattern changes. These vowel changes are brought about by *rules* – not the sort of rules that one might teach to language learners, but more like the instructions that one might build into a machine or write into a computer program. According to Chomsky and Halle, at the abstract phonological level words do not possess stress; stress (of many different levels) is the result of the application of phonological rules, which are simple enough in theory but highly complex in practice. The principles of these rules are explained first on pp. 15–43 of Chomsky and Halle (1968), and in greater detail on pp. 69–162.

There is a clear and thorough introductory account of generative phonology in Clark and Yallop (1995: Chapter 5), and they present a brief account of the generative treatment of stress on pp. 355–7. A briefer review is given in Katamba (1989: Chapter 11, Section l).

Notes for teachers
It should be clear from what is said above that from the purely practical classroom point of view, explaining English word stress in

terms of generative phonology could well create confusion for learners. Finding practice and testing material for word stress is very simple: any modern English dictionary shows word stress patterns as part of word entries, and lists of these can be made either with stress marks for student to read from (as in Exercise 2 of Audio Unit 10), or without stress marks for students to put their own marks on (as in Exercise 1 of the same Audio Unit).

Written exercises (mainly for foreign learners)
Mark the stress on the following words:

1 verbs

a) protect	*e)* bellow
b) clamber	*f)* menace
c) festoon	*g)* disconnect
d) detest	*h)* entering

2 nouns

a) language	*e)* event
b) captain	*f)* jonquil
c) career	*g)* injury
d) paper	*h)* connection

(Native speakers of English should transcribe the words phonemically as well as marking stress.)

11 Complex word stress

11.1 Complex words

In Chapter 10 the nature of stress was explained and some broad general rules were given for deciding which syllable in a word should receive primary stress. The words that were described were called "simple" words; "simple" in this context means "not composed of more than one grammatical unit", so that, for example, the word 'care' is simple while 'careful' and 'careless' (being composed of two grammatical units each) are complex; 'carefully' and 'carelessness' are also complex, and are composed of three grammatical units each. Unfortunately, as was suggested in Chapter 10, it is often difficult to decide on whether a word should be treated as complex or simple. The majority of English words of more than one syllable (**polysyllabic words**) have come from other languages whose way of constructing words is easily recognisable; for example, we can see how combining 'mit' with the prefixes 'per-', 'sub-', 'com-' produced 'permit', 'submit', 'commit', words which have come into English from Latin. Similarly, Greek has given us 'catalogue', 'analogue', 'dialogue', 'monologue', in which the prefixes 'cata-', 'ana-', 'dia-', 'mono-' are recognisable. But we cannot automatically treat the separate grammatical units of other languages as separate grammatical units of English. If we did, we would not be able to study English morphology without first studying the morphology of five or six other languages, and we would be forced into ridiculous analyses such as that the English word 'parallelepiped' is composed of four or five grammatical units (which is the case in Ancient Greek). We must accept, then, that the distinction between "simple" and "complex" words is difficult to draw, and is therefore not always useful.

Complex words are of two major types:

i) words made from a basic word form (which we will call the **stem**), with the addition of an **affix**; and

ii) **compound words**, which are made of two (or occasionally more) independent English words (e.g. 'ice-cream', 'armchair').

We will look first at the words made with affixes. Affixes are of two sorts in English: **prefixes**, which come before the stem (e.g. prefix 'un-' + stem 'pleasant' → 'unpleasant') and **suffixes**, which come after the stem (e.g. stem 'good' + suffix '-ness' → 'goodness').

Affixes have one of three possible effects on word stress:

i) The affix itself receives the primary stress (e.g. 'semi-' + 'circle' **'sɜːkl̩** → 'semicircle' **'semɪsɜːkl̩**; '-ality' + 'person' **'pɜːsn̩** 'person-ality' **pɜːsn̩'æləti**).

ii) The word is stressed just as if the affix were not there (e.g. 'pleasant' **'pleznt̩**, 'unpleasant' **ʌn'pleznt̩**; 'market' **'mɑːkɪt**, 'mar-keting' **'mɑːkɪtɪŋ**).

iii) The stress remains on the stem, not the affix, but is shifted to a different syllable (e.g. 'magnet' **'mægnət**, 'magnetic' **mæg'netɪk**).

11.2 Suffixes

There are so many suffixes that it will only be possible here to examine a small proportion of them; we will concentrate on those which are common and **productive** (that is, are applied to a consider-able number of stems and could be applied to more to make new English words). In the case of the others, foreign learners would probably be better advised to learn the 'stem + affix' combination as an individual item.

One of the problems that will be encountered is that we may find words which are obviously complex but which, when we divide them into stem + affix, turn out to have a stem that is difficult to imagine as an English word. For example, the word 'audacity' seems to be a complex word – but what is its stem? Another problem is that it is difficult in some cases to know whether a word has one, or more than one, suffix (e.g. should we analyse 'personality', from the point of view of stress assignment, as **pɜsn̩** + **æləti** or as **pɜːsn̩** + **æl** + **əti**?). In the study of English word formation at a deeper level than we can go into here, it is necessary for such reasons to distinguish between a stem (which is what remains when affixes are removed), and a **root**, which is the smallest piece of lexical material that a stem can be reduced to. So, in 'personality', we could say that the *suffix* '-ity' is attached to the *stem* 'personal' which contains the *root* 'person'. We will not spend more time here on looking at these problems, but go on to look at some generalisations about suffixes and stress, using only the term 'stem' for the sake of simplicity. The suffixes are referred to in their spelling form.

Suffixes carrying primary stress themselves ◯ AU11, Ex 1

In the examples given, which seem to be the most common, the primary stress is on the first syllable of the suffix. If the stem consists of more than one syllable there will be a secondary stress on one of the syllables of the stem. This cannot fall on the last syllable of the stem and is, if necessary, moved to an earlier syllable. For example, in 'Japan' dʒə'pæn the primary stress is on the last syllable, but when we add the stress-carrying suffix '-ese' the primary stress is on the suffix and the secondary stress is placed not on the second syllable but on the first: 'Japanese' ˌdʒæpə'niːz.

- '-ee': 'refugee' ˌrefjʊ'dʒiː; 'evacuee' ɪˌvækju'iː
- '-eer': 'mountaineer' ˌmaʊntɪ'nɪə; 'volunteer' ˌvɒlən'tɪə
- '-ese': 'Portuguese' ˌpɔːtʃə'giːz; 'journalese' ˌdʒɜːnl̩'iːz
- '-ette': 'cigarette' ˌsɪɡr̩'et; 'launderette' ˌlɔːndr̩'et
- '-esque': 'picturesque' ˌpɪktʃr̩'esk

Suffixes that do not affect stress placement ◯ AU11, Ex 2

- '-able': 'comfort' 'kʌmfət; 'comfortable' 'kʌmftəbl̩
- '-age': 'anchor' 'æŋkə; 'anchorage' 'æŋkərɪdʒ
- '-al': 'refuse' (verb) rɪ'fjuːz; 'refusal' rɪ'fjuːzl̩
- '-en': 'wide' waɪd; 'widen' 'waɪdn̩
- '-ful': 'wonder' 'wʌndə; 'wonderful' 'wʌndəfl̩
- '-ing': 'amaze' ə'meɪz; 'amazing' ə'meɪzɪŋ
- '-ish': 'devil' 'devl̩; 'devilish' 'devl̩ɪʃ

(This is the rule for adjectives; verbs with stems of more than one syllable always have the stress on the syllable immediately preceding 'ish', e.g. 'replenish' rɪ'plenɪʃ, 'demolish' dɪ'mɒlɪʃ.)

- '-like': 'bird' **'bɜːd**; 'birdlike' **'bɜːdlaɪk**
- '-less': 'power' **'paʊə**; 'powerless' **'paʊələs**
- '-ly': 'hurried' **'hʌrɪd**; 'hurriedly' **'hʌrɪdli**
- '-ment' (noun): 'punish' **'pʌnɪʃ**; 'punishment' **'pʌnɪʃmənt**
- '-ness': 'yellow' **'jeləʊ**; 'yellowness' **'jeləʊnəs**
- '-ous': 'poison' **'pɔɪzn̩**; 'poisonous' **'pɔɪzn̩əs**
- '-fy': 'glory' **'glɔːri**; 'glorify' **'glɔːrɪfaɪ**
- '-wise': 'other' **'ʌðə**; 'otherwise' **'ʌðəwaɪz**
- '-y' (adjective or noun): 'fun' **'fʌn**; 'funny' **'fʌni**

Suffixes that influence stress in the stem ◯ AU11, Ex 3
In these examples primary stress is on the last syllable of the stem.

- '-eous': 'advantage' **əd'vɑːntɪdʒ**; 'advantageous' **ˌædvən'teɪdʒəs**
- '-graphy': 'photo' **'fəʊtəʊ**; 'photography' **fə'tɒgrəfi**
- '-ial': 'proverb' **'prɒvɜːb**; 'proverbial' **prə'vɜːbiəl**
- '-ic': 'climate' **'klaɪmɪt**; 'climatic' **klaɪ'mætɪk**
- '-ion': 'perfect' **'pɜːfɪkt**; 'perfection' **pə'fekʃn̩**
- '-ious': 'injure' **'ɪndʒə**; 'injurious' **ɪn'dʒɔːriəs**
- '-ty': 'tranquil' **'træŋkwɪl**; 'tranquillity' **træŋ'kwɪləti**
- '-ive': 'reflex' **'riːfleks**; 'reflexive' **rɪ'fleksɪv**

Finally, when the suffixes '-ance', '-ant' and '-ary' are attached to single-syllable stems, the stress is almost always placed on the stem. When the stem has more than one syllable, the stress is on one of the syllables in the stem. To explain this we need to use a rule based on syllable structure, as was done for simple words in the previous chapter. If the final syllable of the stem is strong, that syllable receives the stress. For example: 'importance' **ɪm'pɔːtn̩s**; 'centenary' **sen'tiːnr̩i**. Otherwise the syllable *before* the last one receives the stress: 'inheritance' **ɪn'herɪtəns**; 'military' **'mɪlɪtri**.

11.3 Prefixes
We will only deal briefly with prefixes. Their effect on stress does not have the comparative regularity, independence and predictability of suffixes, and there is no prefix of one or two syllables that always carries primary stress. Consequently, the best treatment seems to be to say that stress in words with prefixes is governed by the same rules as those for words without prefixes.

11.4 Compound words ⌒ AU11, Ex 4

The words discussed so far in this chapter have all consisted of a stem plus an affix. We now pass on to another type of word. This is called **compound**, and its main characteristic is that it can be analysed into two words, both of which can exist independently as English words. (Some compounds are made of more than two words, but we will not consider these.) As with many of the distinctions being made in connection with stress, there are areas of uncertainty. For example, it could be argued that 'photograph' may be divided into two independent words, 'photo' and 'graph'; yet we usually do not regard it as a compound, but as a simple word. (If, however, someone drew a graph displaying numerical information about photos, this would perhaps be called a 'photo-graph' and the word would be regarded as a compound.) Compounds are written in different ways; sometimes they are written as one word – e.g. 'armchair', 'sunflower' – sometimes with the words separated by a hyphen – e.g. 'gear-change', 'fruit-cake' – and sometimes with two words separated by a space – e.g. 'desk lamp', 'battery charger'. In this last case there would, of course, be no indication to the foreign learner that the pair of words was to be treated as a compound. There is no clear dividing line between two-word compounds and pairs of words that simply happen to occur together quite frequently.

As far as stress is concerned, the question is quite simple. When is primary stress placed on the first constituent word of the compound and when on the second? Both patterns are found. A few rules can be given, although these are not completely reliable. Words which do not receive primary stress normally have secondary stress, although for the sake of simplicity this is not marked here. Perhaps the most familiar type of compound is the one which combines two nouns and which normally has the stress on the first element, as in:

'typewriter' **ˈtaɪpraɪtə**	'suitcase' **ˈsuːtkeɪs**
'car-ferry' **ˈkɑːferi**	'tea-cup' **ˈtiːkʌp**
'sunrise' **ˈsʌnraɪz**	

It is probably safest to assume that stress will normally fall in this way on other compounds; however, a variety of compounds receive stress instead on the second element. For example, compounds with an adjectival first element and the -*ed* morpheme at the end have this pattern (given in spelling only):

bad-'tempered
half-'timbered
heavy-'handed

Compounds in which the first element is a number in some form also tend to have final stress:

three-'wheeler
second-'class
five-'finger

Compounds functioning as adverbs are usually final-stressed:

head-'first
North-'East
down'stream

Finally, compounds which function as verbs and have an adverbial first element take final stress:

down-'grade
back-'pedal
ill-'treat

11.5 Variable stress

It would be wrong to imagine that the stress pattern is always fixed and unchanging in English words. Stress position may vary for one of two reasons: either as a result of the stress on other words occurring next to the word in question, or because not all speakers agree on the placement of stress in some words. The former case is an aspect of connected speech that will be encountered again in Chapter 14: the main effect is that the stress on a final-stressed compound tends to move to a preceding syllable if the following word begins with a strongly stressed syllable. Thus (using some examples from the previous section):

bad-'tempered	but	a 'bad-tempered 'teacher
half-'timbered	but	a 'half-timbered 'house
heavy-'handed	but	a 'heavy-handed 'sentence

The second is not a serious problem, but is one that foreign learners should be aware of. A well-known example is 'controversy', which is pronounced by some speakers as **'kɒntrəvɜːsi** and by others as **kən'trɒvəsi**; it would be quite wrong to say that one version was correct and one incorrect. Other examples of different possibilities are 'ice-cream' (either ˌaɪs'kriːm or 'aɪskriːm), 'kilometre' (either **'kɪləmiːtə** or **kɪ'lɒmɪtə**) and 'formidable' ('fɔːmɪdəbl̩ or fɔː'mɪdəbl̩).

11.6 Word-class pairs

AU11, Ex 5

One aspect of word stress is best treated as a separate issue. There are several dozen pairs of two-syllable words with identical spelling which differ from each other in stress placement, apparently according to word class (noun, verb or adjective). All appear to consist of prefix + stem. We shall treat them as a special type of word and give them the following rule: if a pair of prefix-plus-stem words exists, both members of which are spelt identically, one of which is a verb and the other of which is either a noun or an adjective, then the stress is placed on the second syllable of the verb but on the first syllable of the noun or adjective. Some common examples are given below (V = verb, A = adjective, N = noun):

'abstract'	**'æbstrækt** (A)	æb'strækt (V)
'conduct'	**'kɒndʌkt** (N)	kən'dʌkt (V)
'contract'	**'kɒntrækt** (N)	kən'trækt (V)
'contrast'	**'kɒntrɑːst** (N)	kən'trɑːst (V)
'desert'	**'dezət** (N)	dɪ'zɜːt (V)
'escort'	**'eskɔːt** (N)	ɪs'kɔːt (V)
'export'	**'ekspɔːt** (N)	ɪk'spɔːt (V)
'import'	**'ɪmpɔːt** (N)	ɪm'pɔːt (V)
'insult'	**'ɪnsʌlt** (N)	ɪn'sʌlt (V)
'object'	**'ɒbdʒɪkt** (N)	əb'dʒekt (V)
'perfect'	**'pɜːfɪkt** (A)	pə'fekt (V)
'permit'	**'pɜːmɪt** (N)	pə'mɪt (V)
'present'	**'preznt̩** (N, A)	prɪ'zent (V)
'produce'	**'prɒdjuːs** (N)	prə'djuːs (V)
'protest'	**'prəʊtest** (N)	prə'test (V)
'rebel'	**'rebl̩** (N)	rɪ'bel (V)
'record'	**'rekɔːd** (N)	rɪ'kɔːd (V)
'subject'	**'sʌbdʒɪkt** (N)	səb'dʒekt (V)

Notes on problems and further reading

Most of the reading recommended in the notes for the previous chapter is relevant for this one too. Looking specifically at compounds, it is worth reading Fudge (1984: Chapter 5). See also Cruttenden (1994: 207–9). If you wish to go more deeply into compound-word stress, you should first study English word formation. Recommended reading for this is Bauer (1983). On the distinction between *stem* and *root*, see Radford *et al.* (1999), pp. 67–8.

Written exercises

1   Put stress marks on the following words (try to put secondary stress marks on as well).

a) shop-fitter *b)* open-ended *c)* Javanese

d) birth-mark *e)* anti-clockwise *f)* confirmation

g) eight-sided *h)* fruit-cake *i)* defective

j) roof-timber

2   Write the words in phonemic transcription, including the stress marks.

12 Weak forms

Chapter 9 discussed the difference between strong and weak syllables in English. We have now moved on from looking at syllables to looking at words. We will now consider certain well-known English words that can be pronounced in two different ways; these are called **strong forms** and **weak forms**. As an example, the word 'that' can be pronounced ðæt (strong form) or ðət (weak form). The sentence 'I like that' is pronounced aɪ laɪk ðæt (strong form); the sentence 'I hope that she will' is pronounced aɪ həʊp ðət ʃi wɪl (weak form). There are roughly forty such words in English. It is possible to use only strong forms in speaking, and some foreigners do this. Usually they can still be understood by other speakers of English, so why is it important to learn how weak forms are used? There are two main reasons; first, most native speakers of English find an "all-strong-form" pronunciation unnatural and foreign-sounding, something that most learners would wish to avoid. Second, and more importantly, speakers who are not familiar with the use of weak forms are likely to have difficulty understanding speakers who do use weak forms; since practically all native speakers of British English use them, learners of the language need to learn about these weak forms to help them to understand what they hear.

We must distinguish between weak forms and **contracted forms**. Certain English words are shortened so severely (usually to a single phoneme) and so consistently that they are represented differently in informal writing, e.g. 'it is' – 'it's'; 'we have' – 'we've'; 'do not' – 'don't'. These contracted forms are discussed in a later chapter, and are not included here.

Almost all the words which have both a strong and weak form belong to a category that may be called **function words** – words that do not have a dictionary meaning in the way that we normally expect nouns, verbs, adjectives and adverbs to have. These function words are words such as auxiliary verbs, prepositions, conjunctions, etc., all of which are in certain circumstances pronounced in their strong forms but which are more frequently pronounced in their weak forms. It is important to remember that there are certain contexts where only the strong form is acceptable, and others where the weak form is the normal pronunciation. There are some fairly simple rules; we can say that the strong form is used in the following cases:

i) For many weak-form words, when they occur at the end of a sentence; for example, the word 'of' has the weak form əv in the following sentence:

'I'm fond of chips' **aɪm 'fɒnd əv 'tʃɪps**

However, when it comes at the end of the sentence, as in the following example, it has the strong form **ɒv**:

'Chips are what I'm fond of' **'tʃɪps ə 'wɒt aɪm 'fɒnd ɒv**

Many of the words given below (particularly the first nine) never occur at the end of a sentence, e.g. 'the', 'your'. Some words (particularly the pronouns numbered 10–14 below) do occur in their weak forms in final position.

ii) When a weak-form word is being contrasted with another word; for example:

'The letter's *from* him, not *to* him' **ðə 'letəz 'frɒm ɪm nɒt 'tuː ɪm**

A similar case is what we might call a **co-ordinated** use of prepositions:

'I travel to and from London a lot' **aɪ 'trævl̩ 'tuː ən 'frɒm 'lʌndən ə 'lɒt**
'A work of and about literature' **ə 'wɜːk 'ɒv ən ə'baʊt 'lɪtrɪtʃə**

iii) When a weak-form word is given stress for the purpose of emphasis; for example:

'You *must* give me more money' **ju 'mʌst 'gɪv mi 'mɔː 'mʌni**

iv) When a weak-form word is being "cited" or "quoted"; for example:

'You shouldn't put "and" at the end of a sentence'
ju 'ʃʊdn̩t pʊt 'ænd ət ði 'end əv ə 'sentəns

Another point to remember is that when weak-form words whose spelling begins with 'h' (e.g. 'her', 'have') occur at the beginning of a sentence, the pronunciation is with initial **h**, even though this is usually omitted in other contexts.

◯ AU12, Exs 1–4

In the rest of this chapter, the most common weak-form words will be introduced.

1   'the'
    Weak forms: **ðə** (before consonants)
                  'Shut the door' **'ʃʌt ðə 'dɔː**
                  ði (before vowels)
                  'Wait for the end' **'weɪt fə ði 'end**

2   'a', 'an'
    Weak forms: **ə** (before consonants)
                  'Read a book' **'riːd ə 'bʊk**
                  ən (before vowels)
                  'Eat an apple' **'iːt ən 'æpl̩**

3   'and'
    Weak form: **ən** (sometimes **n** after **t, d, s, z, ʃ**)
                 'Come and see' **'kʌm ən 'siː**
                 'Fish and chips' **'fɪʃ n̩ 'tʃɪps**

4   'but'
    Weak form: **bət**
                 'It's good but expensive' **ɪts 'gʊd bət ɪk'spensɪv**

5   'that'
    This word only has a weak form when used in a relative clause; when used with a demonstrative sense it is always pronounced in its strong form.
    Weak form: **ðət**
                 'The price is the thing that annoys me' **ðə 'praɪs ɪz ðə 'θɪŋ ðət ə'nɔɪz mi**

6   'than'
    Weak form: **ðən**
                 'Better than ever' **'betə ðən 'evə**

7 'his' (when it occurs before a noun)
    Weak form: ɪz (hɪz at the beginning of a sentence)
                     'Take his name' 'teɪk ɪz 'neɪm
                     (Another sense of 'his', as in 'it was his', or 'his was late', always has the strong form.)

8 'her'
    When used with possessive sense, preceding a noun; as an object pronoun, this can also occur at the end of a sentence.
    Weak forms: ə (before consonants)
                     'Take her home' 'teɪk ə 'həʊm
                     ər (before vowels)
                     'Take her out' 'teɪk ər 'aʊt

9 'your'
    Weak forms: jə (before consonants)
                     'Take your time' 'teɪk jə 'taɪm
                     jər (before vowels)
                     'On your own' 'ɒn jər 'əʊn

10 'she', 'he', 'we', 'you'
    This group of pronouns has weak forms pronounced with weaker vowels than the iː and uː of their strong forms. I use the symbols i and u (in preference to ɪ and ʊ) to represent them. There is little difference in the pronunciation in different places in the sentence, except in the case of 'he'.
    Weak forms:

    a) 'she'   ʃi
                     'Why did she read it?' 'waɪ dɪd ʃi 'riːd ɪt
                     'Who *is* she?' 'huː 'ɪz ʃi
    b) 'he'   i (the weak form is usually pronounced without h except at the beginning of a sentence)
                     'Which did he choose?' 'wɪtʃ dɪd i 'tʃuːz
                     'He was late, wasn't he?' hi wəz 'leɪt 'wɒznt i
    c) 'we'   wi
                     'How can we get there?' 'haʊ kən wi 'get ðeə
                     'We need that, don't we?' wi 'niːd ðæt 'dəʊnt wi
    d) 'you'   ju
                     'What do you think?' 'wɒt də ju 'θɪŋk
                     'You like it, do you?' ju 'laɪk ɪt 'duː ju

11 'him'
    Weak form: **ɪm**
        'Leave him alone' **'liːv ɪm ə'ləʊn**
        'I've seen him' **aɪv 'siːn ɪm**

12 'her'
    Weak form: **ə** (**hə** when sentence-initial)
        'Ask her to come' **'ɑːsk ə tə 'kʌm**
        'I've met her' **aɪv 'met ə**

13 'them'
    Weak form: **ðəm**
        'Leave them here' **'liːv ðəm 'hɪə**
        'Eat them' **'iːt ðəm**

14 'us'
    Weak form: **əs**
        'Write us a letter' **'raɪt əs ə 'letə**
        'They invited all of us' **ðeɪ ɪn'vaɪtɪd 'ɔːl əv əs**

The next group of words (some prepositions and other function words) occur in their strong forms when they are final in a sentence; examples of this are given. (Example 19 is a partial exception.)

15 'at'
    Weak form: **ət**
        'I'll see you at lunch' **aɪl 'siː ju ət 'lʌnʃ**
    In final position: **æt**
        'What's he shooting at?' **'wɒts i 'ʃuːtɪŋ æt**

16 'for'
    Weak form: **fə** (before consonants)
        'Tea for two' **'tiː fə 'tuː**
        fər (before vowels)
        'Thanks for asking' **'θæŋks fər 'ɑːskɪŋ**
    In final position: **fɔː**
        'What's that for?' **'wɒts 'ðæt fɔː**

17. 'from'
    Weak form: **frəm**
        'I'm home from work' **aɪm 'həʊm frəm 'wɜːk**
    In final position: **frɒm**
        'Here's where it came from' **'hɪəz weər ɪt 'keɪm frɒm**

18 'of'
    Weak form: əv
                         'Most of all' **'məʊst əv 'ɔːl**
    In final position: **ɒv**
                         'Someone I've heard of' **'sʌmwʌn aɪv 'hɜːd ɒv**

19 'to'
    Weak forms: **tə** (before consonants)
                         'Try to stop' **'traɪ tə 'stɒp**
                         tu (before vowels)
                         'Time to eat' **'taɪm tu 'iːt**
    In final position: **tu** (It is not usual to use the strong form **tuː**, and the pre-consonantal weak form **tə** is never used.)
                         'I don't want to' **aɪ 'dəʊnt 'wɒnt tu**

20 'as'
    Weak form: əz
                         'As much as possible' **əz 'mʌtʃ əz 'pɒsəbl̩**
    In final position: **æz**
                         'That's what it was sold as' **'ðæts 'wɒt ɪt wəz 'səʊld æz**

21 'some'
This word is used in two different ways. In one sense (typically, when it occurs before a countable noun, meaning "an unknown individual") it has the strong form:
      'I think some animal broke it' **aɪ 'θɪŋk sʌm 'ænɪml̩ 'brəʊk ɪt**
It is also used before uncountable nouns (meaning "an unspecified amount of") and before other nouns in the plural (meaning "an unspecified number of"); in such uses it has the weak form **səm**:
      'Have some more tea' **'hæv səm 'mɔː 'tiː**
    In final position: **sʌm**
                    'I've got some' **aɪv 'gɒt sʌm**

22 'there'
When this word has a demonstrative function, it always occurs in its strong form **ðeə** (**ðeər** before vowels), e.g:
                  'There it is' **'ðeər ɪt 'ɪz**
                  'Put it there' **'pʊt ɪt 'ðeə**

Weak forms: ðə (before consonants)

'There should be a rule' ðə 'ʃʊd bi ə 'ruːl

ðər (before vowels)

'There is' ðər 'ɪz

In final position: the pronunciation may be ðə or ðeə.

'There isn't any, is there?' ðər 'ɪzn̩t eni 'ɪz ðə

or ðər 'ɪzn̩t eni 'ɪz ðeə

The remaining weak-form words are all auxiliary verbs, which are always used in conjunction with (or at least implying) another ("full") verb. It is important to remember that in their negative form (i.e. combined with 'not') they never have the weak pronunciation, and some (e.g. 'don't', 'can't') have different vowels from their non-negative strong forms.

23 'can', 'could'

Weak forms: kən, kəd

'They can wait' 'ðeɪ kən 'weɪt

'He could do it' 'hiː kəd 'duː ɪt

In final position: kæn, kʊd

'I think we can' aɪ 'θɪŋk wi 'kæn

'Most of them could' 'məʊst əv ðəm kʊd

24 'have', 'has', 'had'

Weak forms: əv, əz, əd (with initial h in initial position)

'Which have you seen?' 'wɪtʃ əv ju 'siːn

'Which has been best?' 'wɪtʃ əz biːn 'best

'Most had gone home' 'məʊst əd 'gɒn 'həʊm

In final position: hæv, hæz, hæd

'Yes, we have' 'jes wi 'hæv

'I think she has' aɪ 'θɪŋk ʃi 'hæz

'I thought we had' aɪ 'θɔːt wi 'hæd

25 'shall', 'should'

Weak forms: ʃəl or ʃl̩; ʃəd

'We shall need to hurry' wi ʃl̩ 'niːd tə 'hʌri

'I should forget it' 'aɪ ʃəd fə'get ɪt

In final position: ʃæl, ʃʊd

'I think we shall' aɪ 'θɪŋk wi 'ʃæl

'So you should' 'səʊ ju 'ʃʊd

26 'must'

This word is sometimes used with the sense of forming a conclusion or deduction, e.g. 'she left at 8 o'clock, so she must have arrived by now'; when 'must' is used in this way, it is rather less likely to occur in its weak form than when it is being used in its more familiar sense of "obligation".

Weak forms: məs (before consonants)

'You must try harder' ju məs 'traɪ 'hɑːdə

məst (before vowels)

'He must eat more' hi məst 'iːt 'mɔː

In final position: mʌst

'She certainly must' ʃi 'sɜːtn̩li 'mʌst

27 'do', 'does'

Weak forms:

    'do'   də (before consonants)

'Why do they like it?' 'waɪ də ðeɪ 'laɪk ɪt

du (before vowels)

'Why do all the cars stop?' 'waɪ du ɔːl ðə 'kɑːz 'stɒp

    'does'   dəz

'When does it arrive?' 'wen dəz ɪt ə'raɪv

In final position: duː, dʌz

'We don't smoke, but some people do' 'wiː dəʊnt 'sməʊk bət 'sʌm 'piːpl̩ 'duː

'I think John does' aɪ 'θɪŋk 'dʒɒn dʌz

28 'am', 'are', 'was', 'were'

Weak forms: əm

'Why am I here?' 'waɪ əm aɪ 'hɪə

ə (before consonants)

'Here are the plates' 'hɪər ə ðə 'pleɪts

ər (before vowels)

'The coats are in there' ðə 'kəʊts ər ɪn 'ðeə

wəz

'He was here a minute ago' hi wəz hɪər ə 'mɪnɪt ə'gəʊ

wə (before consonants)

'The papers were late' ðə 'peɪpəz wə 'leɪt

wər (before vowels)

'The questions were easy' ðə 'kwestʃənz wər iːzi

In final position: æm, ɑː, wɒz, wɜː

'She's not as old as I am' ʃiz 'nɒt əz 'əʊld əz 'aɪ æm

'I know the Smiths are' aɪ 'nəʊ ðə 'smɪθs ɑː

'The last record was' ðə 'lɑːst 'rekɔːd wɒz

'They weren't as cold as we were' ðeɪ 'wɜːnt əz 'kəʊld əz 'wiː wɜː

Notes on problems and further reading

This chapter is almost entirely practical. All books about English pronunciation devote a lot of attention to these words. Some of them give a great deal of importance to using weak forms, but do not stress the importance of also knowing when to use the strong forms, something which I feel is very important; see Mortimer, 1984.

Written exercises

In the following sentences, the transcription for the weak-form words is left blank. Fill in the blanks, taking care to use the appropriate form (weak or strong).

1 I want her to park that car over there.

   aɪ wɒnt   pɑːk   kɑːr əʊvə

2 Of all the proposals, the one that you made is the silliest.

   ɔːl prəpəʊzlz wʌn   meɪd ɪz   sɪliəst

3 Jane and Bill could have driven them to and from the party.

  dʒeɪn bɪl   drɪvn̩   pɑːti

4 To come to the point, what shall we do for the rest of the week?

    kʌm   pɔɪnt wɒt   rest   wiːk

5 Has anyone got an idea where it came from?

    enɪwʌn gɒt aɪdɪə weər ɪt keɪm

6 Pedestrians must always use the crossings provided.

  pədestrɪənz   ɔːlwɪz juːz krɒsɪŋz prəvaɪdɪd

7 Each one was a perfect example of the art that had been

  iːtʃ wʌn   pɜːfɪkt ɪgzɑːmpl̩   ɑːt   biːn

developed there.

  dɪveləpt

13 Problems in phonemic analysis

The concept of the phoneme was introduced in Chapter 5, and a few theoretical problems connected with phonemic analysis have been mentioned in other chapters. The general assumption (as in most phonetics books) has been that speech is composed of phonemes and that usually whenever a speech sound is produced by a speaker it is possible to identify which phoneme that sound belongs to. While this is often true, we must recognise that there are exceptions which make us consider some quite serious theoretical problems. From the comparatively simple point of view of learning pronunciation, these problems are not particularly important. However, from the point of view of learning about the phonology of English they are too important to ignore.

There are problems of different types. In some cases, we have difficulty in deciding on the overall phonemic system of the accent we are studying, while in others we are concerned about how a particular sound fits into this system. A number of such problems are discussed below.

13.1 Affricates
The affricates **tʃ** and **dʒ** are, phonetically, composed of a plosive followed by a fricative, as explained in Chapter 6. It is possible to treat each of the pair **tʃ**, **dʒ** as a single consonant phoneme; we will call this the **one-phoneme analysis** of **tʃ**, **dʒ**. It is also possible to say that they are composed of two phonemes each – **t** plus **ʃ** and **d** plus **ʒ** respectively – all of which are already established as independent phonemes of English; this will be called the **two-phoneme analysis** of **tʃ** and **dʒ**. If we adopted the two-phoneme analysis, the words 'church' and 'judge' would be composed of five phonemes each, like this:

$$t - \int - 3\colon - t - \int \qquad d - 3 - \Lambda - d - 3$$

instead of the three phonemes that result from the one-phoneme analysis:

$$t\int - 3\colon - t\int \qquad d3 - \Lambda - d3$$

and there would be no separate **tʃ** and **dʒ** phonemes. But how can we decide which analysis is preferable? The two-phoneme analysis has one main advantage: if there are no separate **tʃ** and **dʒ** phonemes, then our total set of English consonants is smaller. Many phonologists have claimed that one should prefer the analysis which is the most "economical" in the number of phonemes it results in. The argument for this might be based on the claim that when we speak to someone we are using a "code", and the most efficient codes do not use unnecessary symbols. Further, it can be claimed that a phonological analysis is a type of scientific theory, and a scientific theory should be stated as economically as possible. However, it is the one-phoneme analysis that is generally chosen by phonologists. Why is this? There are several arguments; no single one of them is conclusive, but added together they are felt to make the one-phoneme analysis seem preferable. We will look briefly at some of these arguments.

i) One argument could be called "phonetic" or "allophonic": if it could be shown that the phonetic quality of the **t** and **ʃ** (or **d** and **ʒ**) in **tʃ**, **dʒ** is clearly different from realisations of **t**, **ʃ**, **d**, **ʒ** found elsewhere in similar contexts, this would support the analysis of **tʃ**, **dʒ** as separate phonemes. As an example, it might be claimed that **ʃ** in 'hutch' **hʌtʃ** was different (perhaps in having shorter duration) from **ʃ** in 'hush' or 'Welsh' **hʌʃ**, **welʃ**; or it might be claimed that the place of articulation of **t** in 'watch apes' **wɒtʃ eɪps** was different from that of **t** in 'what shapes' **wɒt ʃeɪps**. This argument is a weak one: there is no clear evidence that such phonetic differences exist, and even if there were such evidence, it would be easy to produce explanations for the differences that did not depend on phonemic analyses (e.g. the position of the word boundary in 'watch apes', 'what shapes').

ii) It could be argued that the proposed phonemes **tʃ** and **dʒ** (if one were arguing for the one-phoneme analysis) have distributions similar to other consonants, while other combinations of plosive plus fricative do not. It can easily be shown that **tʃ** and **dʒ** are found initially, medially and finally, and that no other combination (e.g. **pf**, **dz**, **tθ**) has such a wide distribution. However, several consonants *are* generally accepted as phonemes of the BBC accent despite *not* being free to occur in all positions (e.g. **r**, **w**, **j**, **h**, **ŋ**, **ʒ**), so this argument, although supporting the one-phoneme analysis, does not actually *prove* that **tʃ**, **dʒ** must be classed with other single consonant phonemes.

iii) If **tʃ** and **dʒ** were able to combine quite freely with other consonants to form consonant clusters, this would support the one-phoneme analysis. In initial position, however, **tʃ** and **dʒ** never occur in clusters with other consonants. In final position in the syllable, we find that **tʃ** can be followed by **t** (e.g. 'watched' **wɒtʃt**) and **dʒ** by **d** (e.g. 'wedged' **wedʒd**). Final **tʃ** and **dʒ** can be preceded by **l** (e.g. 'squelch' **skweltʃ**, 'bulge' **bʌldʒ**); **ʒ** is never preceded by **l**, and **ʃ** is preceded by **l** only in a few words and names, e.g. 'Welsh', 'Walsh' **welʃ**, **wɒlʃ**. A fairly similar situation is found if we ask if **n** can precede **tʃ** and **dʒ**; some BBC speakers have **ntʃ** in 'lunch', 'French', etc., and never pronounce the sequence **nʃ** within a syllable, while other speakers always have **nʃ** in these contexts and never **ntʃ**. It seems, then, that no contrast between syllable-final **lʃ** and **ltʃ** exists in the BBC accent, and the same appears to be true in relation to **nʃ** and **ntʃ** and to **nʒ** and **ndʒ**. There are no other possibilities for final consonant clusters containing **tʃ** and **dʒ**, except that the pre-final **l** or **n** may occur in combination with post-final **t**, **d** as in 'squelched' **skweltʃt**, 'hinged' **hɪndʒd**. It could not, then, be said that **tʃ** and **dʒ** combine freely with other consonants in forming consonant clusters; this is particularly noticeable in initial position.

How would the two-phoneme analysis affect the syllable-structure framework that was introduced in Chapter 8? Initial **tʃ**, **dʒ** would have to be interpreted as initial **t**, **d** plus post-initial **ʃ**, **ʒ**, with the result that the post-initial set of consonants would have to contain **l**, **r**, **w**, **j** and also **ʃ**, **ʒ** – consonants which are rather different from the other four and which could only combine with **t**, **d**. (The only alternative would be to put **t**, **d** with **s** in the pre-initial category, again with very limited possibilities of combining with another consonant.)

iv) Finally, it has been suggested that if native speakers of English who have not been taught phonetics feel that **tʃ** and **dʒ** are each "one sound", we should be guided by their intuitions and prefer the one-phoneme analysis. The problem with this is that discovering what untrained (or "naive") speakers feel about their own language is not as easy as it might sound. It would be necessary to ask questions like this: "Would you say that the word 'chip' begins with one sound – like 'tip' and 'sip' – or with two sounds – like 'trip' and 'skip'?" But the results would be distorted by the fact that two consonant letters are used in the spelling; to do the test properly one should use illiterate subjects, which raises many further problems.

This rather long discussion of the phonemic status of **tʃ** and **dʒ** shows how difficult it can be to reach a conclusion in phonemic analysis.

For the rest of this chapter a number of other phonological problems will be discussed comparatively briefly. I have already mentioned (in Chapter 6) problems of analysis in connection with the sounds usually transcribed **hw** and **hj**. The velar nasal **ŋ**, described in Chapter 7, also raises a lot of analysis problems; many writers have suggested that the correct analysis is one in which there is no **ŋ** phoneme, and this sound is treated as an allophone of the phoneme **n** that occurs when it precedes the phoneme **g**. It was explained in Chapter 7 that in certain contexts no **g** is pronounced, but it can be claimed that at an abstract level there *is* a **g** phoneme, though in certain contexts the **g** is not actually pronounced. The sound **ŋ** is therefore, according to this theory, an allophone of **n**.

13.2 The English vowel system

The analysis of the English vowel system presented in Chapters 2 and 3 contains a large number of phonemes, and it is not surprising that some phonologists (who believe in the importance of keeping the total number of phonemes small) propose different analyses which contain less than ten vowel phonemes and treat all long vowels and diphthongs as composed of two phonemes each. There are different ways of doing this: one way is to treat long vowels and diphthongs as composed of two vowel phonemes. Starting with a set of basic or "simple" vowel phonemes ɪ, e, æ, ʌ, ɒ, ʊ, ə it is possible to make up long vowels by using short vowels twice. Our usual transcription is given in brackets:

ɪɪ (iː) ææ (ɑː) ɒɒ (ɔː) ʊʊ (uː) əə (ɜː)

This can be made to look less unusual by choosing different symbols for the basic vowels. In this approach, diphthongs are made from a simple vowel phoneme followed by one of ɪ, ʊ, ə, and triphthongs are made from a basic vowel plus one of ɪ, ʊ followed by ə, and are therefore composed of three phonemes.

Another way of doing this kind of analysis is to treat long vowels and diphthongs as composed of a vowel plus a consonant; this may seem a less obvious way of proceeding, but it was for many years the choice of most American phonologists. The idea is that long vowels and diphthongs are composed of a basic vowel phoneme followed by one of j, w, h (we should add r for rhotic accents). Thus the diphthongs could be made up like this (our usual transcription is given in brackets):

ej (eɪ)	əw (əʊ)	ɪh (ɪə)
æj (aɪ)	æw (aʊ)	eh (eə)
ɒj (ɔɪ)		ʊh (ʊə)

Long vowels:

ɪj (iː)	æh (ɑː)	ɒh (ɔː)	əh (ɜː)	ʊw (uː)

Diphthongs and long vowels are now of exactly the same phonological composition. An important point about this analysis is that j, w, h do not otherwise occur finally in the syllable. In this analysis, the inequality of distribution is corrected.

In Chapter 9 we saw how, although ɪ and iː are clearly distinct in most contexts, there are other contexts where we find a sound which cannot clearly be said to belong to one or other of these two phonemes. The suggested solution to this problem was to use the symbol i, which does not represent any single phoneme; a similar proposal was made for u. We use the term **neutralisation** for cases where contrasts between phonemes which exist in other places in the language disappear in particular contexts. There are many other ways of analysing the very complex vowel system of English, some of which are extremely ingenious. Each has its own advantages and disadvantages.

13.3 Syllabic consonants

A final analysis problem that we will consider is that mentioned at the end of Chapter 8: how to deal with syllabic consonants. It has to be recognised that syllabic consonants are a problem: they *are* phonologically different from their non-syllabic counterparts. How do we account for the following minimal pairs, which were given in Chapter 9?

Syllabic	*Non-syllabic*
'coddling' kɒdl̩ŋ	'codling' kɒdlɪŋ
'Hungary' hʌŋgr̩i	'hungry' hʌŋgri

One possibility is to add new consonant phonemes to our list. We could invent the phonemes l̩, r̩, n̩, etc. The distribution of these consonants would be rather limited, but the main problem would be fitting them into the pattern of syllable structure. For a word like 'button' bʌtn̩ or 'bottle' bɒtl̩, it would be necessary to add n̩ and l̩ to the first post-final set; the argument would be extended to include the r̩ in 'Hungary'. But if these consonants now form part of a syllable-final consonant cluster, how do we account for the fact that English speakers hear the consonants as extra syllables? The question might be answered by saying that the new phonemes are to be classed as vowels. Another possibility is to set up a phoneme that we might name **syllabicity**, symbolised with the mark ̩. Then the word 'codling' would consist of the following six phonemes: k · ɒ · d · l · ɪ · ŋ, while the word 'coddling' would consist of the following *seven* phonemes: k · ɒ · d · (l and simultaneously ̩) · ɪ · ŋ. This is superficially an attractive theory, but the proposed phoneme is nothing like the other phonemes we have identified up to this point – putting it simply, it doesn't have any sound.

Some phonologists maintain that a syllabic consonant is really a case of a vowel and a consonant that have become combined. Let us suppose that the vowel is ə. We could then say that, for example, 'Hungary' is phonemically hʌŋgəri while 'hungry' is hʌŋgri; it would then be necessary to say that the vowel phoneme in the phonemic representation is not pronounced as a vowel, but instead causes the following consonant to become syllabic. This is an example of the abstract view of phonology where the way a word is represented phonologically may be significantly different from the actual sequence of sounds heard, so that the phonetic and the phonemic levels are quite widely separated.

13.4 Clusters of s plus plosives

Words like 'spill', 'still', 'skill' are usually represented with the phonemes **p**, **t**, **k** following the **s**. But, as many writers have pointed out, it would be quite reasonable to transcribe them with **b**, **d**, **g** instead. For example, **b**, **d**, **g** are unaspirated while **p**, **t**, **k** in syllable-initial position are usually aspirated. However, in **sp**, **st**, **sk** we find an unaspirated plosive, and there could be a strong argument for transcribing them as **sb**, **sd**, **sg**. We do not do this, perhaps because of the spelling, but it is important to remember that the contrasts between **p** and **b**, between **t** and **d** and between **k** and **g** are neutralised in this context.

13.5 Schwa (ə)

It has been suggested that there is not really a contrast between ə and ʌ, since ə only occurs in weak syllables and no minimal pairs can be found to show a clear contrast between ʌ and ə in unstressed syllables (although there have been some ingenious attempts). This has resulted in a proposal that one phoneme symbol (e.g. ə) be used for representing any occurrence of ə or ʌ, so that 'cup' would be transcribed **'kəp** and 'upper' as **'əpə**. This new ə phoneme would have two allophones, one being [ə] and the other [ʌ]; the stress mark would indicate the [ʌ] allophone and in syllables not marked for stress it would be more likely that [ə] would be pronounced.

Other phonologists have suggested that ə is an allophone of several other vowels; for example, compare the middle two syllables in the words 'economy' **ɪ'kɒnəmi** and 'economic' **ˌiːkə'nɒmɪk** – it appears that when the stress moves away from the syllable containing ɒ the vowel becomes ə. Similarly, compare 'Germanic' **dʒɜː'mænɪk** with 'German' **'dʒɜːmən** – when the stress is taken away from the syllable **mæn**, the vowel weakens to ə. Many similar examples could be constructed with other vowels; some possibilities may be suggested by the list of words given in Section 9.2 to show the different spellings that can be pronounced with ə. The conclusion that could be drawn from this argument is that ə is not a phoneme of English, but is an allophone of several different vowel phonemes when those phonemes occur in an unstressed syllable. The argument is in some ways quite an attractive one, but since it leads to a rather complex and abstract phonemic analysis it is not adopted for this course.

13.6 Distinctive features

Many references have been made to phonology in this course, with the purpose of making use of the concepts and analytical techniques of that subject to help explain various facts about English pronunciation as efficiently as possible. One might call this "applied phonology"; however, the phonological analysis of different languages raises a great number of difficult and interesting theoretical problems, and for a long time the study of phonology "for its own sake" has been regarded as an important area of theoretical linguistics. Within this area of what could be called "pure phonology", problems are examined with little or no reference to their relevance to the language learner. Many different theoretical approaches have been developed, and no area of phonology has been free from critical examination. The very fundamental notion of the phoneme, for example, has been treated in many different ways. One approach that has been given a lot of importance is **distinctive feature analysis**, which is based on the principle that phonemes should be regarded not as independent and indivisible units, but instead as combinations of different features. For example, if we consider the English **d** phoneme, it is easy to show that it differs from the plosives **b** and **g** in its place of articulation (alveolar), from **t** in being lenis, from **s** and **z** in not being fricative, from **n** in not being nasal, and so on. If we look at each of the consonants just mentioned and see which of the features each one has, we get a table like this, where + means that a phoneme does possess that feature and – means that it does not:

	d	b	g	t	s	z	n
alveolar	+	−	−	+	+	+	+
bilabial	−	+	−	−	−	−	−
velar	−	−	+	−	−	−	−
lenis	+	+	+	−	−	+	(+)*
plosive	+	+	+	+	−	−	−
fricative	−	−	−	−	+	+	−
nasal	−	−	−	−	−	−	+

* Since there is no fortis/lenis contrast among nasals this could be left blank

If you look carefully at this table, you will see that the combination of + and − values for each phoneme is different; if two sounds were represented by exactly the same +'s and −'s, then by definition they could not be different phonemes. In the case of the limited set of phonemes used for this example, not all the features are needed: if one wished, it would be possible to dispense with, for example, the feature "velar" and the feature "nasal". The **g** phoneme would still be distinguished from **b** and **d** by being neither alveolar nor bilabial, and **n** would be distinct from plosives and fricatives simply by being neither plosive nor fricative. To produce a complete analysis of all the phonemes of English, other features would be needed for representing other types of consonant, and for vowels and diphthongs. In distinctive feature analysis the features themselves thus become important components of the phonology.

It has been claimed by some writers that distinctive feature analysis is relevant to the study of language learning, and that pronunciation difficulties experienced by learners are better seen as due to the need to learn a particular feature or combination of features than as the absence of particular phonemes. For example, English speakers learning French or German have to learn to produce front rounded vowels. In English it is not necessary to be able to consider vowels which are [+front, +round], whereas this is necessary for French and German; it could be said that the major task for the English-speaking learner of French or German in this case is to learn the combination of these features, not to learn the individual vowels **y**, **ø** and (in French) **œ**.[*]

English, on the other hand, has to be able to distinguish dental from labiodental and alveolar places of articulation, for **θ** to be distinct from **f** and **s** and for **ð** to be distinct from **v** and **z**. This requires an additional feature that most languages do not make use of, and learning this could be seen as a specific task for the learner of English. Distinctive feature phonologists have also claimed that when children are learning their first language, they acquire features rather than individual phonemes.

13.7 Conclusion

This chapter is intended to show that there are many ways of analysing the English phonemic system, each with its own advantages and disadvantages. We need to consider the practical goal of teaching or learning about English pronunciation, and for this purpose a very abstract analysis would be unsuitable. This is one criterion for judging the value of an analysis; unless one believes in carrying out phonological analysis for purely aesthetic reasons, the only other important criterion is whether the analysis is likely to correspond to the representation of sounds in the human brain. We do not yet know much about this, but the brain is so powerful and complex that it is very unlikely that any of the analyses proposed so far bear much resemblance to this reality; they are too heavily influenced by the theoretician's preoccupation with economy, elegance and simplicity.

Notes on problems and further reading

The analysis of **tʃ** and **dʒ** is one of the most intractable problems. The general principles in traditional phoneme theory have been set out by Trubetzkoy (1939); the German original has been translated into English (1969), and the relevant section of this translation is reprinted in Fudge (1973: 65–70). The problem is also discussed in Cruttenden (1994, 157–60). The phonemic analysis of the velar nasal has already been discussed above (see Notes in Chapter 7). The 'double vowel' interpretation of English long vowels was put forward

---

[*] The phonetic symbols represent the following sounds: **y** is a close front rounded vowel (e.g. the vowel in French *tu*, German *Bühne*); **ø** is a close-mid front rounded vowel (e.g. French *peu*, German *schön*); **œ** is an open-mid front rounded vowel (e.g. French *oeuf*).

by MacCarthy (1952) and is used by Kreidler (1989). The 'vowel-plus-semivowel' interpretation of long vowels and diphthongs was almost universally accepted by American (and some British) writers from the 1940s to the 1960s, and still pervades contemporary descriptions. It has the advantage of being economical on phonemes and very 'neat and tidy'. The analysis in this form is presented in Trager and Smith (1951). This work was claimed to provide an analysis that could produce a phonologically distinct representation for all English short vowels, long vowels and diphthongs in all accents. An early attack on this view was made by Sledd (1955: 316–24). In generative phonology the claim is that, at the abstract level, English vowels are simply tense or lax. If they are lax they are realised as short vowels, if tense as diphthongs (this category including what I have been calling long vowels). The quality of the first element of the diphthongs/long vowels is modified by some phonological rules, while other rules supply the second element automatically. This is set out in Chomsky and Halle (1968: 178–87). There is a valuable discussion of the interpretation of the English vowel system with reference to several different accents in Giegerich (1992: Chapter 3), followed by an explanation of the distinctive feature analysis of the English vowel system (Chapter 4) and the consonant system (Chapter 5). A more wide-ranging discussion of distinctive features is given in Clark and Yallop (1995: Chapter 10).

On the interpretation of **sp**, **st**, **sk**, see Davidsen-Nielsen (1969). There is an interesting discussion of the ə – ʌ contrast in Wells (1970: 233–5). The idea that ə is an allophone of many English vowels is not a new one. In generative phonology, ə results from vowel reduction in vowels which have never received stress in the process of the application of stress rules. This is explained – in rather difficult terms – in Chomsky and Halle (1968: 110–26). A clearer treatment of the schwa problem is in Giegerich (1992: 68–9 and 285–7).

Note for teachers

Since this is a theoretical chapter it is difficult to come up with practical work. I do not feel that it is helpful for students to do exercises on using different ways of transcribing phonemes – just learning one set of conventions is difficult enough. Some books on phonology give exercises on the phonemic analysis of other languages (e.g. Katamba, 1989; Roca and Johnson, 1999), but although these are useful, I do not feel that it would be appropriate in this book to divert attention from English. The exercises given below therefore concentrate on bits of phonetically transcribed English which involve problems when a phonemic representation is required.

Written exercises

In this exercise you must look at phonetically transcribed material from different English accents and decide on the best way to interpret and transcribe them phonemically. Information is given where necessary about the meaning of the phonetic symbols.

1   a) 'thing'   [θɪŋg]
     b) 'think'   [θɪŋk]
     c) 'thinking'   [θɪŋkɪŋ]
     d) 'finger'   [fɪŋgə]
     e) 'singer'   [sɪŋgə]
     f) 'singing'   [sɪŋgɪŋ]

2   It often happens in rapid speech that a nasal consonant disappears when it comes between a vowel and another consonant (for example, this may happen to the 'n' in 'front': when this happens the preceding vowel becomes **nasalised** (some of the air escapes through the nose). We symbolise a nasalised vowel in phonetic transcription by putting the ~ diacritic above it; for example, the word 'front' may be pronounced [frʌ̃t]. Nasalised vowels are found in the words given in phonetic transcription below. Transcribe them phonemically.

     a) [sãʊ̃d]
     b) [æ̃gə]
     c) [kɑ̃ːt]
     d) [kæ̃pə]
     e) [bõd]

3   When the **t** phoneme occurs between vowels it is sometimes pronounced as a "tap" (the tongue blade strikes the alveolar ridge sharply, producing a very brief voiced plosive: the phonetic symbol is ɾ); this is very common in American English, and is also found in a number of accents in England: think of a typical

American pronunciation of "getting better" [geɾɪŋ beɾə]. Look at the transcriptions of a number of words given below and see if you can work out (for the accent in question) the environment in which [ɾ] is found.

a) 'betting' [beɾɪŋ]
b) 'bedding' [bedɪŋ]
c) 'attend' [əthend]
d) 'attitude' [æɾɪtuːd]
e) 'time' [tham]
f) 'tight' [thaɪt]

4   Distinctive feature analysis looks at different properties of segments and classes of segments. In the following exercise you must mark the value of each feature in the table for each segment listed on the top row with either a '+' or '−'; you will probably find it useful to look at the IPA chart on p. xi.

	p	d	s	m	z
Continuant					
Alveolar					
Voiced					

5   In all the following sets of segments (a–f), all segments in the set possess some characteristic feature which they have in common and which may distinguish them from other segments. Can you identify what this common feature might be for each set?

a) English iː, ɪ, uː, ʊ; Cardinal vowels [i], [e], [u], [o]
b) t d n l s tʃ dʒ ʃ ʒ r
c) b f v k g h
d) p t k f θ s ʃ tʃ
e) uː ɔː əʊ aʊ
f) l r w j

14 Aspects of connected speech

Many years ago scientists tried to develop machines that produced speech from a vocabulary of pre-recorded words; the machines were designed to join these words together to form sentences. For very limited messages, such as those of a "talking clock", this technique was usable, but for other purposes the quality of the speech was so unnatural that it was practically unintelligible. In recent years, developments in computer technology have led to big improvements in this way of producing speech, but the inadequacy of the original "mechanical speech" approach has many lessons to teach us about pronunciation teaching and learning. In looking at connected speech it is useful to bear in mind the difference between the way humans speak and what would be found in "mechanical speech".

14.1 Rhythm

The notion of **rhythm** involves some noticeable event happening at regular intervals of time; one can detect the rhythm of a heart-beat, of a flashing light or of a piece of music. It has often been claimed that English speech is rhythmical, and that the rhythm is detectable in the regular occurrence of stressed syllables; of course, it is not suggested that the timing is as regular as a clock: the regularity of occurrence is only relative. The theory that English has **stress-timed rhythm** implies that stressed syllables will tend to occur at relatively regular intervals whether they are separated by unstressed syllables or not; this would not be the case in "mechanical speech". An example is given below. In this sentence, the stressed syllables are given numbers: syllables 1 and 2 are not separated by any unstressed syllables, 2 and 3 are separated by one unstressed syllable, 3 and 4 by two and 4 and 5 by three.

1	2	3	4	5
'Walk	'down the	'path to	the	'end of the	ca 'nal

'Walk 'down the 'path to the 'end of the ca 'nal

The stress-timed rhythm theory states that the times from each stressed syllable to the next will tend to be the same, irrespective of the number of intervening unstressed syllables. The theory also claims that while some languages (e.g. Russian and Arabic) have stress-timed rhythm similar to that of English, others (such as French, Telugu and Yoruba) have a different rhythmical structure called **syllable-timed rhythm**; in these languages, all syllables, whether stressed or unstressed, tend to occur at regular time-intervals and the time between stressed syllables will be shorter or longer in proportion to the number of unstressed syllables. Some writers have developed theories of English rhythm in which a unit of rhythm, the **foot**, is used (with an obvious parallel in the metrical analysis of verse); the foot begins with a stressed syllable and includes all following unstressed syllables up to (but not including) the following stressed syllable. The example sentence given above would be divided into feet as follows:

1	2	3	4	5
'Walk	'down the	'path to the	'end of the ca	'nal

Some theories of rhythm go further than this, and point to the fact that some feet are stronger than others, producing strong–weak patterns in larger pieces of speech above the level of the foot. To understand how this could be done, let's start with a simple example: the word 'twenty' has one strong and one weak syllable, forming one foot. A diagram of its rhythmical structure can be made, where **s** stands for "strong" and **w** stands for "weak".

s   w
twen   ty

The word 'places' has the same form:

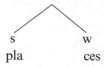

Now consider the phrase 'twenty places', where 'places' normally carries stronger stress than 'twenty', i.e. is rhythmically stronger. We can make our "tree diagram" grow to look like this:

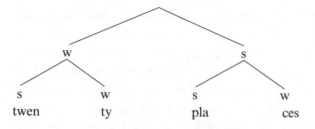

If we then look at this phrase in the context of a longer phrase 'twenty places further back', and build up the 'further back' part in a similar way, we would end up with an even more elaborate structure:

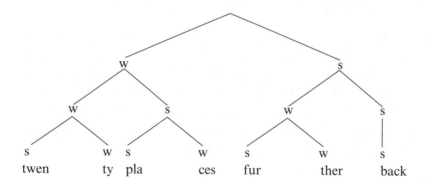

By analysing speech in this way we are able to show the relationships between strong and weak elements, and the different levels of stress that we find. The strength of any particular syllable can be measured by counting up the number of times an s symbol occurs above it; the levels in the sentence shown above can be diagrammed like this (leaving out syllables that have never received stress at any level):

136

						s
	s			s		s
s	s			s		s
twen	ty	pla	ces	fur	ther	back

The above "**metrical grid**" may be correct for very slow speech, but we must now look at what happens to the rhythm in normal speech: many English speakers would feel that, although in 'twenty places' the right-hand foot is the stronger, the word 'twenty' is stronger than 'places' in 'twenty places further back' when spoken in conversational style. It is widely claimed that English speech tends towards a regular alternation between stronger and weaker, and tends to adjust stress levels to bring this about. The effect is particularly noticeable in cases such as the following, which all show the effect of what is called **stress-shift**:

> compact (adjective) **kəm'pækt** *but* compact disc **'kɒmpækt 'dɪsk**
> thirteen **θɜː'tiːn** *but* thirteenth place **'θɜːtiːnθ 'pleɪs**
> Westminster **west'mɪnstə** *but* Westminster Abbey **'westmɪnstər 'æbi**

In brief, it seems that stresses are altered according to context: we need to be able to explain how and why this happens, but this is a difficult question and one for which we have only partial answers.

An additional factor is that in speaking English we vary in how rhythmically we speak: sometimes we speak very rhythmically (this is typical of some styles of public speaking) while at other times we may speak arhythmically (that is, without rhythm) if we are hesitant or nervous. Stress-timed rhythm is thus perhaps characteristic of one style of speaking, not of English speech as a whole; one always speaks with *some* degree of rhythmicality, but the degree varies between a minimum value (arhythmical) and a maximum value (completely stress-timed rhythm).

It follows from what was stated earlier that in a stress-timed language all the feet are supposed to be of roughly the same duration. Many foreign learners of English are made to practise speaking English with a regular rhythm, often with the teacher beating time or clapping hands on the stressed syllables. It must be pointed out, however, that the evidence for the existence of truly stress-timed rhythm is not strong. There are many laboratory techniques for measuring time in speech, and measurement of the time intervals between stressed syllables in connected English speech has not shown the expected regularity; moreover, using the same measuring techniques on different languages, it has not been possible to show a real difference between "stress-timed" and "syllable-timed" languages. Experiments have shown that we tend to hear speech as more rhythmical than it actually is, and one suspects that this is what the proponents of the stress-timed rhythm theory have been led to do in their auditory analysis of English rhythm. However, one ought to keep an open mind on the subject, remembering that the large-scale, objective study of suprasegmental aspects of real speech is difficult to carry out, and much research remains to be done.

What, then, is the practical value of the traditional "rhythm exercise" for foreign learners? The argument about rhythm should not make us forget the very important difference in English between strong and weak syllables. Some languages do not have such a noticeable difference (which may, perhaps, explain the subjective impression of "syllable-timing"), and for native speakers of such languages who are learning English it can be helpful to practise repeating strongly rhythmical utterances since this forces the speaker to concentrate on making unstressed syllables weak. Speakers of languages like Japanese, Hungarian and Spanish – which do not have weak syllables to anything like the same extent as English does – may well find such exercises of some value (as long as they are not overdone to the point where learners feel they have to speak English as though they were reciting verse).

14.2 Assimilation

The device mentioned earlier that produces "mechanical speech" would contain all the words of English, each having been recorded in isolation. A significant difference in natural connected speech is the way that sounds belonging to one word can cause changes in sounds belonging to neighbouring words. Assuming that we know how the phonemes of a particular word would be realised when the word is pronounced in isolation, in cases where we find a phoneme realised differently as a result of being near some other phoneme belonging to a neighbouring word we call this an instance of **assimilation**. Assimilation is something which varies in extent according to speaking rate and style: it is more likely to be found in rapid, casual speech and less likely in slow, careful speech. Sometimes the difference caused by assimilation is very noticeable, and sometimes it is very slight. Generally speaking, the cases that have most often been described are assimilations affecting consonants. As an example, consider a case where two words are combined, the first of which ends with a single final consonant (which we will call C^f) and the second of which starts with a single initial consonant (which we will call C^i); we can construct a diagram like this:

$$- - - - - C^f \mid C^i - - - -$$

       word
      boundary

If C^f changes to become like C^i in some way, then the assimilation is called **regressive** (the phoneme that comes first is affected by the one that comes after it); if C^i changes to become like C^f in some way, then the assimilation is called **progressive**. In what ways can a consonant change? We have seen that the main differences between consonants are of three types:

i) differences in place of articulation;
ii) differences in manner of articulation;
iii) differences in voicing.

In parallel with this, we can identify assimilation of place, of manner and of voicing in consonants. Assimilation of place is most clearly observable in some cases where a final consonant (C^f) with alveolar place of articulation is followed by an initial consonant (C^i) with a place of articulation that is *not* alveolar. For example, the final consonant in 'that' ðæt is alveolar t. In rapid, casual speech the t will become p before a bilabial consonant, as in: 'that person' ðæp pɜːsn̩; 'light blue' laɪp bluː; 'meat pie' miːp paɪ. Before a dental consonant, t will change to a dental plosive, for which the symbol is t̪, as in: 'that thing' ðæt̪ θɪŋ; 'get those' get̪ ðəʊz; 'cut through' kʌt̪ θruː. Before a velar consonant, the t will become k, as in: 'that case' ðæk keɪs; 'bright colour' braɪk kʌlə; 'quite good' kwaɪk gʊd. In similar contexts d would become b, d̪ and g, respectively, and n would become m, n̪ and ŋ. However, the same is not true of the other alveolar consonants: s and z behave differently, the only noticeable change being that **s** becomes **ʃ**, and **z** becomes **ʒ** when followed by **ʃ** or **j**, as in: 'this shoe' **ðɪʃ ʃuː**; 'those years' **ðəʊʒ jɪəz**. It is important to note that the consonants that have undergone assimilation have not disappeared; in the above examples, the duration of the consonants remains more or less what one would expect for a two-consonant cluster. Assimilation of place is only noticeable in this regressive assimilation of alveolar consonants; it is not something that foreign learners need to learn to do.

Assimilation of manner is much less noticeable, and is only found in the most rapid and casual speech; generally speaking, the tendency is again for regressive assimilation and the change in manner is most likely to be towards an "easier" consonant – one which makes less obstruction to the airflow. It is thus possible to find cases where a final plosive becomes a fricative or nasal (e.g. 'that side' **ðæs saɪd**, 'good night' **gʊn naɪt**), but most unlikely that a final fricative or nasal would become a plosive. In one particular case we find progressive assimilation of manner, when a word-initial **ð** follows a plosive or nasal at the end of a preceding word: it is very common to find that the C^i becomes identical in manner to the C^f but with dental place of articulation. For example (the arrow symbol means "becomes"):

'in the'	**ɪn ðə**	→	**ɪn̪n̪ə**
'get them'	**get ðəm**	→	**get̪t̪əm**
'read these'	**riːd ðiːz**	→	**riːd̪d̪iːz**

It seems that the **ð** phoneme frequently occurs with no discernible friction noise.

Assimilation of voice is also found, but again only in a limited way. Only regressive assimilation of voice is found across word boundaries, and then only of one type; since this matter is important for foreign learners we will look at it in some detail. If C^f is a lenis (i.e. "voiced") consonant and C^i is fortis ("voiceless") we often find that the lenis consonant has no voicing; this is not a very noticeable case of assimilation, since, as was explained in Chapter 4, initial and final lenis consonants usually have little or no voicing anyway. When C^f is fortis ("voiceless") and C^i lenis ("voiced"), a context in which in many languages C^f would become voiced, assimilation of voice never takes place; consider the following example: 'I like that black dog' **aɪ laɪk ðæt blæk dɒg**. It is typical of many foreign learners of English that they allow regressive assimilation of voicing to change the final **k** of 'like' to **g**, the final **t** of 'that' to **d** and the final **k** of 'black' to **g**. This creates a very strong impression of a foreign accent, and is something that should obviously be avoided.

Up to this point we have been looking at some fairly clear cases of assimilation across word boundaries. However, similar effects are also observable across morpheme boundaries and to some extent also within the morpheme. Sometimes in the latter case it seems that the assimilation is rather different from the word-boundary examples; for example, if in a syllable-final consonant cluster a nasal consonant precedes a plosive or a fricative in the same morpheme, then the place of articulation of the nasal is always determined by the place of articulation of the other consonant; thus: 'bump' **bʌmp**, 'tenth' **tenθ**, 'hunt' **hʌnt**, 'bank' **bæŋk**. It could be said that this assimilation has become fixed as part of the phonological structure of English syllables, since exceptions are almost non-existent. A similar example of a type of assimilation that has become fixed is the progressive assimilation of voice with the suffixes **s** and **z**; when a verb carries a third person singular '-s' suffix, or a noun carries an '-s' plural suffix or an '-'s' possessive suffix, that suffix will be pronounced as **s** if the preceding consonant is fortis ("voiceless") and as **z** if the preceding consonant is lenis ("voiced"), thus:

'cats' **kæts**	'dogs' **dɒgz**
'jumps' **dʒʌmps**	'runs' **rʌnz**
'Pat's' **pæts**	'Pam's' **pæmz**

Much more could be said about assimilation but, from the point of view of learning or teaching English pronunciation, to do so would not be very useful. It is essentially a natural phenomenon that can be seen in any sort of complex physical activity, and the only important matter is to remember the restriction, specific to English, on voicing assimilation mentioned above.

Assimilation creates something of a problem for phoneme theory; when, for example, **d** in 'good' **gʊd** becomes **g** in the context '. . . girl' (**gʊg gɜːl**) or **b** in the context '. . . boy' (**gʊb bɔɪ**), should we say that one phoneme has been substituted for another? If we do this, how do we describe the assimilation in 'good thing', where **d** becomes dental **d** (**d̪**) before the **θ** of 'thing', or in 'good food', where **d** becomes a labiodental plosive before the **f** in 'food'? English has no dental or labiodental plosive phonemes, so in these cases, although there is clearly assimilation, there could not be said to be a substitution of one phoneme for another. The alternative is to say that assimilation causes a phoneme to be realised by a different allophone; this would mean that, in the case of **gʊg gɜːl** and **gʊb bɔɪ**, the phoneme **d** of 'good' has velar and bilabial allophones. Traditionally, phonemes were supposed not to overlap in their allophones, so that the only plosives that could have allophones with bilabial place of articulation were **p** and **b**; this restriction is no longer looked on as so important.

14.3 Elision

AU14

The nature of **elision** may be stated quite simply: under certain circumstances sounds disappear; one might express this in more technical language by saying that in certain circumstances a phoneme may be realised as **zero**, or have **zero realisation** or be **deleted**. As with assimilation, elision is typical of rapid, casual speech. Producing elisions is something which foreign learners do not need to learn to do, but it is important for them to be aware that when native speakers of English talk to each other, quite a number of phonemes that the foreigner might expect to hear are not actually pronounced. We will look at some examples, although only a small number of the many possibilities can be given here.

i) Loss of weak vowel after **p, t, k**.

    In words like 'potato', 'tomato', 'canary', 'perhaps', 'today', the vowel in the first syllable may disappear; the aspiration of the initial plosive takes up the whole of the middle portion of the syllable, resulting in these pronunciations (where **h** indicates aspiration):

    pʰˈteɪtəʊ tʰˈmɑːtəʊ kʰˈneəri pʰˈhæps tʰˈdeɪ

ii) Weak vowel + **n, l** or **r** becomes syllabic (consonant see Chapter 9 for details of syllabic consonants); for example:

    'tonight' **tn̩aɪt**, 'police' **pl̩iːs**, 'correct' **kr̩ekt**

iii) Avoidance of complex consonant clusters.

It has been said that no normal English speaker would ever pronounce all the consonants between the last two words of the following:

'George the Sixth's throne' dʒɔːdʒ ðə sɪksθs θrəʊn

Though this is not impossible to pronounce, something like sɪksθrəʊn is more likely. In clusters of three plosives or two plosives plus a fricative, the middle plosive may disappear, so that the following pronunciations result:

'acts' æks, 'looked back' lʊk bæk, 'scripts' skrɪps

iv) Loss of final v in 'of' before consonants; for example:

'lots of them' lɒts ə ðəm, 'waste of money' weɪst ə mʌni

It is difficult to know whether **contractions** of grammatical words should be regarded as examples of elision or not. The fact that they are regularly represented with special spelling forms makes them seem rather different from the above examples. The best-known cases are:

- 'had', 'would': spelt 'd, pronounced d (after vowels), əd (after consonants);
- 'is', 'has': spelt 's, pronounced s (after fortis consonants), z (after lenis consonants), except that after s, z, ʃ, ʒ, tʃ, dʒ 'is' is pronounced ɪz and 'has' is pronounced əz in contracted form;
- 'will': spelt 'll, pronounced l (after vowels), l̩ (after consonants);
- 'have': spelt 've, pronounced v (after vowels), əv (after consonants);
- 'not': spelt n't, pronounced nt (after vowels), n̩t (after consonants)
  (there are also vowel changes associated with n't, e.g. 'can' kæn – 'can't' kɑːnt; 'do' duː – 'don't' dəʊnt; 'shall' ʃæl – 'shan't' ʃɑːnt);
- 'are': spelt 're, pronounced ə after vowels, usually with some change in the preceding vowel, e.g. 'you' juː – 'you're' jʊə or jɔː, 'we' wiː – 'we're' wɪə, 'they' ðeɪ – 'they're' ðeə; linking r is used when a vowel follows, as explained in the next section. Contracted 'are' is also pronounced as ə or ər when following a consonant.

14.4 Linking

In our hypothetical "mechanical speech" all words would be separate units placed next to each other in sequence; in real connected speech, however, we sometimes link words together in special ways. The most familiar case is the use of **linking r**; the phoneme **r** does not occur in syllable-final position in the BBC accent, but when a word's spelling suggests a final **r**, and a word beginning with a vowel follows, the usual pronunciation is to pronounce with **r**. For example:

| 'here' **hɪə** | *but* | 'here are' **hɪər ə** |
| 'four' **fɔː** | *but* | 'four eggs' **fɔːr egz** |

BBC speakers often use **r** in a similar way to link words ending with a vowel, even when there is no "justification" from the spelling, as in:

'Formula A' **fɔːmjələr eɪ**
'Australia all out' **ɒstreɪliər ɔːl aʊt**
'media event' **miːdiər ɪvent**

This has been called **intrusive r**; some English speakers and teachers still regard this as incorrect or sub-standard pronunciation, but it is undoubtedly widespread.

"Linking" and "intrusive r" are special cases of **juncture**; this name refers to the relationship between one sound and the sounds that immediately precede and follow it, and it has been given some importance in phonological theory. If we take the two words 'my turn' **maɪ tɜːn**, the relationship between **m** and **aɪ**, between **t** and **ɜː** and between **ɜː** and **n** is said to be one of **close juncture**. The sound **m** is preceded by silence and **n** is followed by silence, and so **m** and **n** are said to be in a position of **external open juncture**. The problem lies in deciding what the relationship is between **aɪ** and **t**; since we do not usually pause between words, there is no silence (or external open juncture) to indicate word division and to justify the space left in the transcription. But if English speakers hear **maɪ tɜːn** they can usually recognise this as 'my turn' and not 'might earn'. This is where the problem of internal open juncture (usually just called "juncture" for short) becomes apparent. What is it that makes perceptible the difference between **maɪ tɜːn** and **maɪt ɜːn**? The answer is that in the one case the **t** is aspirated (initial in 'turn'), and in the other case it is not (being final in 'might'). In addition to this, the **aɪ** diphthong is shorter in 'might', but we will ignore this for the sake of a simpler argument. If a difference in meaning is caused by the difference between aspirated and unaspirated **t**, how can we avoid the conclusion that English has a phonemic contrast between aspirated and unaspirated **t**? The answer is, of course, that the position of a word boundary has some effect on the realisation of the **t** phoneme; this is one of the many cases in which the occurrence of different allophones can only be properly explained by making reference to units of grammar (something which was for a long time disapproved of by many phonologists).

Many ingenious minimal pairs have been invented to show the significance of juncture, a few of which are given below:

- 'might rain' **maɪt reɪn** (**r** voiced when initial in 'rain', **aɪ** short), vs. 'my train' **maɪ treɪn** (**r** voiceless following **t** in 'train')

- 'all that I'm after today' **ɔːl ðət aɪm ɑːftə tədeɪ** (**t** unaspirated when final in 'that')
  'all the time after today' **ɔːl ðə taɪm ɑːftə tədeɪ** (**t** aspirated when initial in 'time')

- 'he lies' **hiː laɪz** ("clear l" initial in 'lies')
  'heal eyes' **hiːl aɪz** ("dark l" final in 'heal')

- 'keep sticking' **kiːp stɪkɪŋ** (**t** unaspirated after **s**; **iː** short)
  'keeps ticking' **kiːps tɪkɪŋ** (**t** aspirated in 'ticking')

Of course, the context in which the words occur almost always makes it clear where the boundary comes, and the juncture information is then redundant.

It should by now be clear that there is a great deal of difference between the way words are pronounced in isolation and in the context of connected speech. It would not be practical or useful to teach all learners of English to produce assimilations; practice in making elisions is more useful, and it is clearly valuable to do exercises related to rhythm and linking. Perhaps the most important consequence of what has been described in this chapter is that learners of English must be made very clearly aware of the problems that they will meet in listening to colloquial, connected speech.

Notes on problems and further reading

14.1 English rhythm is a controversial subject on which widely differing views have been expressed. On one side there are writers such as Abercrombie (1967) and Halliday (1967) who have set out an elaborate theory of the rhythmical structure of English speech (including foot theory). On the other side there are sceptics like Crystal (1969) who reject the idea of an inherent rhythmical pattern. The distinction between physically measurable time intervals and subjective impressions of rhythmicality is discussed in Roach (1982) and Lehiste (1977). Adams (1979) presents a review and experimental study of the subject, and concludes that, despite the theoretical problems, there is practical value in teaching rhythm to learners of English. The treatment of rhythmicality as a matter of degree is presented in Crystal (1969: 161–5). The "stress-timed / syllable-timed" dichotomy is generally agreed in modern work to be an oversimplification; a more common view is that all languages display characteristics of both types of rhythm, but may be closer to one or the other; see Mitchell (1969) and Dauer (1983). Dauer's theory makes possible comparisons between different languages in terms of their relative positions on a scale from maximally stress-timed to maximally syllable-timed (see for example Dimitrova, 1997).

For some writers concerned with English language teaching, the notion of rhythm is a more practical matter of making a sufficiently clear difference between strong and weak syllables, rather than concentrating on a rigid timing pattern, as I suggest at the end of Section 14.1; see, for example, Taylor (1981); also, Mortimer (1984) contains practice material on rhythm.

The treatment of rhythmical hierarchy is based on the theory of metrical phonology. Hogg and McCully (1987) give a full explanation of this, but it is difficult material. Goldsmith (1990: Chapter 4), and Katamba (1989: Chapter 11.1) are briefer and somewhat simpler. A recent paper by Fudge (1999) discusses the relationship between syllables, words and feet. James (1988) explores the relevance of metrical phonology to language learning.

14.2 Assimilation of place with specific reference to alveolar consonants is described in Gimson (1960). It is important to realise that the traditional view of assimilation as a change from one phoneme to another is naive; modern instrumental studies in the broader field of coarticulation show that when assimilation happens one can often show how there is some sort of combination of articulatory gestures. In 'good girl', for example, it is not a simple matter of the first word ending *either* in **d** *or* in **g**, but rather a matter of the extent to which alveolar and/or velar closures are achieved. There may be an alveolar closure immediately preceding and overlapping with a velar closure; there may be simultaneous alveolar and velar closure, or a velar closure followed by slight contact but not closure in the alveolar region. There are many other possibilities.

14.3   An essential part of acquiring fluency in English is learning to produce connected speech without gaps between words, and this is the practical importance of linking. There are several papers on "intrusive r": see Windsor Lewis (1975), Pring (1976), Windsor Lewis (1977) and Fox (1978).

An obvious question to be asked in relation to juncture is whether 'internal open juncture' can actually be heard. Jones (1931) implies that it can, but experimental work (e.g. O'Connor and Tooley, 1964) suggests that in many cases it is not perceptible unless a speaker is deliberately trying to avoid ambiguity. It is interesting to note that some phonologists of the 1950s and 1960s felt it necessary to invent a 'phoneme' of juncture in order to be able to transcribe minimal pairs like 'grey tape' / 'great ape' unambiguously without having to refer to grammatical boundaries; see, for example, Trager and Smith (1951).

Notes for teachers
There is a lot of disagreement about the importance of the various topics in this chapter from the language teacher's point of view. My feeling is that two separate matters are sometimes mixed up: the practice and study of connected speech is agreed by everyone to be of great importance, but this can sometimes result in some relatively unimportant aspects of speech (e.g. assimilation, juncture) being given more emphasis than they should.

In looking at the importance of studying aspects of speech above the segmental level some writers have claimed that learners can come to identify an overall "feel" of the pronunciation of the language being learned. Differences between languages have been described in terms of their **articulatory settings**, that is, overall articulatory posture, by Honikman (1964). She describes such factors as lip mobility and tongue-setting for English, French and other languages. The notion seems a useful one, although it is difficult to confirm these settings scientifically.

Audio Unit 14 is liable to come as something of a surprise to students who have not had the experience of examining colloquial English speech before. The main message to get across is that concentration on selective, analytic listening will help them to recognise what is being said, and that practice usually brings confidence.

Written exercises

1   Divide the following sentences up into feet, using a single vertical line (|) as a boundary symbol. If a sentence starts with an unstressed syllable, leave it out of consideration – it doesn't belong in a foot.

   a)   A bird in the hand is worth two in the bush.
   b)   Over a quarter of a century has elapsed since his death.
   c)   Computers consume a considerable amount of money and time.
   d)   Most of them have arrived on the bus.
   e)   Newspaper editors are invariably underworked.

2   Draw tree diagrams of the rhythmical structure of the following phrases.
   a)   Christmas present
   b)   Rolls Royce
   c)   pet food dealer
   d)   Rolls-Royce rally event

3   The following sentences are given in spelling and in a "slow, careful" phonemic transcription. Rewrite the phonemic transcription as a "broad phonetic" one so as to show likely assimilations, elisions and linking.

a) One   cause   of asthma   is   supposed   to be allergies
   wʌn   kɔːz   əv æsθmə   ɪz   səpəʊzd   tə bi ælədʒiz
   [   ]

b) What the urban population could use is better trains
   wɒt   ði   ɜːbən pɒpjəleɪʃn̩ kʊd   juːz ɪz betə   treɪnz
   [   ]

c) She   acts   particularly   well in the first   scene
   ʃi   ækts   pətɪkjələli   wel ɪn ðə fɜːst   siːn
   [   ]

15 Intonation 1

Many of the previous chapters have been concerned with the description of phonemes, and in Section 5.2 it was pointed out that the subject of phonology includes not just this aspect (which is usually called **segmental phonology**) but also several others. In Chapters 10 and 11, for example, we studied stress. Clearly, stress has linguistic importance and is therefore an aspect of the phonology of English that must be described, but it is not usually regarded as something that is related to individual segmental phonemes; normally, stress is said to be something that is applied to (or is a property of) syllables, and is therefore part of the **suprasegmental phonology** of English. Another part of suprasegmental phonology is **intonation**, and the next five chapters are devoted to this subject.

What is intonation? No definition is completely satisfactory, but any attempt at a definition must recognise that the **pitch** of the voice plays the most important part. Only in very unusual situations do we speak with fixed, unvarying pitch, and when we speak normally the pitch of our voice is constantly changing. One of the most important tasks in analysing intonation is to listen to the speaker's pitch and recognise what it is doing; this is not an easy thing to do, and it seems to be a quite different skill from that acquired in studying segmental phonetics. We describe pitch in terms of **high** and **low**, and some people find it difficult to relate what they hear in someone's voice to a scale ranging from low to high. We should remember that "high" and "low" are arbitrary choices for end-points of the pitch scale. It would be perfectly reasonable to think of pitch as ranging instead from "light" to "heavy", for example, or from "left" to "right", and people who have difficulty in "hearing" intonation patterns are generally only having difficulty in relating what they hear (which is the same as what everyone else hears) to this "pseudo-spatial" representation.

It is very important to make the point that we are not interested in all aspects of a speaker's pitch; the only things that should interest us are those which carry some linguistic information. If a speaker tries to talk while riding fast on a horse, his or her pitch will make a lot of sudden rises and falls as a result of the irregular movement; this is something which is outside the speaker's control and therefore cannot be linguistically significant. Similarly, if we take two speakers at random we will almost certainly find that one speaker typically speaks with lower pitch than the other; the difference between the two speakers is not linguistically significant because their habitual pitch level is determined by their physical structure. But an individual speaker does have control over his or her own pitch, and may choose to speak with a higher than normal pitch; this is something which *is* potentially of linguistic significance.

A word of caution is needed in connection with the word **pitch**. Strictly speaking, this should be used to refer to an auditory sensation experienced by the hearer. The rate of vibration of the vocal folds – something which is physically measurable, and which is related to activity on the part of the speaker – is the **fundamental frequency** of voiced sounds, and should not be called 'pitch'. However, as long as this distinction is understood, it is generally agreed that the term 'pitch' is a convenient one to use informally to refer both to the subjective sensation and to the objectively measurable fundamental frequency.

We have established that for pitch differences to be linguistically significant, it is a necessary condition that they should be under the speaker's control. There is another necessary condition and that is that a pitch difference must be **perceptible**; it is possible to detect differences in the **frequency** of the vibration of a speaker's voice by means of laboratory instruments, but these differences may not be great enough to be heard by a listener as differences in pitch. Finally, it should be remembered that in looking for linguistically significant aspects of speech we must always be looking for *contrasts*; one of the most important things about any unit of phonology or grammar is the set of items it contrasts with. We know how to establish which phonemes are in contrast with **b** in the context -**ɪn**; we can substitute other phonemes (e.g. **p**, **s**) to change the identity of the word from 'bin' to 'pin' to 'sin'. Can we establish such units and contrasts in intonation?

15.1 Form and function in intonation

To summarise what was said above, we want to know the answers to two questions about English speech:

i)   What can we observe when we study pitch variations?
ii) What is the linguistic importance of the phenomena we observe?

These questions might be rephrased more briefly as:

i)   What is the **form** of intonation?
ii) What is the **function** of intonation?

We will begin by looking at intonation in the shortest piece of speech we can find – the single syllable. At this point a new term will be introduced: we need a name for a continuous piece of speech beginning and ending with a clear pause, and we will call this an **utterance**. In this chapter, then, we are going to look at the intonation of one-syllable utterances. These are quite common, and give us a comparatively easy introduction to the subject.

Two common one-syllable utterances are 'yes' and 'no'. The first thing to notice is that we have a choice of saying these with the pitch remaining at a constant level, or with the pitch changing from one level to another. The word we use for the overall behaviour of the pitch in these examples is **tone**; a one-syllable word can be said with either a **level tone** or a **moving tone**. If you try saying 'yes' or 'no' with a level tone (rather as though you were trying to sing them on a steady note) you may find the result does not sound natural, and indeed English speakers do not use level tones on one-syllable utterances very frequently. Moving tones are more common. If English speakers want to say 'yes' or 'no' in a definite, final manner they will probably use a **falling** tone – one which descends from a higher to a lower pitch. If they want to say 'yes?' or 'no?' in a questioning manner they may say it with a **rising** tone – a movement from a lower pitch to a higher one.

Notice that already, in talking about different tones, some idea of function has been introduced; speakers are said to select from a choice of tones according to how they want the utterance to be heard, and it is implied that the listener will hear one-syllable utterances said with different tones as sounding different in some way. During the development of modern phonetics in the twentieth century it was for a long time hoped that scientific study of intonation would make it possible to state what the function of each different aspect of intonation was, and that foreign learners could then be taught rules to enable them to use intonation in the way that native speakers use it. Few people now believe this to be possible. It is certainly possible to produce a few general rules, and some will be given in this course, just as a few general rules for word stress were given in Chapters 10 and 11. However, these rules are certainly not adequate as a complete practical guide to how to use English intonation. My treatment of intonation is based on the belief that foreign learners of English at advanced levels who may use this course should be given training to make them better able to recognise and copy English intonation. The only really efficient way to learn to *use* the intonation of a language is the way a child acquires the intonation of its first language, and the training referred to above should help the adult learner of English to acquire English intonation in a similar (though much slower) way – through listening to and talking to English speakers. It is perhaps a discouraging thing to say, but learners of English who are not able to talk regularly with native speakers of English, or who are not able at least to listen regularly to colloquial English, are not likely to learn English intonation, although they may learn very good pronunciation of the segments and use stress correctly.

15.2. Tone and tone languages ⏵ AU15, Exs 1–3

In the preceding section we mentioned three simple possibilities for the intonation used in pronouncing the one-word utterances 'yes' and 'no'. These were: level, fall and rise. It will often be necessary to use symbols to represent tones, and for this we will use marks placed before the syllable in the following way (phonemic transcription will not be used in these examples – words are given in spelling):

Level	_yes	_no
Falling	ˎyes	ˎno
Rising	ˏyes	ˏno

Obviously, this simple system for tone transcription could be extended, if we wished, to cover a greater number of possibilities. For example, if it were important to distinguish between a high level and low level tone for English we could do it in this way:

High level	ˉyes	ˉno
Low level	_yes	_no

Although in English we do on occasions say ˉyes or ˉno and on other occasions _yes or _no, no speaker of English would say that the meaning of the words 'yes' and 'no' is different with the different tones. (As will be seen below, we will not use the symbols for high and low level tones in the description of English intonation.) But there are many languages in which the tone can determine the meaning of a word, and changing from one tone to another can completely change the meaning. For example, in Kono, a language of West Africa, we find the following (meanings given in brackets):

High level	ˉbɛŋ ('uncle')	ˉbuu ('horn')
Low level	_bɛŋ ('greedy')	_buu ('to be cross')

Similarly, while we can hear a difference between English _yes, ˏyes and ˎyes, and between _no, ˏno and ˎno, there is not a difference in meaning in such a clear-cut way as in Mandarin Chinese, where, for example, ˉma means 'mother', ˏma means 'hemp' and ˎma means 'scold'. Languages such as the above are called **tone languages**; although to most speakers of European languages they may seem strange and exotic, such languages are in fact spoken by a very large proportion of the world's population. In addition to the many dialects of Chinese, many other languages of South-East Asia (e.g. Thai, Vietnamese) are tone languages; so are very many African languages, particularly those of the South and West, and a considerable number of Native American languages. English, however, is not a tone language, and the function of tone is much more difficult to define than in a tone language.

15.3 Complex tones and pitch height

We have introduced three simple tones that can be used on one-syllable English utterances: level, fall and rise. However, other more complex tones are also used. One that is quite frequently found is the **fall–rise** tone, where the pitch descends and then rises again. Another complex tone, much less frequently used, is the **rise–fall** in which the pitch follows the opposite movement. We will not consider any more complex tones, since these are not often encountered and are of little importance.

One further complication should be mentioned here. Each speaker has his or her own normal pitch range: a top level which is the highest pitch normally used by the speaker, and a bottom level that the speaker's pitch normally does not go below. In ordinary speech, the intonation tends to take place within the lower part of the speaker's pitch range, but in situations where strong feelings are to be expressed it is usual to make use of extra pitch height. For example, if we represent the pitch range by drawing two parallel lines representing the highest and lowest limits of the range, then a normal unemphatic 'yes' could be diagrammed like this:

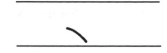

but a strong, emphatic 'yes' like this:

We will use a new symbol ↑ (a vertical upward arrow) to indicate extra pitch height, so that we can distinguish between:

ˌyes   and   ↑ ˌyes

Any of the tones presented in this chapter may be given extra pitch height, but since this course is based on normal, unemotional speech, it will not be necessary to use the symbol very frequently.

15.4 Some functions of English tones   ◯ AU15, Ex 4

In this chapter only a very small part of English intonation has been introduced. We will now see if it is possible to state in what circumstances the different tones are used within the very limited context of the words 'yes' and 'no' said in isolation. We will look at some typical occurrences; no examples of extra pitch height will be considered here, so the examples should be thought of as being said relatively low in the speaker's pitch range.

Fall ˌyes ˌno → neutral, finality

This is the tone about which least needs to be said, and which is usually regarded as more or less "neutral". If someone is asked a

155

question and replies ‚yes or ‚no it will be understood that the question is now answered and that there is nothing more to be said. The fall could be said to give an impression of "finality".

Rise ‚yes ‚no

In a variety of ways, this tone conveys an impression that something more is to follow; a typical occurrence in a dialogue between two speakers whom we shall call A and B might be the following:

> *A (wishing to attract B's attention)*: Excuse me.
> *B*: ‚yes

(B's reply is, perhaps, equivalent to 'what do you want?') Another quite common occurrence would be:

> *A*: Do you know John Smith?

One possible reply from B would be ‚yes, inviting A to continue with what she intends to say about John Smith after establishing that B knows him. To reply instead ‚yes would give a feeling of "finality", of "end of the conversation"; if A did have something to say about John Smith, the response with a fall would make it difficult for A to continue.

We can see similar "invitations to continue" in someone's response to a series of instructions or directions. For example:

> *A*: You start off on the ring road . . .
> *B*: ‚yes
> *A*: turn left at the first roundabout . . .
> *B*: ‚yes
> *A*: and ours is the third house on the left.

Whatever B replies to this last utterance of A, it would be most unlikely to be ‚yes again, since A has clearly finished her instructions and it would be pointless to "prompt" her to continue.

With 'no', a similar function can be seen. For example:

> *A*: Have you seen Ann?

If B replies ‚no, he implies quite clearly that he has no interest in continuing with that topic of conversation. But a reply of ‚no would be an invitation to A to explain why she is looking for Ann, or why she does not know where she is.

Similarly, someone may ask a question that implies readiness to present some new information. For example:

A: Do you know what the longest balloon flight was?

If B replies ˌno he is inviting A to tell him, while a response of ˌno could be taken to mean that he does not know and is not expecting to be told. This is, in fact, a common cause of misunderstanding in English conversation, when a question such as A's above might be a request for information or an offer to provide some.

Fall–rise ˅yes ˅no   *limited agreement* ·

The fall–rise is used a lot in English and has some rather special functions. In the present context we will only consider one fairly simple one, which could perhaps be described as "limited agreement" or "response with reservations". Examples may make this clearer:

A: I've heard that it's a good school.
B: ˅yes

B's reply would be taken to mean that he would not completely agree with what A said, and A would probably expect B to go on to explain why he was reluctant to agree. Similarly:

A: It's not really an expensive book, is it?
B: ˅no

The fall rise in B's reply again indicates that he would not completely agree with A. Fall–rise in such contexts almost always indicates both something "given" or "conceded" and at the same time some "reservation" or "hesitation". This use of intonation will be returned to in Chapter 19.

Rise–fall ˄yes ˄no

This is used to convey rather strong feelings of approval, disapproval or surprise. It is not usually considered to be an important tone for foreign learners to acquire, although it is still useful practice to learn to distinguish it from other tones. Here are some examples:

A: You wouldn't do an awful thing like that, would you?
B: ˄no

A: Isn't the view lovely!

B: ˄yes

A: I think you said it was the best so far.

B: ˄yes

Level _yes _no

This tone is certainly used in English, but in a rather restricted context: it almost always conveys (on single-syllable utterances) a feeling of saying something routine, uninteresting or boring. A teacher calling the names of pupils from a register will often do so using a level tone on each name, and the pupils are likely to respond with _yes when their name is called. Similarly, if one is being asked a series of routine questions for some purpose – such as applying for an insurance policy – one might reply to each question of a series (like 'Have you ever been in prison?', 'Do you suffer from any serious illness?', 'Is your eyesight defective?', etc.) with _no.

A few "meanings" have been suggested for the five tones that have been introduced, but each tone may have many more such meanings. Moreover, it would be quite wrong to conclude that in the above examples only the tones given would be appropriate; it is, in fact, almost impossible to find a context where one could not substitute a different tone. This is not the same thing as saying that any tone can be used in any context: the point is that no particular tone has a unique "privilege of occurrence" in a particular context. When we come to look at more complex intonation patterns, we will see that defining intonational "meanings" does not become any easier.

Notes on problems and further reading

To devote five chapters to intonation may seem excessive, but I feel that this is necessary since the subject is difficult and complex, and needs to be explained at considerable length if the explanation is to be intelligible. The study of intonation went through many changes in the twentieth century. The most intensive theoretical development began during the 1940s. In the United States the theory that evolved was based on 'pitch phonemes' (Pike, 1945): four contrastive pitch levels were established and intonation was described basically in terms of a series of movements from one of these levels to another.

This approach was further developed in Trager and Smith (1951). Although this 'pitch phoneme' theory became an orthodoxy, it was consistently attacked by one American linguist, D. Bolinger (e.g. Bolinger, 1951). In Britain the 'tone-unit' or 'tonetic' approach begun by H. E. Palmer in the 1920s (Palmer, 1924) was developed by (among others) Kingdon (1958), O'Connor and Arnold (1962) and Halliday (1967). These two different theoretical approaches became gradually more elaborate; in the American case perhaps the most elaborate exposition was in Trager (1964), while O'Connor and Arnold produced an extended version of their treatment in their second edition (1973) which was very difficult to learn in full. Since the 1970s it has become clear that, despite their complexity, such frameworks are inadequate for dealing with natural spontaneous speech. In Britain the most influential work leading to this recognition was Crystal (1969). I have tried in this course to reflect some of the more recently developed ideas for dealing with intonation, although the treatment remains essentially within the conventions of the British tradition. A good introduction to the theoretical issues is Cruttenden (1997). A more difficult (though very valuable) book on theory is Ladd (1996).

15.1   The amount of time to be spent on learning about tone languages should depend to some extent on your background. Those whose native language is a tone language should be aware of the considerable linguistic importance of tone in such languages; often it is extremely difficult for people who have spoken a tone language all their life to learn to observe their own use of tone objectively. The study of tone languages when learning English is less important for native speakers of non-tone languages, but most students seem to find it an interesting subject. A good introduction is Ladefoged (1993: 226–32). The classic work on the subject is Pike (1948), while more modern treatments are Hyman (1975: 212–29, Fromkin (1978) and Katamba (1989: Chapter 10).

Many analyses within the British approach to intonation include among tones both 'high' and 'low' varieties. For example, O'Connor and Arnold (1973) distinguished between 'high fall' and 'low fall' (the former starting from a high pitch, the latter from mid), and also between 'low rise' and 'high rise' (the latter rising to a higher point than the former). Some writers have high and low versions of all tones. Compared with the proposed establishing of a separate feature of 'extra pitch height' (which is explained more fully in Section 18.1), this is unnecessary duplication. However, if one adds extra pitch height to a tone, one has not given all possible detail about it. If we take as an example a fall–rise without extra pitch height:

then something symbolised as ↑ ˬ could be any of the following:

It would be possible to extend our framework to distinguish between these possibilities, but I do not believe it would be profitable to do so. Several writers have included in their set of tones **fall–rise–fall** and **rise–fall–rise**; I have seldom felt the need to recognise these as distinct from rise–fall and fall–rise respectively.

Note for teachers

As explained above, some students may be perfectly well able to discriminate between tones, but have difficulty in labelling them as 'fall', 'rise', etc. I find that about five per cent of the students I teach are never able to overcome this difficulty (even though they may have perfect hearing and in some cases a high level of linguistic and musical ability). Of the remainder, a few are especially gifted and cannot understand how anyone could find the task difficult, and most others eventually learn after five or ten hours of practical classes. Many students find it very helpful to work with a computer showing a real-time display of their pitch movements as they speak.

Written exercise

In the following sentences and bits of dialogue, each underlined syllable must be given an appropriate tone mark. Write a tone mark just in front of each of the syllables.

1   This train is for <u>Leeds</u>, <u>York</u>, <u>Darl</u>ington and <u>Dur</u>ham.
2   Can you give me a <u>lift</u>?
     <u>Poss</u>ibly Where <u>to</u>?
3   <u>No</u>! Certainly <u>not</u>! Go a<u>way</u>!
4   Did you know he'd been convicted of drunken <u>driv</u>ing?
     <u>No</u>!
5   If I give him <u>mon</u>ey he goes and <u>spends</u> it
     If I lend him the <u>bike</u> he <u>los</u>es it
     He's completely unrel<u>i</u>able

16 Intonation 2

16.1 The tone-unit

In Chapter 15 it was explained that some of the world's languages are "tone languages", in which substituting one distinctive tone for another on a particular word or morpheme can cause a change in the dictionary ("lexical") meaning of that word or morpheme, or in some aspect of its grammatical categorisation. Although tones or pitch differences are used for other purposes English is one of the languages that do not use tone in this way. Such languages are sometimes called **intonation languages**. In tone languages the main suprasegmental contrastive unit is the tone, which is usually linked to the phonological unit that we call the syllable. It could be said that someone analysing the function and distribution of tones in a tone language would be mainly occupied in examining utterances syllable by syllable, looking at each syllable as an independently variable item. In Chapter 15, five tones found on English one-syllable utterances were introduced, and if English were spoken in isolated monosyllables, the job of tonal analysis would be a rather similar one to that described for tone languages. However, when we look at continuous speech in English utterances we find that these tones can only be identified on a small number of particularly prominent syllables. For the purposes of analysing intonation a unit generally greater in size than the syllable is needed, and this unit is called the **tone-unit**; in its smallest form the tone-unit may consist of only one syllable, so it would in fact be wrong to say that it is always composed of more than one syllable. The tone-unit is difficult to define, and one or two examples may help to make it easier to understand the concept. (As explained in Chapter 15, examples used to illustrate intonation transcription are usually given in spelling form, and you will notice that no punctuation is used; the reason for this is that intonation and stress are the vocal equivalents of written punctuation, so that when these are transcribed it would be unnecessary or even confusing to include punctuation as well.)

◯ AU16, Exs 1 & 2

Let us begin with a one-syllable utterance:

ˌ<u>you</u>

We will underline syllables that carry a tone. Now consider this utterance:

is it ˌ<u>you</u>

The third syllable is more prominent than the other two and carries a rising tone. The other two syllables will normally be much less prominent, and be said on a level pitch. Why do we not say that each of the syllables 'is' and 'it' carries a level tone? This is a difficult question that will be examined more fully later; for the present I will answer it (rather unsatisfactorily) by saying that it is unusual for a syllable said on a level pitch to be so prominent that it would be described as carrying a level *tone*. To summarise the analysis of 'is it ˌ<u>you</u>' so far, it is an utterance of three syllables, consisting of one tone-unit; the only syllable that carries a tone is the third one. From now on, a syllable which carries a tone will be called a **tonic syllable**. It has been mentioned several times that tonic syllables have a high degree of prominence; prominence is, of course, a property of stressed syllables, and a tonic syllable not only carries a tone (which is something related to intonation) but also a type of stress that will be called **tonic stress**. (Some writers use the terms **nucleus** and **nuclear stress** for **tonic syllable** and **tonic stress**.)

The example can now be extended:

ˬ<u>John</u> is it ˌ<u>you</u>

(A fall–rise is used quite commonly in calling someone's name out.) If there is a clear pause (silence) between 'ˬ<u>John</u>' and 'is it ˌ<u>you</u>' then, according to the definition of an utterance given in Chapter 15, there are two utterances; however, it is quite likely that a speaker would say 'ˬ<u>John</u> is it ˌ<u>you</u>' with no pause, so that the four syllables would make up a single utterance. In spite of the absence of any pause, the utterance would normally be regarded as divided into two tone-units: '˷John' and 'is it ˌyou'. Since it is very difficult to lay down the conditions for deciding where the boundaries between tone-units exist, the discussion of this matter must wait until later.

It should be possible to see now that the tone-unit has a place in a range of phonological units that are in a **hierarchical relationship**: speech consists of a number of **utterances** (the largest unit that we shall consider); each utterance consists of one or more **tone-units**; each tone-unit consists of one or more **feet**; each foot consists of one or more **syllables**; each syllable consists of one or more **phonemes**.

16.2 The structure of the tone-unit

In Chapter 8 the structure of the English syllable was examined in some detail. Like the syllable, the tone-unit has a fairly clearly-defined internal structure, but the only component that has been mentioned so far is the tonic syllable. The first thing to be done is to make more precise the role of the tonic syllable in the tone-unit. Most tone-units are of a type that we call **simple**, and the sort that we call **compound** are not discussed in this chapter. Each simple tone-unit has one and only one tonic syllable; this means that the tonic syllable is an obligatory component of the tone-unit. (Compare the role of the vowel in the syllable.) We will now see what the other components may be.

The head

Consider the following one-syllable utterance:

ˌthose

We can find the same tonic syllable in a long utterance (still of one tone-unit):

'give me ˌthose

The rest of the tone-unit in this example is called the **head**. Notice that the first syllable has a stress mark; this is important. A head is all of that part of a tone-unit that extends from the first stressed syllable up to (but not including) the tonic syllable. It follows that if there is no stressed syllable before the tonic syllable, there cannot be a head. In the above example, the first two syllables (words) are the head of the tone-unit. In the following example, the head consists of the first five syllables:

'Bill 'called to 'give me ˌthese

As was said a little earlier, if there is no stressed syllable preceding the tonic syllable, there is no head. This is the case in the following example:

in an ˌhour

Neither of the two syllables preceding the tonic syllable is stressed. The syllables 'in an' form a **pre-head**, which is the next component of the tone-unit to be introduced.

The pre-head

The pre-head is composed of all the unstressed syllables in a tone-unit preceding the first stressed syllable. Thus pre-heads are found in two main environments:

i)   when there is no head (i.e. no stressed syllable preceding the tonic syllable), as in this example:

in an ˌhour

ii) when there is a head, as in this example:

in a 'little 'less than an ˌhour

In this example, the pre-head consists of 'in a', the head consists of "little 'less than an', and the tonic syllable is 'ˌhour'.

The tail

It often happens that some syllables follow the tonic syllable. Any syllables between the tonic syllable and the end of the tone-unit are called the **tail**. In the following examples, each tone-unit consists of an initial tonic syllable and a tail:

ˌlook at it   ˌwhat did you say
ˌboth of them were here

When it is necessary to mark stress in a tail, we will use a special symbol, a raised dot · for reasons that will be explained later. The above examples should, then, be transcribed as follows:

ˌlook at it   ˌwhat did you ·say
ˌboth of them were ·here

This completes the list of tone-unit components. If we use brackets to indicate optional components (that is, components which may be present or may be absent), we can summarise tone-unit structure as follows:

(pre-head)   (head)   tonic syllable   (tail)

or, more briefly, as:

(PH)   (H)   TS   (T)

To illustrate this more fully, let us consider the following passage, which is transcribed from a tape-recording of spontaneous speech (the speaker is describing a picture). When we analyse longer stretches of speech, it is necessary to mark the places where tone-unit boundaries occur (that is, where one tone-unit ends and another begins, or where a tone-unit ends and is followed by a pause, or where a tone-unit begins following a pause). It was mentioned above that tone-units are sometimes separated by silent pauses and sometimes not; pause-type boundaries can be marked by double vertical lines (‖) and non-pause boundaries with a single vertical line (|). In practice it is not usually important to mark pauses at the beginning and end of a passage. In the rest of the book I put no lines on short examples and only single lines around longer ones; the boundaries within a passage are much more important.

‖ and then 'nearer to the ˅front ‖ on the ˌleft | theres a 'bit of ˌforest | 'coming 'down to the ˌwaterside ‖ and then a 'bit of a ˌbay ‖

We can mark their structure as follows:

‖	PH		H		TS	‖ PH		TS		PH	
‖	and then		'nearer to the		˅front	‖ on the		ˌleft		there's a	

H	TS	T		H		TS	T	‖
'bit of	ˌfor	est		'coming 'down to the		ˌwa	terside	‖

PH		H		TS	‖
and then a		'bit of a		ˌbay	‖

The above passage contains five tone-units. Notice that in the third tone-unit, since it is the tonic syllable rather than the word that carries the tone, it is necessary to divide the word 'forest' into two parts, 'for' **fɔr** and 'est' ɪst (it could be argued that the syllables should be divided 'fo' and 'rest', but this is not important here). This example shows clearly how the units of phonological analysis can sometimes be seen to differ from those of grammatical analysis.

16.3 Pitch possibilities in the simple tone-unit

It has been said several times in this chapter that tone is carried by the tonic syllable, and it is now necessary to examine this statement more carefully. Before doing this, another general statement will be made (and will also need further explanation): intonation is carried by the tone-unit.

In a one-syllable utterance, the single syllable must have one of the five tones described in Chapter 15. In a tone-unit of more than one syllable, the tonic syllable must have one of those tones. If the tonic syllable is the final syllable, the tone will not sound much different from that of a corresponding one-syllable tone-unit. For example, the word 'here' will be said in much the same way in the following:

ˌhere   'shall we 'sit ˌhere

However, if there are other syllables following the tonic syllable (i.e. there is a tail), we find that the pitch movement of the tone is not completed on the tonic syllable. If a tail follows a tonic syllable that has a rising tone, it will almost always be found that the syllable or syllables of the tail will continue to move upwards from the pitch of the tonic syllable. For example, if the word 'what' is said on a rising tone, 'ˌwhat', it might have a pitch movement that could be diagrammed like this:

The four syllables in 'ˌwhat did you say' might be said like this:

with the pitch of the syllables in the tail getting progressively higher. In such cases, the tonic syllable is the syllable on which the pitch movement of the tone begins, but that pitch movement is completed over the rest of the tone-unit (i.e. the tail). If, in rising progressively higher, the pitch reaches the highest part of the speaker's normal pitch range, subsequent syllables will continue at that top level.

We find a similar situation with the falling tone. On a single syllable '͵why', the pitch movement might be of this sort:

but if there are syllables following, the fall may not be completed on the tonic syllable: ͵why did you go

Again, if the speaker's lowest pitch is reached before the end of the tail, the pitch continues at the bottom level. In the case of a level tone, syllables following in the tail will, of course, continue at the same level; since level tone is to be treated as a rather unusual type of tone, we will not examine it in more detail at this stage. The situation is more complicated when we have a tail following a fall–rise or a rise–fall, and this is described in Chapter 17.

Notes on problems and further reading

Almost all British analyses use a unit similar or identical to what I call a tone-unit, and link intonation to higher-level grammatical units. Different writers use different names: 'tone-group', 'sense-group', 'intonation unit' and 'tone-unit' are all more or less synonymous. It is possible to represent intonation as a simple sequence of tonic and non-tonic stressed syllables, and pauses, with no higher-level organisation; an example of this is the transcription used in the Spoken English Corpus (Williams, 1996). An early attempt at defining intonation units was that of Jones (1975: Chapter 30), where stretches of speech between pauses were called 'breath-groups' and marked with double vertical lines (‖), and smaller stretches within these – called 'sense-groups' – bounded by places where 'pauses *may* be made' and consisting of 'a few words in close grammatical connexion'. Trim (1959)* criticises this proposal, saying that Jones' 'sense-group' is defined in semantic terms and the 'breath-group' in physiological terms, whereas we should be concerned with phonetic and phonological units and definitions. Instead, he proposes that the unit used should be the 'tone-group', defined in terms of rhythm and pitch movements, and that we should distinguish between 'major' and 'minor' tone-groups. The minor tone-group corresponds to the tone-unit used in this course, and the idea of a larger unit (the major tone-unit) is a valuable one that will be discussed further in the notes on Chapter 19.

Note for teachers
The move from tones to tone-units is a difficult one, and I feel it is advisable at this stage to use only slow, careful speech for exercises (Audio Units 15 and 16). More difficult exercises follow later (Audio Units 18 and 19).

Written exercises
1   Here is a list of single tonic syllables. Add a number of extra syllables (as specified by the number in brackets) to make a tail. Example: go (2); Answer: go for it

   a) buy (3)
   b) hear (1)
   c) talk (2)
   (The answers section gives some possible versions.)

2   Now expand the following tonic syllables by putting heads in front of them, containing the number of stressed syllables indicated in brackets. Example: (2) dark; Answer: 'John was a'fraid of the dark

   a) (1) step
   b) (3) train
   c) (2) hot

* Not surprisingly, the fact that Trim's article is written in phonemic transcription with many words not separated by spaces makes it hard to read.

3   The following sentences are given with intonation transcribed. Draw underneath them a diagram of the pitch movements, leaving a gap between each syllable. Example:

'would you 'like some 'more ˌmilk

a) 'Only when the ˌwind blows

b) ˌWhen did you say

c) 'What was the ˌname of the place

17 Intonation 3

In Chapter 16 the structure of the tone-unit was introduced and it was explained that when a tonic syllable is followed by a tail, that tail continues and completes the tone begun on the tonic syllable. Examples were given to show how this happens in the case of rising and falling tones. We now go on to consider the rather more difficult cases of fall–rise and rise–fall tones.

17.1 Fall–rise and rise–fall tones followed by a tail

⌒ AU17, Exs 1 & 2

A rising or a falling tone is quite easy to identify, whether it falls on a single syllable or extends over more syllables in the case of a tonic syllable followed by a tail. Fall–rise and rise–fall tones, however, can be quite difficult to recognise when they are extended over tails, since their characteristic pitch movements are often broken up or distorted by the structure of the syllables they occur on. For example, the pitch movement on 'ˇsome' will be something like this:

If we add a syllable, the "fall" part of the fall–rise is usually carried by the first syllable and the "rise" part by the second. The result may be a continuous pitch movement very similar to the one-syllable case, if there are no voiceless medial consonants to cause a break in the voicing. For example:

ˇsome ˈmen

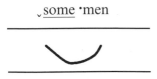

If the continuity of the voicing is broken, however, the pitch pattern might be more like this:

ˏsome ˈchairs

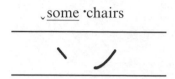

In this case it would be possible to say that there is a falling tone on 'some' and a rise on 'chairs'. However, most English speakers seem to feel that the pitch movement in this case is the same as that in the previous two examples; it can be said that there is a parallel with rhyming. Just as 'balloon' rhymes with 'moon', so we might say that 'ˏsome ˈchairs' has what could be called a **tonal rhyme** with 'ˏsome'.

If there is a tail of two or more syllables, the normal pitch movement is for the pitch to fall on the tonic syllable and to remain low until the last stressed syllable in the tail. The pitch then rises from that point up to the end of the tone-unit. If there is *no* stressed syllable in the tail, the rise happens on the final syllable. Here are some examples:

i) I ˏmight ˈbuy it

I ˏmight have ˈthought of ˈbuying it

ii) ˏmost of them

ˏmost of it was for them

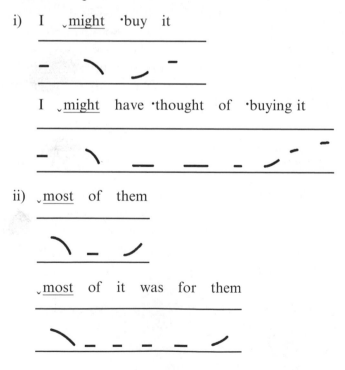

With the rise–fall tone we find a similar situation: if the tonic syllable is followed by a single syllable in the tail, the "rise" part of the tone takes place on the first (tonic) syllable and the "fall" part is on the second. Thus:

When there are two or more syllables in the tail, the syllable immediately following the tonic syllable is always higher and any following syllables are low. For example:

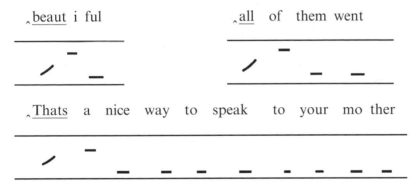

It should be clear by now that the speaker does not have a choice in the matter of the pitch of the syllables in the tail. This is completely determined by the choice of tone for the tonic syllable.

17.2 High and low heads

AU17, Ex 3

The head was defined in Chapter 16 as "all that part of a tone-unit that extends from the first stressed syllable up to, but not including, the tonic syllable". In our description of intonation up to this point, the only pitch contrasts found in the tone-unit are the different possible choices of tone for the tonic syllable. However, we can identify different pitch possibilities in the head, although these are limited to two which we will call **high head** and **low head**. In the case of the high head, the stressed syllable which begins the head is high in pitch; usually it is higher than the beginning pitch of the tone on the tonic syllable. For example:

The   'bus   was   <u>ˌlate</u>   Is   'that   the   <u>ˌend</u>

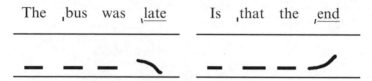

In the low head the stressed syllable which begins the head is low in pitch; usually it is lower than the beginning pitch of the tone on the tonic syllable. To mark this stressed syllable in the low head we will use a different symbol, ˌ as in 'ˌlow'. As an example, the heads of the above sentences will be changed from high to low:

The   ˌbus   was   <u>ˌlate</u>   Is   ˌthat   the   <u>ˌend</u>

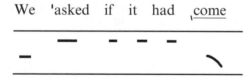

The two different versions (high and low head) will usually sound slightly different to English listeners, although it is not easy to say just what the difference *is*, as will be made clear in Chapter 18.

It is usual for unstressed syllables to continue the pitch of the stressed syllable that precedes them. In the following example, the three unstressed syllables 'if it had' continue at the same pitch as the stressed syllable 'asked'.

i)   with high head

    We   'asked   if   it   had   <u>ˌcome</u>

ii)   with low head

    We   ˌasked   if   it   had   <u>ˌcome</u>

When there is more than one stressed syllable in the head there is usually a slight change in pitch from the level of one stressed syllable to that of the next, the change being in the direction of the beginning pitch of the tone on the tonic syllable. We will use some long examples to illustrate this, although heads of this length are not very frequently found in natural speech. In the first example the stressed syllables in the high head step downwards progressively to approach the beginning of the tone:

The 'rain was 'com ing 'down 'fair ly ˌhard

In the next example the head is low; since the tone also starts low, being a rise, there is no upward movement in the head:

ˌThats ˌnot the ˌsto ry you ˌtold in ˌcourt

When there is a low head followed by a falling tone, successive stressed syllables in the head tend to move upwards towards the beginning pitch of the tone:

ˌI could have ˌbought it for ˌless than a ˌpound

When a high head is followed by a rise the stressed syllables tend to move downwards, as one would expect, towards the beginning pitch of the tone:

'Will there be a'nother 'train ˌlater

Of course, when we examine the intonation of polysyllabic heads we find much greater variety than these simple examples suggest. However, the division into high and low heads as general types is probably the most basic that can be made, and it would be pointless to set up a more elaborate system to represent differences if these differences were not recognised by most English speakers. Some writers on intonation claim that the intonation pattern starting at a fairly high pitch, with a gradual dropping down of pitch during the utterance, is the most basic, normal, "unmarked" intonation pattern; this movement is often called **declination**. The claim that declination is universally unmarked in English, or even in all languages, is a strong one. As far as English is concerned, it would be good to see more evidence from the full range of regional and national varieties in support of the claim.

It should be noted that the two marks ' and ˌ are being used for two different purposes in this course, as they are in many phonetics books. When stress is being discussed, the ' mark indicates primary stress and ˌ indicates secondary stress. For the purposes of marking intonation, however, the mark ' indicates a stressed syllable in a high head and the mark ˌ indicates a stressed syllable in a low head. In practice this is not usually found confusing as long as one is aware of whether one is marking stress levels or intonation. When the high and low marks ' and ˌ are being used to indicate intonation it is no longer possible to mark two different levels of stress within the word. However, when looking at speech at the level of the tone-unit we are not usually interested in this; a much more important difference here is that between tonic stress (marked by underlining the tonic syllable and placing before it one of the five tone-marks) and non-tonic stressed syllables (marked ' or ˌ in the head or · in the tail).

It needs to be emphasised that in marking intonation, only stressed syllables are marked; this implies that intonation is carried entirely by the stressed syllables of a tone-unit and that the pitch of unstressed syllables is either predictable from that of stressed sylla-bles or is of so little importance that it is not worth marking. Remember that the additional information given in the examples above by drawing pitch levels and movements between lines is only included here to make the examples clearer and is not normally given with our system of transcription; all the important information about intonation must, therefore, be given by the marks placed in the text.

17.3 Problems in analysing the form of intonation

The analysis of intonational form presented in this chapter and in Chapters 15 and 16 is similar in most respects to the approaches used in many British studies of English intonation. There are certain difficulties that all of these studies have had to confront, and it is useful to give a brief summary of what the major difficulties are.

Identifying the tonic syllable

It is often said that the tonic syllable can be identified because it is the only syllable in the tone-unit that carries a movement in pitch; this is in fact not always true. We have seen how when the tonic syllable is followed by a tail the tone is carried by the tonic plus tail together in such a way that in some cases practically no pitch movement is detectable on the tonic syllable itself. In addition it has been claimed that one of the tones is the *level* tone, which by definition may not have any pitch movement. It is therefore necessary to say in this particular case that the tonic syllable is identified simply as the most prominent syllable.

In addition, it sometimes seems as if some tone-units (though only a small number) contain not one but two tonic syllables, almost always with the first syllable having a fall on it and the other a rise. An example is:

In this example there seems to be equal prominence on 'seen' and 'him'. Of course, it could be claimed that this is the same thing as:

Ive ˬseen him

ii) — ＼ ／

It has, however, been pointed out that the two versions are different in several ways. Since 'him' has greater prominence in (i), it cannot occur in its weak form ɪm, but must be pronounced hɪm, whereas in (ii) the pronunciation is likely to be aɪv ˬsiːn ɪm. The two versions are said to convey different meanings, too. Version (i) might be said in conversation on hearing someone's name, as in this example:

A: John Cleese is a very funny actor.
B: 'Oh ˎyes | Ive ˌseen ˌhim

In version (ii), on the other hand, the word 'seen' is given the greatest prominence, and it is likely to sound as though the speaker has some reservation, or has something further to say:

A: Have you seen my father yet?
B: Ive ˎseen him | but I 'havent had 'time to ˌtalk to him

The same is found with 'her', as in

Ive ˌseen ˌher
aɪv ˌsiːn ˌhɜː

compared with

Ive ˎseen her
aɪv ˎsiːn ə

This is a difficult problem, since it weakens the general claim made earlier that each tone-unit contains only one tonic syllable.

Identifying tone-unit boundaries

It is a generally accepted principle in the study of grammar that utterances may contain one or more sentences, and that one can identify on grammatical grounds the places where one sentence ends and another begins. In a similar way, in suprasegmental phonology it is claimed that utterances may be divided up into tone-units, and that one can identify on phonetic or phonological grounds the places where one tone-unit ends and another tone-unit begins. However, giving rules for determining where the boundaries are placed is not easy, except in cases where a clear pause separates tone-units. Two principles are usually mentioned: one is that it is possible in most cases to detect some sudden change from the pitch level at the end of one tone-unit to the pitch level that starts the following tone-unit, and recognition of the start of the following tone-unit is made easier by the fact that speakers tend to "return home" to a particular pitch level at the beginning of a tone-unit. The second principle used in tone-unit boundary identification is a rhythmical one: it is claimed that within the tone-unit, speech has a regular rhythm, but that rhythm is broken or interrupted at the tone-unit boundary. Both the above principles are useful guides, but one regularly finds, in analysing natural speech, cases where it remains difficult or impossible to make a clear decision; the principles may well be factually correct, but it should be emphasised that at present there is no conclusive evidence from instrumental study in the laboratory that they are.

Anomalous tone-units

However comprehensive one's descriptive framework may be (and the one given in this course is very limited), there will inevitably be cases which do not fit within it. For example other tones such as fall–rise–fall or rise–fall–rise are occasionally found. In the head, we sometimes find cases where the stressed syllables are not all high or all low, as in the following example:

,After ,one of the 'worst 'days of my ˬlife

It can also happen that a speaker is interrupted and leaves a tone-unit incomplete – for example, lacking a tonic syllable. To return to the analogy with grammar, in natural speech one often finds sentences which are grammatically anomalous or incomplete, but this does not deter the grammarian from describing "normal" sentence structure. Similarly, although there are inevitably problems and exceptions, we continue to treat the tone-unit as something that can be described, defined and recognised.

17.4 Autosegmental treatment of intonation

In recent years a rather different way of analysing intonation, sometimes referred to as **autosegmental**, has become quite widely used, especially in American work. In this approach, all intonational phenomena can be reduced to just two basic phonological elements: H (high tone) and L (low tone). A movement of pitch from high to low (a fall) is treated as the sequence HL. Individual stressed ("accented") syllables must all be marked as H or L, or with a combination marking a pitch movement. In addition to this process, H and L tones are associated with boundaries. A major tone-unit boundary (equivalent to what we have been marking with ‖) is given the symbol %, but it must also be given a H or a L tone. Let us take an utterance like 'It's time to leave', which might be pronounced its 'time to ˌleave   (using our usual transcription)

In a simple version the alternative transcription will look like this:

    H   H L%
    its time to leave

Instead of marking a falling tone on the word 'leave', the high-pitched part of the word is shown by the H and the low part by the L associated with the boundary %. There is another boundary (corresponding to the minor tone-unit boundary |) which is marked with –, and again this must be marked with either a H or a L. There must always be one of these boundaries marked before a % boundary. So, the following utterance would be transcribed like this in the system used in this book:

        we ˌlooked at the ˌsky | and 'saw the ˌclouds

and in this way using autosegmental transcription:

      L   L H–   H   H L– L%
      we looked at the sky   and saw the clouds

How would this approach deal with complex tones spread over several syllables?

                                            H   L– H%
    ˇmost of them   could be transcribed   most of them

Although this type of analysis has some attractions, especially in the way it fits with contemporary phonological theory, it seems unlikely that it would be more useful to learners of English than the traditional analysis presented here.

Notes on problems and further reading

The main concern of this chapter is to complete the description of intonational form, including analysis of perhaps the most difficult aspect: that of recognising fall–rise and rise–fall tones when they are extended over a number of syllables. This is necessary since no complete analysis of intonation can be done without having studied these "extended tones".

Cruttenden (1997: Chapters 3 and 4) gives a good introduction to the problems of analysing tones both within the traditional British framework and in autosegmental terms. A very detailed discussion of the difference between fall–rise and the "compound" fall-plus-rise is given in Sharp (1958), although this is not easy reading and some of the examples are difficult to follow. On tone-unit boundaries, there is a clear explanation of the problems in Cruttenden (1997: Section 3.2), and in more detail in Crystal (1969: 204–7). The study of Scottish English by Brown *et al.* (1980) gives ample evidence that tone-units in real life are not as easy to identify as tone-units in textbooks. There has recently been a growth of interest in the comparative study of intonation in different languages and dialects: see Cruttenden (1997: Chapter 5); Hirst and di Cristo (1998); Ladd (1996: Chapter 4).

On declination, see Cruttenden (1997: 121–3).

For reading on autosegmental analysis (which is often also given the name **ToBI**), a good introduction is Cruttenden (1997: 56–67). A fuller and more critical analysis can be read in Ladd (1996: Chapters 2 and 3); see also Roca and Johnson (1999: Chapter 14). A short account of the problems found in trying to compare this approach with the traditional British analysis is given in Roach (1994).

Note for teachers

I would like to emphasise how valuable an exercise it is for students and teachers to attempt to analyse some recorded speech for themselves. For beginners it is best to start on slow, careful speech – such as that of newsreaders – before attempting conversational speech. One can learn more about intonation in an hour of this work than in days of reading textbooks on the subject, and one's interest in and understanding of theoretical problems becomes much more profound.

Written exercises

1   The following sentences are given with intonation marks. Sketch the pitch within the lines below, leaving a gap between each syllable.

a) 'Which was the ˌcheap one did you say

———————————————————————

———————————————————————

b) I 'only 'want to ˎtaste it

———————————————————————

———————————————————————

c) ˌShe would have ˌthought it was ˌ˅obvious

_____

_____

d) There 'wasnt 'even a 'piece of ˌbread in the ˈhouse

_____

_____

e) ˌNow will you be ˈlieve me

_____

_____

2   This exercise is similar, but here you are given polysyllabic words
    and a tone. You must draw an appropriate pitch movement
    between the lines.

a) (rise)   opportunity

_____

_____

b) (fall–rise)   actually

_____

_____

c) (fall)   confidently

_____

_____

d) (rise–fall)   magnificent

_____

_____

e) (rise)   relationship

_____

_____

f) (fall–rise)   afternoon

_____

_____

18 Functions of intonation 1

The form of intonation has now been described in some detail, and we will move on to look more closely at its functions. Perhaps the best way to start is to ask ourselves what would be lost if we were to speak *without* intonation: you should try to imagine speech in which every syllable was said on the same level pitch, with no pauses and no changes in speed or loudness. This is the sort of speech that would be produced by a "mechanical speech" device (as described at the beginning of Chapter 14) that made sentences by putting together recordings of isolated words. To put it in the broadest possible terms, we can see that intonation makes it easier for a listener to understand what a speaker is trying to convey. The ways in which intonation does this are very complex, and many suggestions have been made for ways of isolating different functions. Among the most often proposed are the following:

i) Intonation enables us to express emotions and attitudes as we speak, and this adds a special kind of "meaning" to spoken language. This is often called the **attitudinal function** of intonation.

ii) Intonation helps to produce the effect of prominence on syllables that need to be perceived as stressed, and in particular the placing of tonic stress on a particular syllable marks out the word to which it belongs as the most important in the tone-unit. This has been called the **accentual function** of intonation.

iii) The listener is better able to recognise the grammar and syntactic structure of what is being said by using the information contained in the intonation; for example, such things as the placement of boundaries between phrases, clauses or sentences, the difference between questions and statements and the use of grammatical subordination may be indicated. This has been called the **grammatical function** of intonation.

iv) Looking at the act of speaking in a broader way, we can see that intonation can signal to the listener what is to be taken as "new" information and what is already "given", can suggest when the speaker is indicating some sort of contrast or link with material in another tone-unit and, in conversation, can convey to the listener what kind of response is expected. Such functions are examples of intonation's **discourse function.**

The attitudinal function has been given so much importance in past work on intonation that it will be discussed separately in this chapter, although it should eventually become clear that it overlaps considerably with the discourse function. In the case of the other three functions, it will be argued that it is difficult to see how they could be treated as separate; for example, the placement of tonic stress is closely linked to the presentation of "new" information, while the question/statement distinction and the indication of contrast seem to be equally important in grammar and discourse. What seems to be common to accentual, grammatical and discourse functions is the indication, by means of intonation, of the relationship between some linguistic element and the context in which it occurs. The fact that they overlap with each other to a large degree is not so important if one does not insist on defining watertight boundaries between them.

The rest of this chapter is concerned with a critical examination of the attitudinal function.

18.1 The attitudinal function of intonation

Many writers have expressed the view that intonation is used to convey our feelings and attitudes; for example, the same sentence can be said in different ways, which might be labelled "angry", "happy", "grateful", "bored" and so on. It has also been widely observed that the form of intonation is different in different languages; for example, the intonation of languages such as Swedish, Italian or Hindi is instantly recognisable as being different from that of English. Not surprisingly, it has often been said that foreign learners of English need to learn English intonation. Some have gone further than this and claimed that, unless the foreign learner learns the appropriate way to use intonation in a given situation, there is a risk that he or she may unintentionally give offence; for example, the learner might use an intonation suitable for expressing boredom or discontent when what is needed is an expression of gratitude or affection. This misleading view of intonation must have caused unnecessary anxiety to many learners of the language.

Let us begin by considering how one might analyse the attitudinal function of intonation. One possibility would be for the analyst to invent a large number of sentences and to try saying them with different intonation patterns (i.e. different combinations of head and tone), noting what attitude was supposed to correspond to the intonation in each case; of course, the results are then very subjective, and based on an artificial performance that has little resemblance to conversational speech. Alternatively, the analyst could say these different sentences to a group of listeners and ask them all to write down what attitudes they thought were being expressed; however, we have a vast range of adjectives available for labelling attitudes and the members of the group would probably produce a very large number of such adjectives, leaving the analyst with the problem of deciding whether pairs such as 'pompous' and 'stuck-up', or 'obsequious' and 'sycophantic' were synonyms or represented different attitudes. To overcome this difficulty, one could ask the members of the group to choose among a small number of adjectives (or "labels") given by the analyst; the results would then inevitably be easier to quantify (that is, the job of counting the different responses would be simpler) but the results would no longer represent the listeners' free choices of label. An alternative procedure would be to ask a lot of speakers to say a list of sentences in different ways according to labels provided by the analyst, and see what intonational features are found in common (for example, one might count how many speakers used a low head in saying something in a "hostile" way). The results of such experiments are usually very variable and difficult to interpret, not least because the range of acting talent in a randomly selected group is considerable.

A much more useful and realistic approach is to study recordings of different speakers' natural, spontaneous speech and try to make generalisations about attitudes and intonation on this basis. Many problems remain, however. In the method described previously, the analyst tries to select sentences (or passages of some other size) whose meaning is fairly "neutral" from the emotional point of view, and will tend to avoid material such as 'Why don't you leave me alone?' or 'How can I ever thank you enough?' because the lexical meaning of the words used already makes the speaker's attitude pretty clear, whereas sentences such as 'She's going to buy it tomorrow' or 'The paper has fallen under the table' are less likely to prejudice the listener. The choice of material is much less free for someone studying natural speech. Nevertheless, if we are ever to make new discoveries about intonation, it will be as a result of studying what people actually say rather than inventing examples of what they *might* say.

The notion of "expressing an emotion or attitude" is itself a more complex one than is generally realised. First, an emotion may be expressed involuntarily or voluntarily; if I say something in a "happy" way, this may be because I *feel* happy, or because I want to convey to you the *impression* that I am happy. Second, an attitude that is expressed could be an attitude towards the listener (e.g. if I say something in a "friendly" way), towards what is being said (e.g. if I say something in a "sceptical" or "dubious" way) or towards some external event or situation (e.g. "regretful" or "disapproving").

However, one point is much more important and fundamental than all the problems discussed above. To understand this point you should imagine (or even actually perform) your pronunciation of a sentence in a number of different ways for example, if the sentence was 'I want to buy a new car' and you were to say it in the following ways: "pleading", "angry", "sad", "happy", "proud", it is certain that at least some of your performances will be different from some others, but it is also certain that the technique for analysing and transcribing intonation introduced earlier in the course will be found inadequate to represent the different things you do. You will have used variations in loudness and speed, for example; almost certainly you will have used different voice qualities for different attitudes. You may have used your pitch range (which was introduced in Section 15.3) in different ways: your pitch movements may have taken place within quite a narrow range (**narrow pitch range**) or using the full range between high and low (**wide pitch range**); if you did not use wide pitch range, you may have used different **keys**: **high key** (using the upper part of your pitch range), **mid key** (using the middle part of the range) or **low key** (the lower part). It is very likely that you will have used different facial expressions and even gestures and body movements. These factors are all of great importance in conveying attitudes and emotions, yet the traditional handbooks on English pronunciation have almost completely ignored them.

If we accept the importance of these factors it becomes necessary to consider how they are related to intonation, and what intonation itself consists of. We can isolate three distinct types of suprasegmental variable: sequential, prosodic and paralinguistic.

Sequential

These components of intonation are found as elements in sequences of other such elements occurring one after another (never simultaneously). These are:

i) pre-heads, heads, tonic syllables and tails (with their pitch possibilities);
ii) pauses;
iii) tone-unit boundaries.

These have all been introduced in previous chapters.

Prosodic

These components are characteristics of speech which are constantly present and observable while speech is going on. The most important are:

i) width of pitch range;
ii) key;
iii) loudness;
iv) speed;
v) voice quality.

It is not possible to speak without one's speech having some degree or type of pitch range, loudness, speed and voice quality (with the possible exception that pitch factors are largely lost in whispered speech). Different speakers do, of course, have their own typical pitch range, loudness, voice quality, etc., and contrasts among prosodic components should be seen as relative to these "background" speaker characteristics.

Each of these prosodic components needs a proper framework for categorisation, and this is an interesting area of current research. One example of the prosodic component "width of pitch range" has already been mentioned in Section 15.3, when "extra pitch height" was introduced, and the "rhythmicality" discussed in Section 14.1 could be regarded as another prosodic component. Prosodic components should be regarded as part of intonation along with sequential components.

Paralinguistic

Mention was made above of facial expressions, gestures and body movements. People who study human behaviour often use the term **body language** for such activity. One could also mention certain vocal effects such as laughs and sobs. These paralinguistic effects are obviously relevant to the act of speaking but could not themselves properly be regarded as components of speech. Again, they need a proper descriptive and classificatory system, but this is not something that comes within the scope of this course, nor in my opinion should they be regarded as components of intonation.

What advice, then, can be given to the foreign learner of English who wants to learn "correct intonation"? It is certainly true that a few generalisations can be made about the attitudinal functions of some components of intonation. Within tone, for example, most books agree on some basic meanings; here are some examples:

1. Fall
   Finality, definiteness: That is the end of the ˋnews
   I'm absolutely ˋcertain
   Stop ˋtalking
2. Rise
   Most of the functions attributed to rises are nearer to grammatical than attitudinal, as in the first three examples given below; they are included here mainly to give a fuller picture of intonational function.
   General questions: Can you ˏhelp me
   Is it ˏover

Listing: ˌRed ˌbrown ˌyellow or ˌblue
         (fall is normal on the last item)
"More to follow": I phoned them right a ˌway
         (and they agreed to come)
         You must write it a ˌgain
         (and this time, get it right)
Encouraging: It wont ˌhurt

3. Fall–rise
Uncertainty, doubt: You ˅may be right
         Its ˅possible
Requesting: Can I ˅buy it
         Will you ˅lend it to me

4. Rise–fall
Surprise, being impressed: You were ˄first
         ˄All of them

Generalisations such as these are, however, very broad, and foreign learners do not find it easy to learn to use intonation through studying them. Similarly, within the area of prosodic components most generalisations tend to be rather obvious: wider pitch range tends to be used in excited or enthusiastic speaking, slower speed is typical of the speech of someone who is tired or bored, and so on. Most of the generalisations one could make are probably true for a lot of other languages as well. In short, of the rules and generalisations that could be made about conveying attitudes through intonation, those which are not actually wrong are likely to be too trivial to be worth learning. I have witnessed many occasions when foreigners have unintentionally caused misunderstanding or even offence in speaking to a native English speaker, but can remember only a few occasions when this could be attributed to "using the wrong intonation"; most such cases have involved native speakers of different varieties of English, rather than learners of English. Sometimes an intonation mistake can cause a difference in apparent grammatical meaning (something that is dealt with in Chapter 19). It should not be concluded that intonation is not important for conveying attitudes. What is being claimed here is that, although it is of great importance, the complexity of the total set of sequential and prosodic components of intonation and of paralinguistic features makes it a very difficult thing to teach or learn. One might compare the difficulty with that of trying to write rules for how one might indicate to someone that one finds him or her sexually attractive; while psychologists and biologists might make detailed observations and generalisations about how human beings of a particular culture behave in such a situation, most people would rightly feel that studying these generalisations would be no substitute for practical experience, and that relying on a textbook could lead to hilarious consequences. The attitudinal use of intonation is something that is best acquired through talking with and listening to English speakers, and this course aims simply to train learners to be more aware of and sensitive to the way English speakers use intonation.

Notes on problems and further reading

Perhaps the most controversial question concerning English intonation is what its function is; pedagogically speaking, this is a very important question, since one would not wish to devote time to teaching something without knowing what its value is likely to be. At the beginning of this chapter I list four commonly cited functions; it is possible to construct a longer list; Lee (1958), for example, proposed ten.

For general introductory reading on the functions of intonation, there is a good survey in Cruttenden (1997: Chapter 4). Critical views are expressed in Brazil *et al.* (1980: 98–103) and Crystal (1969: 282–308). There are many useful examples in Brazil (1994). Few people have carried out experiments on listeners' perception of attitudes through intonation, probably because it is extremely difficult to design properly controlled experiments.

Once one has recognised the importance of features other than pitch, it is necessary to devise a framework for categorising these features. There are many different views about the meaning of the term "paralinguistic". In the framework presented in Crystal and Quirk (1964), paralinguistic features of the "vocal effect" type are treated as part of intonation, and it is not made sufficiently clear how these are to be distinguished from prosodic features. Crystal (1969) defines paralinguistic features as: 'vocal effects which are primarily the result of physiological mechanisms other than the vocal cords, such as the direct results of the workings of the pharyngeal, oral or nasal cavities' but this does not seem to me to fit the facts. In my view, "paralinguistic" implies 'outside the system of contrasts used in spoken language' – which does not, of course, necessarily mean 'non-vocal'. I would therefore treat prosodic variables as linguistic – and consequently part of intonation – while I would treat vocal effects like laughs or sobs as non-linguistic vocal effects to be classed with gestures and facial expressions. Brown (1990), on the other hand, uses "paralinguistic" to include what I call "prosodic", and appears to have no separate term for non-linguistic vocal effects. A recent paper on transcription of prosodie and paralinguistic features is Roach *et al.* (1998).

The term 'voice quality' needs comment, as it tends to be used with different meanings: sometimes the term is used to refer to the personal, "background" characteristics that make one person's voice recognisably different from another, mainly as a result of the complex interaction of laryngeal and supralaryngeal features (Crystal, 1969: 100–4; Laver, 1980; 1994); for some writers, however, "voice quality" is the auditory result of different types of vocal fold vibration. A better name for this is **phonation type** (Catford, 1964).

Note for teachers
Audio Unit 18 consists of extracts from a recording of spontaneous dialogue. Students usually feel that listening to these unfamiliar voices chopped up into small pieces is hard work, but generally the transcription exercise is not found nearly as difficult as expected.

Written exercises
In the following bits of conversation, you are supplied with an "opening line" and a response that you must imagine saying. You are given an indication in brackets of the feeling or attitude expressed, and you must mark on the text the intonation you think is appropriate (mark only the response). As usual in intonation work in this book, punctuation is left out, since it can cause confusion.

1	It looks nice for a ˌswim	Its rather cold (*doubtful*)
2	Why not get a ˌcar	Because I cant afford it (*impatient*)
3	Ive lost my ˌticket	Youre silly then (*stating the obvious*)

4 You cant have an ice ˌcream   Oh please (*pleading*)
5 What times are the ˌbuses   Seven o'clock seven thirty and
                                eight (*listing*)
6 She got four ˌ'A' levels   Four (*impressed*)
7 How much ˌwork have you   Ive got to do the shopping
   got to do   (*and more things after that*)
8 Will the ˇchildren go   Some of them might (*uncertain*)

19 Functions of intonation 2

In the previous chapter a distinction was made between the attitudinal function of intonation and several other functions that were given the collective name of syntagmatic functions. They include accentual, grammatical and discourse functions, and these are discussed below.

19.1 The accentual function of intonation

The term accentual is derived from "accent", a word used by some writers to refer to what in this course is called "stress". When writers say that intonation has accentual function they imply that the placement of stress is something that is determined by intonation. It is possible to argue against this view: in Chapters 10 and 11 word stress is presented as something quite independent of intonation, and subsequently (p. 176) it was said that 'intonation is carried entirely by the stressed syllables of a tone-unit'. This means that the presentation so far has implied that the placing of stress is independent of and prior to the choice of intonation. However, one particular aspect of stress *could* be regarded as part of intonation: this is the placement of the tonic stress within the tone-unit. It would be reasonable to suggest that while word stress is independent of intonation, the placement of tonic stress is a function (the accentual function) of intonation. Some older pronunciation handbooks refer to this area as "sentence stress", which is not an appropriate name: the sentence is a unit of grammar, while the location of tonic stress is a matter which concerns the tone unit, a unit of phonology.

The location of the tonic syllable is of considerable linguistic importance. The most common position for this is on the last lexical word (e.g. noun, adjective, verb, adverb as distinct from the function words introduced in Chapter 12, pp. 112–13) of the tone-unit. For contrastive purposes, however, any word may become the bearer of the tonic syllable. It is frequently said that the placement of the tonic syllable indicates the **focus** of the information. In the following pairs of examples, (i) represents normal placement and (ii) contrastive:

i) | I ˌwant to ˌknow ˌwhere hes ˌtravelling to |
     (The word 'to', being a preposition and not a lexical word, is not stressed.)
ii) (I 'dont want to 'know where hes 'travelling ˎfrom)
     | I ˌwant to ˌknow ˌ where hes ˌ travelling ˌto |

i) | She was 'wearing a 'red ˌdress |
ii) (She 'wasnt 'wearing a ˎgreen ·dress) | She was 'wearing a ˌred ·dress |

Similarly, for the purpose of emphasis we may place the tonic stress in other positions; in these examples, (i) is non-emphatic and (ii) is emphatic:

i) | It was 'very ˌboring |
ii) | It was ˌvery ·boring |

i) | You 'mustnt 'talk so ˌloudly |
ii) | You ˌmustnt ·talk so ·loudly |

However, it would be wrong to say that the only cases of departure from putting tonic stress on the last lexical word were cases of contrast or emphasis. There are quite a few situations where it is normal for the tonic syllable to come earlier in the tone-unit. A well-known example is the sentence 'I have plans to leave'; this is ambiguous:

i) | I have 'plans to ˌleave |
     (i.e. I am planning to leave.)
ii) | I have ˌplans to ·leave |
     (i.e. I have some plans/diagrams/drawings that I have to leave.)

Version (ii) could not be described as contrastive or emphatic. There are many examples similar to (ii); perhaps the best rule to give is that the tonic syllable will *tend* to occur on the last lexical word in the tone-unit, but may be placed earlier in the tone-unit if there is a word there with greater importance to what is being said. This can quite often happen as a result of the last part of the tone-unit being already "given" (i.e. something which has already been mentioned or is completely predictable); for example:

i) | 'Heres that ˌbook you ·asked me to ·bring |
     (The fact that you asked me to bring it is not new.)

ii) | Ive ˌgot to ˌtake the ˌdog for a ·walk |
     ('For a walk' is by far the most probable thing to follow 'I've got to take the dog'; if the sentence ended with 'to the vet' the tonic syllable would probably be 'vet'.)

Placement of tonic stress is, therefore, important and is closely linked to intonation. A question that remains, however, is whether one can and should treat this matter as separate from the other functions described below.

19.2 The grammatical function of intonation

The word "grammatical" tends to be used in a very loose sense in this context. It is usual to illustrate the grammatical function by inventing sentences which when written are ambiguous, and whose ambiguity can only be removed by using differences of intonation. A typical example is the sentence 'Those who sold quickly made a profit'. This can be said in at least two different ways:

i) | 'Those who 'sold ˅quickly | ˌmade a ˌprofit

ii) | 'Those who ˅sold | ˌquickly ˌmade a ˌprofit |

The difference caused by the placement of the tone-unit boundary is seen to be equivalent to giving two different paraphrases of the sentences, as in:

i)   A profit was made by those who sold quickly.

ii) A profit was quickly made by those who sold.

Let us look further at the role of tone-unit boundaries, and the link between the tone-unit and units of grammar. There is a strong tendency for tone-unit boundaries to occur at boundaries between grammatical units of higher order than words; it is extremely common to find a tone-unit boundary at a sentence boundary, as in:

| I 'wont have any ˌtea | I 'dont ˌlike it |

In sentences with a more complex structure, tone-unit boundaries are often found at phrase and clause boundaries as well, as in:

| In ˇFrance | where ˌfarms ˌtend to be ˇsmaller | the 'subsidies are 'more imˌportant

It is very unusual to find a tone-unit boundary at a place where the only grammatical boundary is a boundary between words. It would, for example, sound distinctly odd to have a tone-unit boundary between an article and a following noun, or between auxiliary and main verbs if they are adjacent (although we may, on occasions, hesitate or pause in such places within a tone-unit; it is interesting to note that some people who do a lot of arguing and debating, notably politicians and philosophers, develop the skill of pausing for breath in such intonationally unlikely places because they are less likely to be interrupted than if they pause at the end of a sentence). Tone-unit boundary placement can, then, indicate grammatical structure to the listener and we can find minimal pairs such as the following:

i)   The Con'servatives who ˇlike the pro ·posal | are ˌpleased
ii) The Con ˇservatives | who ˇlike the pro ·posal | are ˌpleased

The intonation makes clear the difference between (i) "restrictive" and (ii) "non-restrictive" relative clauses; (i) implies that only *some* Conservatives like the proposal, while (ii) implies that *all* the Conservatives like it.

   Another component of intonation that can be said to have grammatical significance is the choice of tone on the tonic syllable. One example that is very familiar is the use of a rising tone with questions. Many languages have the possibility of changing a statement into a question simply by changing the tone from falling to rising. This is, in fact, not used very much by itself in the variety of English being described here, where questions are usually grammatically marked. The sentence 'The price is going up' can be said as a statement like this:

| The ˌprice is going up |

(the tonic stress could equally well be on 'up'). It would be quite acceptable in some dialects of English (e.g. many varieties of American English) to ask a question like this:

(Why do you want to buy it now?) | The ˌprice is going up |

But speakers in Britain would be more likely to ask the question like this:

(Why do you want to buy it now?) | 'Is the ˌprice going up |

It is by no means true that a rising tone is always used for questions in English; it is quite usual, for example, to use a falling tone with questions beginning with one of the "wh-question-words" like 'what', 'which', 'when', etc. Here are two examples with typical intonations, where (i) does not start with a "wh-word" and has a rising tone and (ii) begins with 'where' and has a falling tone.

i) | 'Did you 'park the ˌcar |
ii) | 'Where did you 'park the ˌcar |

However, the fall in (ii) is certainly not obligatory, and a rise is quite often heard in such a question. A fall is also possible in (i).

The intonation of **question-tags** (e.g. 'isn't it', 'can't he', 'should she', 'won't they', etc.) is often quoted as a case of a difference in meaning being due to the difference between falling and rising tone. In the following example, the question-tag is 'aren't they'; when it has a falling tone, as in (i), the implication is said to be that the speaker is comparatively certain that the information is correct, and simply expects the listener to provide confirmation, while the rising tone in (ii) is said to indicate a lesser degree of certainty, so that the question-tag functions more like a request for information.

i) | They 'are 'coming on ˌTuesday | ˌarent they |
ii) | They 'are 'coming on ˌTuesday | ˌarent they |

The difference illustrated here could reasonably be said to be as much attitudinal as grammatical. Certainly there is overlap between these two functions.

19.3 The discourse function of intonation

If we think of linguistic analysis as usually being linked to the sentence as the maximum unit of grammar, then the study of discourse attempts to look at the larger contexts in which sentences occur. For example, consider the four sentences in the following:

A: Have you got any free time this morning?
B: I might have later on if that meeting's off.
A: They were talking about putting it later.
B: You can't be sure.

Each sentence could be studied in isolation and be analysed in terms of grammatical construction, lexical content and so on. But it is obvious that the sentences form part of some larger act of conversational interaction between two speakers; the sentences contain several references that presuppose shared knowledge (e.g. 'that meeting' implies that both speakers know which meeting is being spoken about), and in some cases the meaning of a sentence can only be correctly interpreted in the light of knowledge of what has preceded it in the conversation (e.g. 'You can't be sure').

If we consider how intonation may be studied in relation to discourse, we can identify two main areas: one of them is the use of intonation to focus the listener's attention on aspects of the message that are most important, and the other is concerned with the regulation of conversational behaviour. We will look at these in turn.

In the case of "attention focusing", the most obvious use has already been described: this is the placing of tonic stress on the appropriate syllable of one particular word in the tone-unit. In many cases it is easy to demonstrate that the tonic stress is placed on the word that is in some sense the "most important", as in:

| She 'went to ˌScotland |

Sometimes it seems more appropriate to describe tonic stress placement in terms of "information content": the more predictable a word's occurrence is in a given context, the lower its information content is. Tonic stress will tend to be placed on words with high information content, as suggested above when the term *focus* was introduced. This is the explanation that would be used in the case of the sentences suggested in Section 9.1:

i) | Ive ˌgot to ˌtake the ˌdog for a ·walk |
ii) | Ive ˌgot to ˌtake the ˌdog to the ˌvet |

The word 'vet' is less predictable (has a higher information content) than 'walk'. However, we still find many cases where it is difficult to explain tonic placement in terms of "importance" or "information". For example, in messages like:

Your coat's on fire   The wing's breaking up
The radio's gone wrong   Your uncle's died

probably the majority of English speakers would place the tonic stress on the subject noun, although it is difficult to see how this is more important than the last lexical word in each of the sentences. The placement of tonic stress is still to some extent an unsolved mystery; it is clear, however, that it is at least partly determined by the larger context (linguistic and non-linguistic) in which the tone-unit occurs.

We can see at least two other ways in which intonation can assist in focusing attention. The tone chosen can indicate whether the tone-unit in which it occurs is being used to present new information or to refer to information which is felt to be already possessed by speaker and hearer. For example, in the following sentence:

| 'Since the ˌlast time we ·met | when we had that 'huge ˌdinner |
Ive 'been on a ˌdiet |

the first two tone-units present information which is relevant to what the speaker is saying, but which is not something new and unknown to the listener. The final tone-unit, however, does present new information. Writers on discourse intonation have proposed that the falling tone indicates new information while rising (including falling–rising) tones indicate "shared" or "given" information.

Another use of intonation connected with the focusing of attention is **intonational subordination**; we can signal that a particular tone-unit is of comparatively low importance and as a result give correspondingly greater importance to adjacent tone-units. For example:

i) | As I ex ˌpect youve ˌheard | theyre ˈonly ad ˈmitting eˌmergency ·cases |

ii) | The ˌJapa ˌnese | for ˌsome ˌreason or ˌother | ˈdrive on the ˌleft | like ˌus |

In a typical conversational pronunciation of these sentences, the first tone-unit of (i) and the second and fourth tone-units of (ii) might be treated as intonationally subordinate; the prosodic characteristics marking this are usually:

i) a drop to a lower part of the pitch range ("low key");
ii) increased speed;
iii) narrower range of pitch; and
iv) lower loudness, relative to the non-subordinate tone-unit(s).

The use of these components has the result that the subordinate tone-units are less easy to hear. Native speakers can usually still understand what is said, if necessary by guessing at inaudible or unrecognisable words on the basis of their knowledge of what the speaker is talking about. Foreign learners of English, on the other hand, having in general less "common ground" or shared knowledge with the speaker, often find that these subordinate tone-units – with their "throwaway", parenthetic style – cause serious difficulties in understanding.

We now turn to the second main area of intonational discourse function: the regulation of conversational behaviour. We have already seen how the study of sequences of tone-units in the speech of one speaker can reveal information carried by intonation which would not have been recognised if intonation were analysed only at the level of individual tone-units. Intonation is also important in the conversational interaction of two or more speakers. Most of the research on this has been on conversational interaction of a rather restricted kind – such as between doctor and patient, teacher and pupil or between the various speakers in court cases. In such material it is comparatively easy to identify what each speaker is actually doing in speaking – for example, questioning, challenging, advising, encouraging, disapproving, etc. It is likely that other forms of conversation can be analysed in the same way, although this is considerably more difficult. In a more general way, it can be seen that speakers use various prosodic components to indicate to others that they have finished speaking, that another person is expected to speak, that a particular type of response is required and so on. A very familiar example is that quoted above (p. 197), where the difference between falling and rising intonation on question-tags is supposed to indicate to the listener what sort of response is expected. It seems that key (the part of the pitch range used) is important in signalling information about conversational interaction. We can observe many examples in non-linguistic behaviour of the use of signals to regulate turn-taking: in many sports, for example, it is necessary to do this – footballers can indicate that they are looking for someone to pass the ball to, or that they are ready to receive the ball, and doubles partners in tennis can indicate to each other who is to play a shot. Intonation, in conjunction with "body language" such as eye contact, facial expression, gestures and head-turning, is used for similar purposes in speech, as well as for establishing or confirming the status of the participants in a conversation.

19.4 Conclusions

It seems clear that studying intonation in relation to discourse makes it possible to explain much more comprehensively the uses that speakers make of intonation. Practically all the separate functions traditionally attributed to intonation (attitudinal, accentual and grammatical) could be seen as different aspects of discourse function. The risk, with such a broad approach, is that one might end up making generalisations that were too broad and had little power to predict with any accuracy the intonation that a speaker would use in a particular context. It is still too early to say how useful the discourse approach will be, but even if it achieves nothing else, it can at least be claimed to have shown the inadequacy of attempting to analyse the function of intonation on the basis of isolated sentences or tone-units, removed from their linguistic and situational context.

Notes on problems and further reading

Important work was done on the placement of tonic stress by Halliday (1967); his term for this is 'tonicity', and he adopts the widely-used linguistic term 'marked' for tonicity that deviates from what I have called (for the sake of simplicity) 'normal'. Within generative phonology there has been much debate about whether one can determine the placing of tonic ('primary') stress without referring to the non-linguistic context in which the speaker says something. This debate was very active in the 1970s, well summarised and criticised in Schmerling (1976), but see Bolinger (1972). For more recent accounts, see Couper-Kuhlen (1986: Chapters 7 and 8) and Ladd (1996: 221–35).

One of the most interesting developments of recent years has been the emergence of a theory of discourse intonation. Readers unfamiliar with the study of discourse may find some initial difficulty in understanding the principles involved; the best introduction is Brazil *et al.* (1980), while the ideas set out there are given more practical expression in Brazil (1994). I have not been able to do more than suggest the rough outline of this approach.

The treatment of intonational subordination is based not on the work of Brazil but on Crystal and Quirk (1964: 52–6) and Crystal (1969: 235–52). The basic philosophy is the same, however, in that both views illustrate the fact that there is in intonation some organisation at a level higher than the isolated tone-unit; this was pointed out in the discussion of Trim (1959; see the notes on Chapter 16 above); see also Fox (1973). A parallel might be drawn with the relationship between the sentence and the paragraph in writing. It seems likely that a considerable amount of valuable new research on pronunciation will grow out of the study of discourse.

Note for teachers

The comment about Audio Unit 18 at the end of Chapter 18 applies also to Audio Unit 19: at first hearing it seems very difficult, but when worked on step by step it is far from impossible. In fact, although this passage sounds rapid and colloquial it is still easier to analyse than a full-speed conversational interchange.

Written exercises

1   In the following exercise, read the "opening line" and then decide the most suitable place for tonic stress placement (underline the syllable) in the response.

a) I'd like you to ˌhelp me   (right) can I do the shopping for you

b) I hear you're offering to do the ˌshopping for someone   (right) can I do the shopping for you

c) What was the first thing that ˌhappened   first the professor explained her theory

d) Was the theory explained by ˌstudents   no first the professor explained her theory

e) Tell me how the ˌtheory was presented   first she explained her theory

f) I think it starts at ten to ˌthree   no ten past three

g) I think it starts at quarter past ˌthree   no ten past three

h) I think it starts at ten past ˌfour   no ten past three

2 The following sentences are given without punctuation. Underline the appropriate tonic syllable places and mark tone-unit boundaries where you think they are appropriate.

a) (*he wrote the letter in a sad way*) he wrote the letter sadly

b) (*it's regrettable that he wrote the letter*) he wrote the letter sadly

c) four plus six divided by two equals five

d) four plus six divided by two equals seven

e) we broke one thing after another fell down

f) we broke one thing after another that night

20 Further areas of study in phonetics and phonology

This chapter completes the course by looking at two further areas of study. Each is important in its own way, and each is an area on which students working at an advanced level in phonetics and phonology spend a considerable amount of time.

20.1 Laboratory phonetics

Experimental phonetics has been an important part of phonetics for most of the twentieth century, and experimental work in phonetics laboratories has produced many important discoveries about how speech is produced and perceived. Too often, however, this area of the subject has been regarded as a mysterious world where incomprehensible things are done with expensive equipment. This situation is changing rapidly, and one consequence of the easier availability of instrumental speech analysis techniques is that the fields of descriptive phonetics, pronunciation teaching and experimental phonetics have become much more closely linked. Computers and the software needed to analyse speech are becoming much cheaper, and the increasing accessibility of the internet is adding to the availability of suitable technology.

In explaining the subject matter of experimental phonetics it is helpful to start by looking at the **speech chain**, which may be diagrammed in simplified form like this:

speaker's brain		speaker's vocal tract		transmission of sound through air		listener's ear		listener's brain
1	→	2	→	3	→	4	→	5
		articulatory phonetic level		**acoustic phonetic level**		**auditory phonetic level**		

With currently available technology we are not able to discover what goes on in detail in the brain when someone is speaking (Stage 1), although we can make informed guesses based on evidence such as speech errors ("slips of the tongue"), the effects on speech production of different sorts of brain damage and the evidence of brain scanning.

Much more is known about Stage 2, the articulatory aspect of speech production. Many special instruments have been developed to help us to find out about such things as the pressure of air in the lungs and the vocal tract, the flow of air out of the mouth and nose, the opening and closing of the vocal folds and of the soft palate, and the movement of articulators like the lips and the lower jaw. X-ray techniques were used extensively for examining the movements of articulators until the 1970s, and produced very important discoveries, but it later became clear that there were serious health risks in using normal radiographic and cineradiographic technology (in the early 1970s I received – at my own request – a large amount of radiation through cineradiographic recording of my larynx for my research, which I now find a little worrying!). Safer "microbeam" techniques with much lower doses of radiation were developed in the 1980s, but even those are now little used. Contact between the tongue and the palate can be measured electrically by means of **electropalatography** (EPG), where a piece of moulded plastic is fitted to the hard palate. This false palate is similar to the palate that holds false teeth for those who have them but, instead of having teeth, this palate contains small electrodes that can detect the contact of the tongue with the hard palate. This technique can reveal a great deal of interesting information about the working of the tongue during speech. Additionally, it is possible to detect the electrical activity that is produced when muscles contract, through **electromyography** (EMG), and we can thus observe the complex co-ordination of activity in the muscles controlling speech production. Although most of these techniques are expensive and difficult to use, it is possible that at least some of them may become more easily available. They can be very useful both for discovering in detail how English speakers produce their speech sounds, and for demonstrating to learners of English their pronunciation errors in a way that helps them to correct them. To give a simple example, recording the airflow from speakers' mouths can show how successfully they are producing the aspiration appropriate for syllable-initial **p**, **t** and **k**.

Stage 3, the transmission of sound waves through the air, is studied by **acoustic analysis**. Much has been discovered about the sounds of speech in this way. We can discover the physical events that produce the perceptual characteristics of speech sounds, including the **duration** of sounds or syllables (we often refer to duration as "length"), the **intensity** of different sounds (which is closely related to the loudness that we perceive), and the fundamental frequency of voiced sounds (which is closely related to pitch). Until recently, the acoustic analysis of speech was such a slow and laborious business that only small samples of speech could be analysed; however, developments in computer technology have made it possible to carry out analysis on a much larger scale. Software for acoustic analysis and spectrographic displays of speech is available at little or no cost via the internet, and it is now possible to get a computer to produce a simple phonetic transcription of what is said to it.

Computers can provide additional pronunciation training at times when a human teacher is not available, and can help children with hearing and speech disorders to improve their speech. Since (as mentioned above) it is possible to produce an accurate computer analysis of the fundamental frequency of speech, this can be displayed on a screen to help someone in practising the production of prosodic features of speech.

Finally, it is of great importance to discover more about how the listener's brain identifies what it receives from the ear (Stages 4 and 5). Many experiments have shown how sensitive human beings are to very slight acoustic differences and how flexible they are in being able to adjust to very different speakers. We are also very strongly influenced by our expectations: if we have heard and understood half a sentence, it seems that our brain is already guessing at what the rest of it will be before it is heard, and is certainly not acting in a passive way like a simple machine. To help in discovering the organisation and the capabilities of our ability for perceiving speech, we need to be able to produce very small and finely-controlled differences in speech sounds. Experimental phonetics has made much use of speech produced through the technique of **speech synthesis**. The best speech synthesis is capable of producing speech of such high quality that

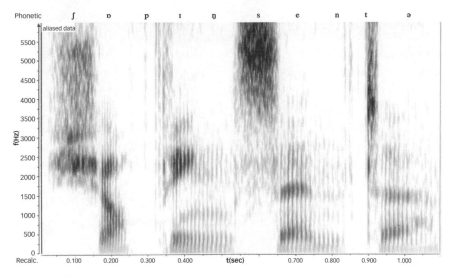

Fig. 15 Spectrogram of phrase 'shopping centre'

only an expert can distinguish it from a recording of a human being's speech; less sophisticated synthesisers are now often provided at no cost with ordinary personal computers. It is possible that synthetic speech may have a useful role to play in testing language learners' ability to perceive important segmental and suprasegmental distinctions in the language they are learning. We can also make many discoveries about perception by modifying and manipulating recordings of real speech. Tricks such as cutting sounds out of words, playing sounds backwards, lengthening or shortening syllables and modifying the intonation of a sentence are all relatively easy to do and can provide surprising results.

One of the major problems in the experimental study of speech is the enormous amount of **variability** found both within the speech of an individual and among different speakers. This means that if we study only one or two speakers, it is likely that our results will not be typical of other speakers. Much modern speech research makes use of collections of very large amounts of spoken data stored in digital form on computers in a form which allows the computer to search and process examples of particular types of phonetic data. Such collections are known as **speech databases**. Examples from my own research include searching for all fall–rise intonation patterns in six hours of BBC speech (producing several thousand examples), and comparing the durations of different types of sound in a database comprising a number of different languages to look for cross-language differences and similarities.

20.2 The study of variety

The previous section ended with a brief introduction to the subject of variability in speech. One type of variability is seen in the differences among accents of English, and this is a subject that many students of English find interesting and wish to know more about. For a long time, the study of accents was part of the subject of **dialectology**, which aimed to identify all the ways in which a language differed from place to place. Dialectology in its traditional form is therefore principally interested in geographical differences; its best-known data-gathering technique was to send researchers (usually called "field-workers") mainly into rural areas (where the speakers were believed to be less likely to have been influenced by other accents), to find elderly speakers (whose speech was believed to have been less influenced by other accents and to preserve older forms of the dialect) and to use lists of questions to find information about vocabulary and pronunciation, the questions being chosen to concentrate on items known to vary a lot from region to region. Surveys of this kind can provide the basis for many generalisations about geographical variation, but they have serious weaknesses.

Differences between accents are of two main sorts: **phonetic** and **phonological**. When two accents differ from each other only phonetically, we find the same set of phonemes in both accents, but some or all of the phonemes are realised differently. There may also be differences in stress or intonation, but not such as would cause a change in meaning. As an example of phonetic differences at the segmental level, it is said that Australian English has the same set of phonemes and phonemic contrasts as BBC pronunciation, yet Australian pronunciation is so different from that accent that it is easily recognised. A word of caution should be given here: it is all too easy to talk about such things as "Australian English", "American English" and so on, and to ignore the variety that inevitably exists within a large community of speakers. Each individual's speech is different from any other's; it follows from this that no one speaker can be taken to represent a particular accent or dialect, and it also follows that the idea of a standard pronunciation is a convenient fiction, not a scientific fact.

Many accents of English also differ noticeably in intonation without the difference being such as would cause a difference in meaning; some Welsh accents, for example, have a tendency for unstressed syllables to be higher in pitch than stressed syllables. Such a difference is, again, a phonetic one. An example of a phonetic (non-phonological) difference in stress would be the stressing of the final syllable of verbs ending in '-ise' in some Scottish and Northern Irish accents (e.g. 'realise' **rɪəˈlaɪz**).

Phonological differences are of various types: again, we can divide these into segmental and suprasegmental. Within the area of segmental phonology the most obvious type of difference is where one accent has a different number of phonemes (and hence of phonemic contrasts) from another. Many speakers with Northern English accents, for example, do not have a contrast between ʌ and ʊ, so that 'luck' and 'look' are pronounced identically (both as **lʊk**); in the case of consonants, many accents do not have the phoneme **h**, so that there is no difference in pronunciation between 'art' and 'heart'. The phonemic system of such accents is therefore different from that of the BBC accent. On the other hand, some accents differ from others in having *more* phonemes and phonemic contrasts. For example, many Northern English accents have a long **eː** sound as the realisation of the phoneme symbolised **eɪ** in BBC (which is a simple phonetic difference); but in some Northern accents there is both an **eɪ** diphthong phoneme and also a contrasting long vowel phoneme that can be symbolised as **eː**. Words like 'eight' and 'reign' are pronounced **eɪt**, **reɪn**, while 'late', 'rain' (with no 'g' in the spelling) are pronounced **leːt**, **reːn**.

A more complicated kind of difference is where, without affecting the overall set of phonemes and contrasts, a phoneme has a distribution in one accent that is different from the same phoneme's distribution in another accent. The obvious example is **r**, which is restricted to occurring in pre-vocalic position in BBC pronunciation, but in many other accents is not restricted in this way. Another example is the occurrence of **j** between a consonant and **uː**, **ʊ** or **ʊə**;

in BBC pronunciation we can find the following: 'pew' **pjuː**, 'tune' **tjuːn**, 'queue' **kjuː**. However, in many American accents and in some English accents of the South and East we find that, while 'pew' is pronounced **pjuː** and 'queue' as **kjuː**, 'tune' is pronounced **tuːn**; this absence of **j** is found after the other alveolar consonants, hence: 'due' **duː**; 'new' **nuː**.

We also find another kind of variation: in the example just given above, the occurrence of the phonemes being discussed is determined by their phonological context; however, sometimes the determining factor is lexical rather than phonological. For example, in many accents of the Midlands and North-Western England a particular set of words containing a vowel (represented by 'o' in the spelling) is pronounced as ʌ in BBC but as ɒ in these other accents; the list of words includes 'one', 'none', 'nothing', 'tongue', 'mongrel' and 'constable'. One result of this difference is that such accents have different pronunciations for the two members of pairs of words that are pronounced identically (i.e. are homophones) in BBC, e.g. 'won' and 'one', 'nun' and 'none'. For example, in my own pronunciation when I was young, I had ɒ instead of ʌ in these words, so that 'won' was pronounced **wʌn** and 'one' as **wɒn**, 'nun' as **nʌn** and 'none' as **nɒn**.

It would be satisfying to be able to list examples of phonological differences between accents in the area of stress and intonation but, unfortunately, straightforward examples are not available. We do not yet know enough about the phonological functions of stress and intonation, and not enough work has been done on comparing accents in terms of these factors. It will be necessary to show how one accent is able to make some difference in meaning with stress or intonation that another accent is unable to make. It is very probable that such differences do exist, and that they will in due course be identified by suitable research work.

It was mentioned earlier in this section that there were weaknesses in the description of accents in terms of geographical variation alone; the study of sociolinguistics has shown the importance of considering other sources of variation. We can find differences in pronunciation (as well as in other fields of linguistic analysis) resulting from various factors that we could call "static" influences including (in addition to geographical origin) one's age and sex, social class, educational background, occupation and personality. In addition, various situational factors influence pronunciation, such as the social relationship between speaker and hearer, whether one is speaking publicly or privately and the purposes for which one is using language. Some people (who usually turn out to do well in phonetic training) find that in speaking to someone with a different accent their pronunciation gets progressively more like that of the person they are speaking to, like a chameleon adapting its colour to its environment.

Among the situational factors influencing variation, it is possible to pick out some which could be described as stylistic, and many linguists have attempted to produce frameworks for the analysis of style in language. There is not space for us to consider this in detail, but we should note that, for foreign learners, a typical situation – regrettably, an almost inevitable one – is that they learn a style of pronunciation which could be described as careful and formal. Probably their teachers speak to them in this style, although what the learners are likely to encounter when they join in conversations with native speakers is what we have referred to previously as a "rapid, casual" style. An additional problem is that young foreign students tend to be taught the pronunciation of an older generation; even if they should learn to speak like young English people, it is likely that they will face the problem of being evaluated by examiners whose standard is that of an older generation.

Young children have an enviable ability to acquire the rapid, casual pronunciation of a language apparently without effort if they are provided with the necessary social contact with native speakers and meaningful communication situations. It has been claimed that adults can also "pick up" spoken language in this way (second language acquisition) better than by the traditional classroom approach (second language learning) if the conditions are similar to those experienced by young children. This is an attractive idea, but for most adults the goal of learning through communicating naturally in the language throughout the day will, sadly, never be a practical one. We have to continue to make use of something like formal classroom teaching because of the limited time and resources available.

It should now be clear that the pronunciation described in this course is only one of a vast number of possible varieties. The choice of a slow, careful style is made for the sake of convenience and simplicity; learners of English need to be aware of the fact that this style is far from being the only one they will meet, and teachers of English to foreigners should do their best to expose their pupils to other varieties.

Notes on problems and further reading

20.1   There are few satisfactory books that explain the principles of experimental phonetics, in the sense of how to design and carry out experiments and to interpret the results in terms that are meaningful to other phoneticians. I would recommend Lass (1996), although some of it is difficult. There is a useful review of modern instrumental techniques in Ball and Code (1997) or, more briefly, in Chapter 12 of Ball and Rahilly (1999). A recent addition to the list is Hayward (2000).

There are some good books that explain the speech chain and the aspects of speech that are measurable. *The Speech Chain* by Denes and Pinson (1993) is clear and interesting. Basic introductions to acoustic phonetics are given in many phonetics textbooks including Ladefoged (1993), Clark and Yallop (1995) and Ball and Rahilly (1999). Fuller treatment is given in Johnson (1996), Borden and Harris (1994) and Lieberman and Blumstein (1988).

20.2   On the study of accent variety, the list of references could become enormous. Those given in the section "Recommendations for general reading" (pp. 270) should be enough for most readers. The same is true for sociolinguistics, but I feel that any reading beyond basic introductory material ought to include some work by Labov, whose influence on the subject has been profound; see, for example, Labov (1972).

Note for teachers
Audio Unit 20 is short and intensive. It is meant primarily to give a final reminder that English spoken at something like full conversational speed is very different from the slow, careful pronunciation of the early Audio Units. If there is time, students should now be encouraged to go back to some of the more difficult Audio Units

dealing with connected speech (say from Audio Unit 12 onwards, missing out Audio Unit 15); they will probably discover a lot of things they did not notice before.

Written exercises
Phonological differences between accents are of various types. For each of the following sets of data, based on non-BBC accents, say what you can conclude about the phonology of that accent.

1 'sing' sɪŋ   'finger' fɪŋgə
   'sung' sʌŋ   'running' rʌnɪn
   'singing' sɪŋɪn   'ring' rɪŋ
2 'day' deː   'you' juː
   'buy' baɪ   'me' miː
   'go' goː   'more' mɔː
   'now' naʊ   'fur' fɜː
3 'mother' mʌvə   'father' fɑːvə
   'think' fɪŋk   'breath' bref
   'lip' lɪp   'pill' pɪw
   'help' ewp   'hill' ɪw
4 'mother' mʌðər   'father' fɑːðər
   'car' kɑːr   'cart' kɑːrt
   'area' eːriəl   'aerial' eːriəl
   'idea' aɪdɪəl   'ideal' aɪdɪəl
   'India' ɪndɪəl   'Norma' nɔːrməl
5 'cat' kat   'plaster' plaːstər
   'cart' kɑːrt   'grass' graːs
   'calm' kɑːm   'gas' gas

Recorded exercises

These exercises are mainly intended for students whose native language is not English; however, those exercises which involve work with transcription (exercises 2.2, 3.3, 3.5, 3.7, 4.5, 5.3, 5.4, 6.2, 7.6, 9.5, 10.1, 10.2, 10.3, 11.5, 12.3, 13.1, 13.2, 13.3, all of Audio Unit 14 and exercise 20.2) and those which give practice in intonation (Audio Units 15, 16, 17, 18, and 19, and exercise 20.3) will be useful to native speakers as well.

Each Audio Unit corresponds to a chapter of this book, with the exception that there is no Audio Unit 1 to correspond to Chapter 1. As far as possible, I have tried to relate the contents of each Audio Unit to the subject matter of the chapter; however, where the chapter is devoted to theoretical matters I have taken advantage of this to produce revision exercises going back over some of the subjects previously worked on.

In some of the exercises you are asked to put stress or intonation marks on the text. It would obviously be sensible to do this in a way that will make it possible for you, or someone else, to erase these marks and use the exercise again.

As with the chapters of the book, the CDs and tapes are intended to be worked through from first to last. Those at the beginning are concerned with individual vowels and consonants, and the words containing them are usually pronounced in isolation in a slow, careful style. Pronouncing isolated words in this way is, of course, a very artificial practice, but the recorded exercises are designed to lead the student towards the study of comparatively natural and fluent speech by the end of the course. In some of the later exercises you will find it necessary to stop the CD or tape in order to allow yourself enough time to write a transcription.

After Audio Unit 20, there is an answers section. Two symbols are used throughout the Audio Units: **||** means "Pause the CD or tape" and ▶ means "Start the CD or tape".

Audio Unit 2   English short vowels

The exercises in this Audio Unit practise the six short vowels introduced in Chapter 2. When pronouncing them, you should take care to give the vowels the correct length *and* the correct quality.

Exercise 1   Repetition
Listen and repeat:

ɪ

| bit **bɪt** | bid **bɪd** | him **hɪm** | miss **mɪs** |

e

| bet **bet** | bed **bed** | hen **hen** | mess **mes** |

æ

| bat **bæt** | bad **bæd** | ham **hæm** | mass **mæs** |

ʌ

| cut **kʌt** | bud **bʌd** | bun **bʌn** | bus **bʌs** |

ɒ

| pot **pɒt** | cod **kɒd** | Tom **tɒm** | loss **lɒs** |

ʊ

| put **pʊt** | wood **wʊd** | pull **pʊl** | push **pʊʃ** |

Exercise 2   Identification
Write the symbol for the vowel you hear in each word. (1 . . . 10)
Check your answers.   **||**

Exercise 3   Production   ▶
When you hear the number, pronounce the word (which is given in spelling and in phonetic symbols). Repeat the correct pronunciation when you hear it. *Example*: 1. 'mad'

1 mad **mæd**	7 put **pʊt**
2 mud **mʌd**	8 pot **pɒt**
3 bit **bɪt**	9 men **men**
4 bet **bet**	10 man **mæn**
5 cut **kʌt**	11 fun **fʌn**
6 cot **kɒt**	12 fan **fæn**

Exercise 4   Short vowels contrasted
Listen and repeat (words given in spelling):

ɪ and e		e and æ		æ and ʌ	
bit	bet	hem	ham	lack	luck
tin	ten	set	sat	bad	bud
fill	fell	peck	pack	fan	fun
built	belt	send	sand	stamp	stump
lift	left	wreck	rack	flash	flush

ʌ and ɒ		ɒ and ʊ	
dug	dog	lock	look
cup	cop	cod	could
rub	rob	pot	put
stuck	stock	shock	shook
luck	lock	crock	crook?tpb=2pt>

Audio Unit 3   Long vowels, diphthongs and triphthongs

Long vowels

Exercise 1   Repetition
Listen and repeat:

iː
| beat **biːt** | bead **biːd** | been **biːn** | beef **biːf** |

ɑː
| heart **hɑːt** | hard **hɑːd** | harm **hɑːm** | hearth **hɑːθ** |

ɔː
| caught **kɔːt** | cord **kɔːd** | corn **kɔːn** | course **kɔːs** |

uː
| root **ruːt** | rude **ruːd** | room **ruːm** | roof **ruːf** |

ɜː
| hurt **hɜːt** | heard **hɜːd** | earn **ɜːn** | earth **ɜːθ** |

Exercise 2   Production
When you hear the number, pronounce the word. Repeat the correct pronunciation when you hear it.

1 heard **hɜːd**   6 heart **hɑːt**
2 been **biːn**   7 cord **kɔːd**

3 root **ruːt**   8 beef **biːf**
4 hearth **hɑːθ**   9 rude **ruːd**
5 caught **kɔːt** 10 earn **ɜːn**

Exercise 3 Transcription
Write the symbol for the vowel you hear in each word. (1 . . . 10)

Check your answers.   **II**

Exercise 4 Long–short vowel contrasts   ▶
Listen and repeat (words given in spelling):

iː and ɪ		ɑː and ʌ		ɑː and æ	
feel	fill	calm	come	part	pat
bead	bid	cart	cit	lard	lad
steel	still	half	huff	calm	Cam
reed	rid	lark	luck	heart	hat
been	bin	mast	must	harms	hams

ɔː and ɒ		uː and ʊ		ɜː and ʌ		ɑː and ɒ	
caught	cot	pool	pull	hurt	hut	dark	dock
stork	stock	suit	soot	turn	ton	part	pot
short	shot	Luke	look	curt	cut	lark	lock
cord	cod	wooed	wood	girl	gull	balm	bomb
port	pot	fool	full	bird	bud	large	lodge

Exercise 5 Transcription
Write the symbol for the vowel (long or short) you hear in each word. (1 . . . 10)

Check your answers.   **II**

Exercise 6 Repetition   ▶
Listen and repeat, making sure that the second part of the diphthong is weak.

eɪ
mate **meɪt**   made **meɪd**   main **meɪn**   mace **meɪs**
aɪ
right **raɪt**   ride **raɪd**   rhyme **raɪm**   rice **raɪs**

ɔɪ

quoit **kɔɪt**	buoyed **bɔɪd**	Boyne **bɔɪn**	Royce **rɔɪs**

əʊ

coat **kəʊt**	code **kəʊd**	cone **kəʊn**	close **kləʊs**

aʊ

gout **gaʊt**	loud **laʊd**	gown **gaʊn**	louse **laʊs**

ɪə

	feared **fɪəd**	Ian **ɪən**	fierce **fɪəs**

eə

	cared **keəd**	cairn **keən**	scarce **skeəs**

ʊə

	moored **mʊəd**	fuel **fjʊəl**

Exercise 7   Transcription
Write the symbol for the diphthong you hear in each word. (1 . . . 12)

Check your answers.   ‖

Triphthongs

Exercise 8   Repetition   ▶
Listen and repeat:

eɪə	layer **leɪə**	əʊə	lower **ləʊə**
aɪə	liar **laɪə**	aʊə	tower **taʊə**
ɔɪə	loyal **lɔɪəl**		

Audio Unit 4   Plosives

Exercise 1   Repetition of initial plosives

INITIAL FORTIS **p**, **t**, **k**
Each word begins with a fortis plosive; notice that the plosive is aspirated. Listen and repeat:

paw **pɔː**	care **keə**
tea **tiː**	two **tuː**
car **kɑː**	key **kiː**
pie **paɪ**	tar **tɑː**
toe **təʊ**	pay **peɪ**

218

INITIAL LENIS **b**, **d**, **g**
Each word begins with a lenis plosive; notice that there is practically no voicing of the plosive. Listen and repeat:

bee **biː**	gear **gɪə**
door **dɔː**	boy **bɔɪ**
go **gəʊ**	dear **dɪə**
bear **beə**	bough **baʊ**
do **duː**	day **deɪ**

INITIAL **sp**, **st**, **sk**
The plosive must be unaspirated. Listen and repeat:

spy **spaɪ**	score **skɔː**
store **stɔː**	spear **spɪə**
ski **skiː**	stay **steɪ**
spare **speə**	sky **skaɪ**
steer **stɪə**	spar **spɑː**

Exercise 2 Repetition of final plosives

In the pairs of words in this exercise one word ends with a fortis plosive and the other ends with a lenis plosive. Notice the length difference in the vowel. Listen to each pair and repeat:

FORTIS FOLLOWED BY LENIS

mate made	**meɪt meɪd**
rope robe	**rəʊp rəʊb**
leak league	**liːk liːg**
cart card	**kɑːt kɑːd**
back bag	**bæk bæg**

LENIS FOLLOWED BY FORTIS

code coat	**kəʊd kəʊt**
bid bit	**bɪd bɪt**
lobe lope	**ləʊb ləʊp**
heard hurt	**hɜːd hɜːt**
brogue broke	**brəʊg brəʊk**

Exercise 3   Identification of final plosives
You will hear the twenty words of Exercise 2. Each will be one of a
pair. You must choose whether the word is the one ending with a
fortis plosive or the one ending with a lenis plosive; when you hear
the word, say "fortis" if you heard the word on the left, or "lenis" if
you heard the word on the right. You will then hear the correct
answer and the word will be said again for you to repeat.
Example: 'coat'

Fortis	Lenis	Fortis	Lenis
coat **kəʊt**	code **kəʊd**	mate **meɪt**	made **meɪd**
leak **liːk**	league **liːg**	coat **kəʊt**	code **kəʊd**
hurt **hɜːt**	heard **hɜːd**	leak **liːk**	league **liːg**
bit **bɪt**	bid **bɪd**	rope **rəʊp**	robe **rəʊb**
mate **meɪt**	made **meɪd**	hurt **hɜːt**	heard **hɜːd**
lope **ləʊp**	lobe **ləʊb**	broke **brəʊk**	brogue **brəʊg**
back **bæk**	bag **bæg**	lope **ləʊp**	lobe **ləʊb**
cart **kɑːt**	card **kɑːd**	bit **bɪt**	bid **bɪd**
broke **brəʊk**	brogue **brəʊg**	back **bæk**	bag **bæg**
rope **rəʊp**	robe **rəʊb**	cart **kɑːt**	card **kɑːd**

Each of the words which follow ends with a plosive. Write the
symbol for each plosive when you hear the word. Each will be said
twice.
(1 . . . 10)

Check your answers.   ❚❚

Exercise 4   Repetition of words containing plosives   ▶
The following words contain several plosives. They are given in
spelling and in transcription. Listen and repeat:

potato **pəteɪtəʊ**	carpeted **kɑːpɪtɪd**
topic **tɒpɪk**	bodyguard **bɒdɪgɑːd**
petticoat **petɪkəʊt**	tobacco **təbækəʊ**
partake **pɑːteɪk**	doubted **daʊtɪd**
cupboard **kʌbəd**	decode **diːkəʊd**
decapitated **dɪkæpɪteɪtɪd**	bigoted **bɪgətɪd**
pocket **pɒkɪt**	about **əbaʊt**

Exercise 5   Reading of words in transcription
When you hear the number, pronounce the word given in transcription taking care to pronounce the plosives correctly and putting the strongest stress on the syllable preceded by the stress mark '. You will then hear the correct pronunciation which you should repeat.

1 dɪˈbeɪt	6 ˈgɑːdɪd
2 ˈkɒpɪd	7 ˈdedɪkeɪtɪd
3 ˈbʌtəkʌp	8 ˈpædək
4 ˈkʊkuː	9 buːˈtiːk
5 dɪˈkeɪd	10 ˈæpɪtaɪt

(You will find these words in spelling form in the answers section)

Audio Unit 5   Revision

Exercise 1   Vowels and diphthongs
Listen and repeat (words given in spelling):

ɑː and ɜː		eɪ and e		aɪ and ɑː	
barn	burn	fade	fed	life	laugh
are	err	sale	sell	tight	tart
fast	first	laid	led	pike	park
cart	curt	paste	pest	hide	hard
lark	lurk	late	let	spike	spark

ɔɪ and ɔː		əʊ and ɔː		ɪə and iː	
toy	tore	phone	fawn	fear	fee
coin	corn	boat	bought	beard	bead
boil	ball	code	cord	mere	me
boy	bore	stoke	stork	steered	steed
foil	fall	bowl	ball	peer	pea

eə and eɪ		eə and ɪə		ʊə and ɔː	
dare	day	fare	fear	poor	paw
stared	stayed	pair	pier	sure	shore
pairs	pays	stare	steer	moor	more
hair	hay	air	ear	dour	door
mare	may	snare	sneer	tour	tore

Exercise 2   Triphthongs
Listen and repeat:

eɪə   player **pleɪə**

aɪə   tyre **taɪə**

ɔɪə   loyal **lɔɪəl**

əʊə   mower **məʊə**

aʊə   shower **ʃaʊə**

Exercise 3   Transcription of words
You should now be able to recognise all the vowels, diphthongs and triphthongs of English, and all the plosives. In the next exercise you will hear one-syllable English words composed of these sounds. Each word will be said twice. You must transcribe these words using the phonetic symbols that you have learned in the first three chapters. When you hear the word, write it with phonetic symbols. (1 . . . 20) Now check your answers.   ▮▮

Exercise 4   Production   ▶
The following are all English words; they are given only in phonemic transcription. When you hear the number you should say the word; you will then hear the correct pronunciation, which you should repeat. If you want to see how these words are spelt when you have finished the exercise, you will find them in the answers section.

1 **kiːp**	11 **dʌk**
2 **bəʊt**	12 **kəʊp**
3 **kʌp**	13 **dɒg**
4 **dɜːt**	14 **kaʊəd**
5 **baɪk**	15 **beɪk**
6 **kæb**	16 **taɪd**
7 **geɪt**	17 **bɪəd**
8 **keəd**	18 **pʊt**
9 **taɪəd**	19 **bʌg**
10 **bɜːd**	20 **daʊt**

Exercise 5   Fortis/lenis discrimination

When you hear the word, say "fortis" if you hear it as ending with a fortis consonant, and "lenis' if you hear it as ending with a lenis consonant. You will then hear the correct answer and the word will be said again for you to repeat.

Fortis	Lenis
1 right **raɪt**	ride **raɪd**
2 bat **bæt**	bad **bæd**
3 bet **bet**	bed **bed**
4 leak **liːk**	league **liːg**
5 feet **fiːt**	feed **fiːd**
6 right **raɪt**	ride **raɪd**
7 tack **tæk**	tag **tæg**
8 rope **rəʊp**	robe **rəʊb**
9 mate **meɪt**	made **meɪd**
10 beat **biːt**	bead **biːd**

Audio Unit 6   Fricatives and affricates

Exercise 1   Repetition of words containing fricatives

Listen and repeat (words given in spelling and transcription):

f	fin **fɪn**	offer **ɒfə**	laugh **lɑːf**
v	vat **væt**	over **əʊvə**	leave **liːv**
θ	thing **θɪŋ**	method **meθəd**	breath **breθ**
ð	these **ðiːz**	other **ʌðə**	breathe **briːð**
s	sad **sæd**	lesser **lesə**	moss **mɒs**
z	zoo **zuː**	lazy **leɪzi**	lose **luːz**
ʃ	show **ʃəʊ**	washing **wɒʃɪŋ**	rush **rʌʃ**
ʒ		measure **meʒə**	rogue **ruːʒ**
h	hot **hɒt**	beehive **biːhaɪv**	

Exercise 2   Identification

Write the symbol for the fricative you hear in each word.

a) initial position: (1 . . . 5)

b) medial position (6 . . . 10)

c) final position (11 . . . 15)

Now check your answers.   ‖

Exercise 3   Production   ▶

When you hear the number, pronounce the word, giving particular attention to the fricatives. You will then hear the correct pronunciation, which you should repeat.

1 **ðiːz** these	6 **fɪfθ** fifth
2 **feɪθ** faith	7 **ʃɪvəz** shivers
3 **heðə** heather	8 **bɪheɪv** behave
4 **siːʃɔː** seashore	9 **siːʒə** seizure
5 **feðəz** feathers	10 **læʃɪz** lashes

Exercise 4   Repetition of fricative and affricate pairs

Listen and repeat:

a) Initial **ʃ** and **tʃ**
   ʃɒp tʃɒp (shop, chop)
   ʃiːt tʃiːt (sheet, cheat)
   ʃuːz tʃuːz (shoes, choose)

b) Medial **ʃ** and **tʃ**
   liːʃɪz liːtʃɪz (leashes, leaches)
   wɒʃɪŋ wɒtʃɪŋ (washing, watching)
   bæʃɪz bætʃɪz (bashes, batches)

c) Final **ʃ** and **tʃ**
   mæʃ mætʃ (mash, match)
   kæʃ kætʃ (cash, catch)
   wɪʃ wɪtʃ (wish, witch)

d) Medial **ʒ** and **dʒ**
   leʒə ledʒə (leisure, ledger)
   pleʒə pledʒə (pleasure, pledger)
   liːʒən liːdʒən (lesion, legion)

Exercise 5   Discrimination between fricatives and affricates

You will hear some of the words of Exercise 4. When you hear the word, say "A" if you hear the word on the left, or "B" if you hear the word on the right. You will then hear the correct answer and the word will be said again for you to repeat.

A	B
ʃɒp	tʃɒp
kæʃ	kætʃ
wɒʃɪŋ	wɒtʃɪŋ
ʃuːz	tʃuːz
liːʒən	liːdʒən
bæʃɪz	bætʃɪz
ʃiːt	tʃiːt
leʒə	ledʒə
liːʃɪz	liːtʃɪz
wɪʃ	wɪtʃ
pleʒə	pledʒə
mæʃ	mætʃ

Audio Unit 7   Further consonants

Exercise 1   Repetition of words containing a velar nasal

Listen and repeat; take care not to pronounce a plosive after the velar nasal.

hæŋ	hæŋə
sɪŋɪŋ	rɒŋ
rʌŋ	bæŋɪŋ
θɪŋ	rɪŋ

Exercise 2   ŋ with and without g

WORDS OF ONE MORPHEME
Listen and repeat:

fɪŋgə	finger
æŋgə	anger
bæŋgə	Bangor
hʌŋgə	hunger
æŋgl̩	angle

225

WORDS OF TWO MORPHEMES
Listen and repeat:

sɪŋə	singer
hæŋə	hanger
lɒŋɪŋ	longing
rɪŋɪŋ	ringing
bæŋə	banger

Exercise 3   "Clear" and "dark" 1

"CLEAR l" BEFORE VOWELS
Listen and repeat:

laɪ lie	ləʊ low
luːs loose	laʊd loud
liːk leak	lɔː law

"DARK l" BEFORE PAUSE
Listen and repeat:

fɪl fill	peɪl pale
bel bell	maɪl mile
niːl kneel	kɪl kill

"DARK l" BEFORE CONSONANTS
Listen and repeat:

help help	feɪld failed
fɪlθ filth	mɪlk milk
belt belt	welʃ Welsh

Exercise 4   The consonant r
Listen and repeat, concentrating on not allowing the tongue to make contact with the roof of the mouth in pronouncing this consonant:

eərɪŋ airing	reərə rarer
riːraɪt rewrite	herɪŋ herring
terərɪst terrorist	mɪrə mirror
ærəʊ arrow	rɔːrɪŋ roaring

Exercise 5   The consonants **j** and **w**

Listen and repeat:

juː you	**weɪ** way
jɔːn yawn	**wɔː** war
jɪə year	**wɪn** win
jʊə your	**weə** wear

Exercise 6   Dictation of words

When you hear the word, write it down using phonemic symbols. Each word will be said three times; you should pause your CD or tape if you need more time for writing.
(1 . . . 12)

Check your answers.   ▐▐

Audio Unit 8   Consonant clusters

Exercise 1   Devoicing of **l, r, w, j**

When **l, r, w, j** follow **p, t** or **k** in syllable-initial position they are produced as voiceless, slightly fricative sounds.
Listen and repeat:

pleɪ play	**treɪ** tray	**klɪə** clear
preɪ pray	**twɪn** twin	**kraɪ** cry
pjuː pew	**tjuːn** tune	**kjuː** queue

Exercise 2   Repetition of initial clusters

TWO CONSONANTS
Listen and repeat:

spɒt spot	**plaʊ** plough
stəʊn stone	**twɪst** twist
skeɪt skate	**kriːm** cream
sfɪə sphere	**pjʊə** pure
smaɪl smile	**fleɪm** flame
snəʊ snow	**ʃrɪŋk** shrink
slæm slam	**vjuː** view
swɪtʃ switch	**θwɔːt** thwart

THREE CONSONANTS
Listen and repeat:

spleɪ splay	streɪ stray	skruː screw
spreɪ spray	stjuː stew	skwɒʃ squash
spjuː spew		skjuː skew

Exercise 3 Final plosive-plus-plosive clusters

a) When one plosive is followed by another at the end of a syllable, the second plosive is usually the only one that can be clearly heard. In this exercise, take care not to make an audible release of the first plosive.
Listen and repeat:

pækt packed	rɪgd rigged
bægd bagged	dʌkt duct
drɒpt dropped	lept leapt
rɒbd robbed	græbd grabbed

b) It is difficult to hear the difference between, for example, 'dropped back' and 'drop back', since in the normal pronunciation only the last plosive of the cluster (the **b** of **bæk**) is audibly released. The main difference is that the three-consonant cluster is longer.
Listen and repeat:

A	B
græbd bəʊθ grabbed both	græb bəʊθ grab both
laɪkt ðəm liked them	laɪk ðəm like them
hɒpt bæk hopped back	hɒp bæk hop back
lʊkt fɔːwəd looked forward	lʊk fɔːwəd look forward
pegd daʊn pegged down	peg daʊn peg down
wɪpt kriːm whipped cream	wɪp kriːm whip cream

Exercise 4 Recognition

Look at the items of Exercise 3(b) above. When you hear one of them, say "A" if you hear an item from the left-hand column, or "B" if you hear one from the right-hand column. You will then hear the correct answer and the item will be said again for you to repeat.
(1 . . . 6)

Exercise 5   *Final clusters of three and four consonants*

Listen and repeat:

helps helps	**nekst** next
sɪksθ sixth	**reɪndʒd** ranged
θæŋkt thanked	**rɪsks** risks
edʒd edged	**riːtʃt** reached
twelfθs twelfths	**teksts** texts

Exercise 6   *Pronouncing consonant clusters*

When you hear the number, say the word. You will then hear the correct pronunciation which you should repeat.

1 **skreɪpt**	5 **krʌnʃt**
2 **grʌdʒd**	6 **θrəʊnz**
3 **kləʊðz**	7 **plʌndʒd**
4 **skrɪpts**	8 **kwenʃ**

(The spelling of these words is given in the answers section.)   **▌▌**

Audio Unit 9   Weak syllables

Exercise 1   *"Schwa" ə*

TWO-SYLLABLE WORDS WITH WEAK FIRST SYLLABLE
AND STRESS ON THE SECOND SYLLABLE
Listen and repeat:

Weak syllable spelt 'a'
about ə'baʊt	ahead ə'hed	again ə'gen

Spelt 'o'
obtuse əb'tjuːs	oppose ə'pəʊz	offend ə'fend

Spelt 'u'
suppose sə'pəʊz	support sə'pɔːt	suggest sə'dʒest

Spelt 'or'
forget fə'get	forsake fə'seɪk	forbid fə'bɪd

Spelt 'er'
perhaps pə'hæps	per cent pə'sent	perceive pə'siːv

Spelt 'ur'
survive sə'vaɪv	surprise sə'praɪz	survey (verb) sə'veɪ

229

TWO-SYLLABLE WORDS WITH WEAK SECOND SYLLABLE AND STRESS ON THE FIRST SYLLABLE
Listen and repeat:

Weak syllable spelt 'a'

ballad 'bæləd	Alan 'ælən	necklace 'nekləs

Spelt 'o'

melon 'melən	paddock 'pædək	purpose 'pɜːpəs

Spelt 'e'

hundred 'hʌndrəd	sullen 'sʌlən	open 'əupən

Spelt 'u'

circus 'sɜːkəs	Autumn 'ɔːtəm	album 'ælbəm

Spelt 'ar'

tankard 'tæŋkəd	custard 'kʌstəd	standard 'stændəd

Spelt 'or'

juror 'dʒuərə	major 'meɪdʒə	manor 'mænə

Spelt 'er'

longer 'lɒŋgə	eastern 'iːstən	mother 'mʌðə

Spelt 'ure'

nature 'neɪtʃə	posture 'pɒstʃə	creature 'kriːtʃə

Spelt 'ous'

ferrous 'ferəs	vicious 'vɪʃəs	gracious 'greɪʃəs

Spelt 'ough'

thorough 'θʌrə	borough 'bʌrə	

Spelt 'our'

saviour 'seɪvjə	succour 'sʌkə	colour 'kʌlə

THREE-SYLLABLE WORDS WITH WEAK SECOND SYLLABLE AND STRESS ON THE FIRST SYLLABLE
Listen and repeat:

Weak syllable spelt 'a'

workaday 'wɜːkədeɪ	roundabout 'raundəbaut

Spelt 'o'

customer 'kʌstəmə	pantomime 'pæntəmaɪm

Spelt 'u'

perjury 'pɜːdʒəri	venturer 'ventʃərə

Spelt 'ar'

standardize 'stændədaɪz	jeopardy 'dʒepədi

Spelt 'er'

wonderland 'wʌndəlænd	yesterday 'jestədeɪ

Exercise 2　Close front vowels

WEAK INITIAL SYLLABLES
Listen and repeat:

excite ɪk'saɪt	resume rɪ'zjuːm
exist ɪg'zɪst	relate rɪ'leɪt
inane ɪ'neɪn	effect ɪ'fekt
device dɪ'vaɪs	ellipse ɪ'lɪps

WEAK FINAL SYLLABLES
Listen and repeat:

city 'sɪti	many 'meni
funny 'fʌni	lazy 'leɪzi
easy 'iːzi	only 'əʊnli
busy 'bɪzi	lady 'leɪdi

Exercise 3　Syllabic ḷ
Listen and repeat:

bottle 'bɒtḷ	bottled 'bɒtḷd	bottling 'bɒtḷɪŋ
muddle 'mʌdḷ	muddled 'mʌdḷd	muddling 'mʌdḷɪŋ
tunnel 'tʌnḷ	tunnelled 'tʌnḷd	tunnelling 'tʌnḷɪŋ
wrestle 'resḷ	wrestled 'resḷd	wrestling 'resḷɪŋ

Exercise 4　Syllabic ṇ
Listen and repeat:

burden 'bɜːdṇ	burdened 'bɜːdṇd	burdening 'bɜːdṇɪŋ
frighten 'fraɪtṇ	frightened 'fraɪtṇd	frightening 'fraɪtṇɪŋ
listen 'lɪsṇ	listened 'lɪsṇd	listening 'lɪsṇ

Exercise 5　Transcription
Transcribe the following words when you hear them, giving particular attention to the weak syllables. Each word will be said twice. If you need more time for writing, pause your CD or tape and restart it when you are ready for the next word.
(1 . . . 10)

Now check your answers.　　　　　　　　　　　　　　■■

Audio Unit 10   Word stress

Exercise 1   Stress marking
When you hear the word, repeat it, then place a stress mark (') before
the stressed syllable.

enɪmi enemy	səbtrækt subtract
kəlekt collect	elɪfənt elephant
kæpɪtl̩ capital	əbzɜːvə observer
kɑːneɪʃn̩ carnation	prɒfɪt profit
pærədaɪs paradise	entəteɪn entertain

Now check your marking with the correct version. **▌▌**

Exercise 2   Pronouncing from transcription ▶
The following are British place names. When you hear the number,
pronounce them with the stress as marked. You will then hear the
correct pronunciation, which you should repeat.

1 'ʃrəʊzbr̩i	6 'bɜːmɪŋəm
2 pɒl'perəʊ	7 nɔː'θæmptən
3 æbə'diːn	8 dʌn'diː
4 wʊlvə'hæmptən	9 'kæntəbr̩i
5 æbə'rɪstwəθ	10 'beɪzɪŋstəʊk

(The spelling for these names is given in the answers section.)

Exercise 3   Placing stress on verbs, adjectives and nouns
When you hear the number, pronounce the word with the appropriate stress. You will then hear the correct pronunciation, which you
should repeat.

TWO-SYLLABLE WORDS

VERBS

1 dɪsiːv deceive	6 əbʒekt object
2 ʃɑːpən sharpen	7 kɒŋkə conquer
3 kəlekt collect	8 rɪkɔːd record
4 prənaʊns pronounce	9 pɒlɪʃ polish
5 kɒpi copy	10 dɪpend depend

ADJECTIVES

1 iːzi easy
2 kəmpliːt complete
3 meɪdʒə major
4 ələʊn alone
5 bɪləʊ below

6 jeləʊ yellow
7 ɜːli early
8 səblaɪm sublime
9 hevi heavy
10 əlaɪv alive

NOUNS

1 bɪʃəp bishop
2 æspekt aspect
3 əfeə affair
4 kɑːpɪt carpet
5 dɪfiːt defeat

6 ɒfɪs office
7 əreɪ array
8 pətrəʊl patrol
9 dentɪst dentist
10 ɔːtəm Autumn

THREE-SYLLABLE WORDS

VERBS

1 entəteɪn entertain
2 rezərekt resurrect
3 əbændən abandon
4 dɪlɪvə deliver
5 ɪntərʌpt interrupt

6 ɪlɪsɪt elicit
7 kɒməndɪə commandeer
8 ɪmædʒɪn imagine
9 dɪtɜːmɪn determine
10 sepəreɪt separate

ADJECTIVES

1 ɪmpɔːtn̩t important
2 ɪnɔːməs enormous
3 derɪlɪkt derelict
4 desɪml̩ decimal
5 æbnɔːml̩ abnormal

6 ɪnsl̩ənt insolent
7 fæntæstɪk fantastic
8 negətɪv negative
9 ækjərət accurate
10 ʌnlaɪkli unlikely

NOUNS

1 fɜːnɪtʃə furniture
2 dɪzɑːstə disaster
3 dɪsaɪpl̩ disciple
4 æmbjələns ambulance
5 kwɒntɪti quantity

6 kəθiːdrəl cathedral
7 hɒləkɔːst holocaust
8 trænzɪstə transistor
9 æksɪdn̩t accident
10 təmɑːtəʊ tomato

Audio Unit 11   Complex word stress

Exercise 1   Stress-carrying suffixes

When you hear the number, pronounce the word with stress on the suffix. You will then hear the correct pronunciation which you should repeat.

1 -ain: entertain ˌentə'teɪn   4 -ese: Portuguese ˌpɔːtʃə'giːz
2 -ee: refugee ˌrefjʊ'dʒiː   5 -ette: cigarette ˌsɪgə'ret
3 -eer: mountaineer   6 -esque: picturesque
   ˌmaʊntɪ'nɪə   ˌpɪktʃə'resk

When you hear the stem word, say the word with the given suffix, putting the stress on that suffix. In these examples, a secondary stress comes on the penultimate syllable of the stem.

employ+-ee   absent+-ee
engine+-eer   profit+-eer
Sudan+-ese   Pekin+-ese
usher+-ette   statue+-ette (statuette)

Exercise 2   Neutral suffixes

When you hear the stem word, add the suffix, without changing the stress.

comfort+-able   power+-less
anchor+-age   hurried+-ly
refuse+-al (refusal) punish+-ment
wide+-en (widen)   yellow+-ness
wonder+-ful   poison+-ous
amaze+-ing (amazing) glory+-fy (glorify)
devil+-ish   other+-wise
bird+-like   fun+-y (funny)

Exercise 3   Stress-moving suffixes

When you hear the stem word, say it with the suffix added and put the stress on the last syllable of the stem.

advantage+-ous   injure+-ious (injurious)
photo+-graphy   tranquil+-ity (tranquillity)
proverb+-ial   hurried+-ly

climate+-ic (climatic)   reflex+-ive
                                embryo+-logy

Exercise 4   Compound words

When you hear the number, say the item.

a) First element adjectival, stress on second element.

    1 loudspeaker   4 second-class

    2 bad-tempered   5 three-wheeler

    3 headquarters

b) First element nominal, stress on first element.

    1 typewriter   4 suitcase

    2 car-ferry   5 tea-cup

    3 sunrise

c) Mixture of type (a) and (b).

    1 long-suffering   4 red-blooded

    2 gunman   5 gear-box

    3 shoelace   6 overweight

Exercise 5   Word-class pairs

You will hear the number of the item and its word-class. Stress the second syllable if it is a verb; stress the first syllable if it is a noun or adjective.

1 abstract (Adjective)	10 object (Noun)
2 conduct (Verb)	11 perfect (Adjective)
3 contract (Noun)	12 permit (Verb)
4 contrast (Verb)	13 present (Adjective)
5 desert (Noun)	14 produce (Verb)
6 escort (Noun)	15 protest (Noun)
7 export (Verb)	16 rebel (Verb)
8 import (Noun)	17 record (Noun)
9 insult (Verb)	18 subject (Noun)

Audio Unit 12   Weak forms

Words occurring in their weak forms are printed in smaller type than stressed words and strong forms, e.g. 'We can wait' **'wɪː** kən **'weɪt**

Exercise 1   Sentences for repetition

Listen and repeat:

'We can 'wait for the 'bus   wi kən 'weɪt fə ðə 'bʌs

'How do the 'lights 'work   'haʊ də ðə 'laɪts 'wɜːk

There are some 'new 'books I must 'read   ðər ə səm 'njuː 'bʊks aɪ məs 'riːd

She 'took her 'aunt for a 'drive   ʃi 'tʊk ər 'ɑːnt fər ə 'draɪv

The 'basket was 'full of 'things to 'eat   ðə 'bɑːskɪt wəz 'fʊl əv 'θɪŋz tu 'iːt

'Why should a 'man 'earn 'more than a 'woman?   'waɪ ʃəd ə 'mæn 'ɜːn 'mɔː ðən ə 'wʊmən

You 'ought to 'have your 'own 'car   ju 'ɔːt tə 'hæv jər 'əʊn 'kɑː

He 'wants to 'come and 'see us at 'home   hi 'wɒnts tə 'kʌm ən 'siː əs ət 'həʊm

'Have you 'taken them from 'that 'box?   'hæv ju 'teɪkən ðəm frəm 'ðæt 'bɒks

It's 'true that he was 'late, but his 'car could have 'broken 'down   ɪts 'truː ðət i wəz 'leɪt bət ɪz 'kɑː kəd əv 'brəʊkən 'daʊn

I shall 'take as 'much as I 'want   aɪ ʃl̩ 'teɪk əz 'mʌtʃ əz aɪ 'wɒnt

'Why am I 'too 'late to 'see him to'day?   'waɪ əm aɪ 'tuː 'leɪt tə 'siː ɪm tə'deɪ

Exercise 2   Weak forms with pre-vocalic and pre-consonantal forms

DIFFERENT VOWELS
When you hear the number, say the phrase, using the appropriate weak form:

the	1 the apple **ði æpļ**	2	the pear **ðə peə**
to	3 to Edinburgh **tu edņbrə**	4	to Leeds **tə liːdz**
do	5 so do I **səʊ du aɪ**	6	so do they **səʊ də ðeɪ**

LINKING CONSONANT
a/an   7 an ear **ən ɪə**   8 a foot **ə fʊt**
(the other words in this section have "linking r".)

her	9 Her eyes **hər aɪz**	10	her nose **hə nəʊz**
your	11 your uncle **jər ʌŋkļ**	12	your friend **jə frend**
for	13 for Alan **fər ælən**	14	for Mike **fə maɪk**
there	15 there aren't **ðər ɑːnt**	16	there couldn't **ðə kʊdņt**
are	17 these are ours **ðiːz ər aʊəz**	18	these are mine **ðiːz ə maɪn**
were	19 you were out **juː wər aʊt**	20	you were there **juː wə ðeə**

Exercise 3   Transcription
(Note: this exercise is a long one, and it is possible to go directly to Exercise 4 if wished.)
Write the following sentences in transcription, taking care to give the correct weak forms for the words printed in smaller type.

1   'Leave the 'rest of the 'food for 'lunch
2   'Aren't there some 'letters for her to 'open?
3   'Where do the 'eggs come from?
4   'Read his 'book and 'write some 'notes
5   At 'least we can 'try and 'help

Now correct your transcription, using the version in the answers section.   ❚❚

Exercise 4   Pronunciation of weak forms   ▶
This exercise uses the sentences of Exercise 3. When you hear the
number, say the sentence, giving particular attention to the weak
forms.
(1 . . . 5)

Audio Unit 13   Revision

Exercise 1   Reading unfamiliar words from transcription   ▶
The following are British place names written in transcription.*
When you hear the number, say the word, making sure that the stress
is correctly placed. You will then hear the correct pronunciation,
which you should repeat.

1	ˈkəʊltʃɪstə	6	ˌhɒliˈhed
2	kɑːˈlaɪl	7	ˈfræmlɪŋəm
3	ˈherɪfəd	8	saʊθˈend
4	ˈskʌnθɔːp	9	ˈtʃeltn̩əm
5	gləˈmɔːgən	10	ˌɪnvəˈnes

Exercise 2   Transcription of unfamiliar words
The following are also place names. Each will be said twice; write
what you hear in transcription, including stress marks.
(1 . . . 10)

Now check your transcriptions with the correct version.   ▌▌

Exercise 3   Stress placement in sentences
Put a stress mark ' before each syllable you would expect to be
stressed in the following sentences. For example, given the sentence 'I
think I'll be late for work' you should mark the words 'think', 'late'
and 'work' like this:

　　I 'think Ill be 'late for 'work

1   James decided to type the letter himself
2   The plane was approaching the runway at high speed
3   Try to see the other persons point of view

---
* Spelling is given in the answers section.

4   You put your brakes on when the light turns to red
5   In a short time the house was full of children

Now correct your stress marking by looking at the versions given in the answers section.

Exercise 4   Pronunciation of stressed syllables   ▶
When you hear the number, say the sentence from the list in Exercise 3 taking care to stress the correct syllables. You will then hear the correct version, which you should repeat.
(1 . . . 5)

Exercise 5   Weak forms
In the following sentences, those words which are not stressed must be pronounced in their weak forms. When you hear the number, say the sentence:

1   'Heres a 'present for your 'brother
2   'These are 'all the 'pictures that are 'left
3   There 'could be a 'bit of 'rain at the 'end of the 'morning
4   A 'few 'people 'asked him a 'question
5   Col'lect your 'luggage be'fore 'leaving the 'train

Audio Unit 14   Elisions

Read this before starting this exercise
This Audio Unit gives you practice in recognising places where elision occurs in natural speech (i.e. where one or more phonemes which would be pronounced in careful speech are not pronounced). The examples are extracted from dialogues between speakers who are discussing differences between two similar pictures. Each extract is given three times. You must transcribe each item, using phonemic symbols so that the elision can be seen in the transcription. For example, if you heard 'sixth time' pronounced without the θ fricative at the end of the first word you would write **sɪks taɪm**, and the elision would be clearly indicated in this way. You can use the ʰ symbol to indicate a devoiced weak vowel, as in 'potato' **pʰteɪtəʊ**.

   You will probably need to pause your CD or tape to give yourself more time to write the transcription. This is a difficult exercise, but explanatory notes are given in the answers section.

Transcription ▶

ONE ELISION

1 a beautiful girl
2 we seem to have a definite one there
3 could it be a stool rather than a table
4 a fifth in
5 any peculiarities about that
6 and how many stripes on yours
7 well it appears to button up its got three
8 or the what do you call it the sill

TWO ELISIONS

9 by column into columns all right
10 diamond shaped patch
11 and I should think from experience of kitchen knives
12 what shall we do next go down

THREE ELISIONS

13 the top of the bottle is projecting outwards into the room

Now check your transcriptions. ▮▮

Audio Unit 15   Tones

Exercise 1   Repetition of tones
Listen and repeat:

Fall:	ˌyes	ˌno	ˌwell	ˌfour
Rise:	ˌyes	ˌno	ˌwell	ˌfour
Fall–rise:	ˬyes	ˬno	ˬwell	ˬfour
Rise–fall:	˄yes	˄no	˄well	˄four
Level:	_yes	_no	_well	_four

Exercise 2   Production of tones
When you hear the number, say the syllable with the tone indicated:

1 ˌthem	5 ˌwhat	9 ˌnow
2 ˌwhy	6 ˄no	10 ˌend
3 ˅well	7 ˌhere	
4 ˌJohn	8 ˅you	

Exercise 3   Identification
You will hear each syllable twice. Write an appropriate tone symbol.
with the tone indicated.
(1 . . . 10)

Now check your answers.   ▮▮

Exercise 4   Production in context
When you hear the sentence, say the response with the tone
indicated.

Hello, is that 661071?	ˌyes
Do you know any scientists?	˅some
Keep away from that road!	ˌwhy
How many dogs have you got?	ˌtwo
Have you ever heard such a terrible thing?	˄no
What colour is your car?	ˌred
Do you want my plate?	ˌplease
Don't you like it?	˅yes
You haven't seen my watch, have you?	ˌno
What was the weather like?	ˌwet

Audio Unit 16   The tone-unit

Exercise 1   Identifying the tonic syllable
Listen and repeat, then underline the tonic syllable.

1 We could go by bus
2 Of course its broken
3 The car was where Id left it
4 How much is the biggest one
5 I knew it would go wrong

   6 It was too cold

   7 Here it is

   8 That was a loud noise

   9 We could go from Manchester

10 Have you finished

Now check your answers. ▮▮

Exercise 2   Pronouncing the tonic syllable ▶

When you hear the number, say the item with the tonic syllable in the place indicated, using a falling tone:

1 Dont do <u>that</u>

2 Dont <u>do</u> that

3 <u>Dont</u> do that

4 Write your <u>name</u>

5 Write <u>your</u> name

6 <u>Write</u> your name

7 Heres my <u>pen</u>

8 Heres <u>my</u> pen

9 <u>Heres</u> my pen

10 Why dont you <u>try</u>

11 Why dont <u>you</u> try

12 Why <u>dont</u> you try

13 <u>Why</u> dont you try

Exercise 3   Repetition of tone-units

Listen and repeat, trying to copy the intonation exactly; no transcription is given.

> What time will they come
> A day return to London
> The North Pole would be warmer
> Have you decided to buy it
> I recorded them on cassette

Exercise 4   Partial analysis of tone-units

The items of Exercise 3 will now be said again twice, and you must do the following things:

a) Identify the tonic syllable and underline it.

b) Identify the tone (in these items the only tones used are fall and rise).

c) Identify any stressed syllables preceding the tonic syllable and place a stress mark ' before each.

You may need to pause your CD or tape to allow enough time to complete the analysis of each item.

1   What time will they come
2   A day return to London
3,   The North Pole would be warmer
4   Have you decided to buy it
5   I recorded them on cassette

Now check your transcription.   ▮▮

Audio Unit 17   Intonation

Exercise 1   Repetition of tonic syllable plus tail
Listen and repeat, taking care to continue the pitch movement of the tone over the tail:

ˌ<u>Bill</u> ·bought it   ˌ<u>Four</u> of them ·came   ˌ<u>Why</u> do you ·do it
ˊ<u>Bill</u> ·bought it   ˊ<u>Four</u> of them ·came   ˊ<u>Why</u> do you ·do it
ˬ<u>Bill</u> ·bought it   ˬ<u>Four</u> of them ·came   ˬ<u>Why</u> do you ·do it
ˆ<u>Bill</u> ·bought it   ˆ<u>Four</u> of them ·came   ˆ<u>Why</u> do you ·do it

Exercise 2   Production of tonic syllable plus tail
The items from Exercise 1 will be used again. When you hear the number, say the item with the tone that is marked.
(1 . . . 12)

Exercise 3   High and low head
The following tone-units will be repeated with high and low heads. Listen and repeat:

'Taxes have 'risen by 'five per ˌ<u>cent</u>
ˌTaxes have ˌrisen by ˌfive per ˌ<u>cent</u>

'Havent you 'asked the 'boss for ˌ<u>more</u>
ˌHavent you ˌasked the ˌboss for ˌ<u>more</u>

We 'dont have 'time to 'read the ˌ<u>paper</u>
We ˌdont have ˌtime to ˌread the ˌ<u>paper</u>

'Wouldnt you 'like to 'read it on the ˌ<u>train</u>
ˌWouldnt you ˌlike to ˌread it on the ˌ<u>train</u>

Exercise 4   Transcription of tone-units

Each item will be pronounced as one tone-unit, and will be heard three times. You must do the following things:

a) Identify the tonic syllable and underline it.

b) Decide which tone carries (only ˏ, ˏ and ˇ are used in this exercise) and put the appropriate tone-mark before the tonic syllable.

c) Listen for stressed syllables preceding the tonic syllable and mark them high (') or low (ˌ).

d) Listen for stressed syllables in the tail and mark them (if there are any) with a raised dot (·).

You will probably need to pause your CD or tape to complete the transcription of each item.

1   Now heres the weather forecast
2   You didnt say anything about rates
3   A few years ago they were top
4   No-one could say the cinema was dead
5   Is there anything you wouldnt eat
6   Have you ever considered writing
7   That was what he claimed to be
8   We try to do our shopping in the market
9   But I never go there now
10   It wouldnt be difficult to find out

▌▌

Now check your transcriptions. If there is time, you will find it useful to go back to the start of Exercise 4 and practise repeating the items while looking at the transcriptions.

Audio Unit 18   Intonation: extracts from conversation

The following extracts are from the same recorded conversations as were used in Audio Unit 14. Each extract will be heard three times, with four or five seconds between repetitions. Mark the intonation; the instructions for how to do this are given in the text for Audio Unit 17, Exercise 4. In addition, for numbers 10–16 you will need to use the vertical line | to separate tone-units. You should expect this tape to be more difficult than previous intonation tapes!

Transcription ▶

ONE TONE-UNIT

1 it looks like a French magazine
2 the television is plugged in
3 does your colander have a handle
4 ('s) a flap on it
5 you tell me about yours
6 well dark hair
7 more than half way
8 but er not in the other corners
9 a sort of Daily Sketch format newspaper

TWO TONE-UNITS

10 on the top on the lid
11 well theyre on alternate steps theyre not on every step
12 what about the vent at the back
13 and a ladys handbag hanging on a nail on the wall
14 you do the left hand bit of the picture and Ill do the right hand bit
15 were being very particular but we just havent hit upon one of the differences yet

THREE TONE-UNITS

16 and what about your television two knobs in the front

Now check your intonation marking. ❚❚

Audio Unit 19 Transcription of connected speech

Listen to the recording on which this exercise is based:

> it was rather frightening because there there are scores of these bicycles and er you really have to have your wits about you all the time because the you know they stop suddenly and it's awkward because the traffic regulations are more honoured in the breach than the observance I'm not in not really sure what regulations there are er for instance the er traffic lights red red

lights do not apply if you're turning right erm which means that if you're coming up to a traffic light and there's erm someone stopped who wants to go straight on or turn left and you want to turn right then you pull out overtake them and then cut across in front

II

The above passage will now be heard divided up into 27 tone-units, each of which will be heard three times. Incomplete tone-units (those without a nucleus) are omitted. The main object of the exercise is to transcribe the intonation; however, for a harder exercise taking more time, you can also write a transcription using phonemic symbols plus any non-phonemic symbols you may need. The transcription given in the answers section is in this form.

▶

it was rather frightening
because there there are scores
of these bicycles
you really have to
have your wits about you
all the time
because the you know they stop suddenly
its awkward
because the traffic regulations
are more honoured in the breach
than the observance
Im not in not really sure what
regulations there are
for instance
the er traffic lights
red red lights
do not apply
if youre turning right
which means that
if you're coming up to a traffic light
someone stopped
who wants to go straight on
or turn left
and you want to turn right
then you pull out

> overtake them
> and then cut across
> in front

Now check your transcription.   **II**

Audio Unit 20   Further practice on connected speech

Exercise 1   Dictation
You will hear five sentences spoken rapidly. Each will be given three times. Write each sentence down in *normal spelling*.
(1 . . . 5)

Compare what you have written with the correct version.   **II**

Exercise 2   Transcription   ▶
Now skip back to the previous track on the CD or wind your tape back and listen to the above sentences again; this time *transcribe* what you hear, using mainly phonemic symbols but also using raised **h** (ʰ) to indicate a weak voiceless vowel, as in **pʰteɪtəʊ**. Do not mark intonation.
(1 . . . 5)

Exercise 3   Reading intonation
When you hear the number, say the sentence with the intonation indicated. You will then hear the correct pronunciation, which you should repeat.

1   I ˌthought you were on ˌholiday this ·week
2   ᷅Some ·day | Im ˌgoing to get ˌround to ˌmending the ˌfuse
3   There were a ˌlot | 'not just 'one or ᷅two
4   'Didnt 'anyone 'try to ˌstop them
5   'Leave it till 'after youve 'had some ˌtea | ˌotherwise youll be ˌtoo ˌfull to ˌeat

Answers to written exercises

Chapter 2

1. a) Soft palate or velum
   b) Alveolar ridge
   c) Front of tongue
   d) Hard palate
   e) Lower lip
2. a) Close back rounded
   b) Close-mid front unrounded
   c) Open front unrounded
   d) Close front unrounded
   e) Close-mid back rounded
3.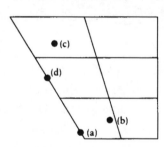

4. a) e   e) ʊ
   b) ʌ   f) ɒ
   c) ʊ   g) æ
   d) ɪ   h) e

Chapter 3

1

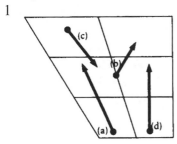

2	a) ɔː	d) ɜː	g) ɜː
	b) ɔː	e) uː	h) iː
	c) ɑː	f) iː	i) ɜː
3	a) əʊ	d) eɪ	g) eə
	b) aɪ	e) ɪə	h) aɪ
	c) aʊ	f) ɔɪ	i) eɪ

Chapter 4

1   You will obviously not have written descriptions identical to the ones given below. The important thing is to check that the sequence of articulatory events is more or less the same.

a) goat

Starting from the position for normal breathing, the back of the tongue is raised to form a closure against the velum (soft palate). The lungs are compressed to produce higher air pressure in the vocal tract and the vocal folds are brought together in the voicing position. The vocal folds begin to vibrate, and the back of the tongue is lowered to allow the compressed air to escape. The tongue is moved to a mid central vowel and then moves in the direction of a closer, backer vowel: the lips are moderately rounded for the second part. The tongue blade is raised to make a closure against the alveolar ridge, the vocal folds are separated and voicing ceases. Then the compressed air is released quietly and the lips return to an unrounded shape.

b) ape

The tongue is moved slightly upward and forward and the vocal folds are brought together to begin voicing. The tongue glides to a slightly closer and more central vowel postion. Then the lips are pressed together making a closure and at the same time the vocal folds are separated so that voicing ceases. The lips are then opened and the compressed air is released quietly, while the tongue is lowered to the position for normal breathing.

2   a) beɪk   d) bɔːt   g) bɔːd

     b) gəʊt   e) tɪk   h) gɑːd

     c) daʊt   f) baʊ   i) piː

Chapter 5

a) 'speed'   spiːd   [spiːd̥]

b) 'partake'   paːteɪk   [pʰɑˑtʰĕɪk]

c) 'book'   bʊk   [b̥ŭk]

d) 'goat'   gəʊt   [g̊ə̆ʊt]

e) 'car'   kɑː   [k̊ʰɑː]

f) 'bad'   bæd   [b̥æd̥]

g) 'appeared'   əpɪəd   [əpʰɪəd̥]

h) 'toast'   təʊst   [tʰə̆ʊst]

i)   'stalk'   stɔːk   [stɔˑk]

Chapter 6

1   a) fɪʃɪz   e) ətʃiːvz

     b) ʃeɪvə   f) ʌðəz

     c) sɪksθ   g) meʒə

     d) ðiːz   h) əhed

2 Starting from the position for normal breathing, the lower lip is brought into contact with the upper teeth. The lungs are compressed, causing air to flow through the constriction producing fricative noise. The tongue moves to the position for ɪ. The vocal folds are brought together, causing voicing to begin, and at the same time the lower lip is lowered. Then the tongue blade is raised to make a fairly wide constriction in the palato-alveolar region and the vocal folds are separated to stop voicing; the flow of air causes fricative noise. Next, the vocal folds are brought together to begin voicing again and at the same time the tongue is lowered from the constriction position into the ɪ vowel posture. The tongue blade is then raised against the alveolar ridge forming a constriction which results in fricative noise. This is initially accompanied by voicing, which then dies away. Finally, the

tongue is lowered from the alveolar constriction, the vocal folds are separated and normal breathing is resumed.

Chapter 7

1   Plosives: p t k b d g
    Fricatives: f θ s ʃ h v ð z ʒ
    Affricates: tʃ dʒ
    Nasals: m n ŋ
    Lateral: l
    Approximants: r w j
    (This course has also mentioned the possibility of ç and ʍ)

2   a) səʊfə   e) skweə
    b) vɜːs   f) æŋgə
    c) stɪərɪŋ   g) bɔɪt
    d) bredkrʌm   h) naɪntiːn

3   a) The soft palate is raised for the **b** plosive and remains raised for **æ**. It is lowered for **n**, then raised again for the final **ə**.
    b) The soft palate remains lowered during the articulation of **m**, and is then raised for the rest of the syllable.
    c) The soft palate is raised for the **æ** vowel, then lowered for **ŋ**. It is then raised for the **g** plosive and remains raised for the **l**.

Chapter 8

a)

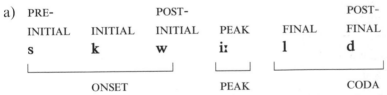

PRE-INITIAL	INITIAL	POST-INITIAL	PEAK	FINAL	POST-FINAL
s	k	w	iː	l	d

ONSET   PEAK   CODA

(It would be possible to treat **l** as pre-final and **d** as final, but the above analysis is slightly preferable in that **d** here is a suffix and we know that **l** occurs finally in 'squeal' **skwiːl**.)

b)

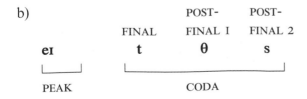

	FINAL	POST-FINAL I	POST-FINAL 2
eɪ	t	θ	s

PEAK   CODA

c)

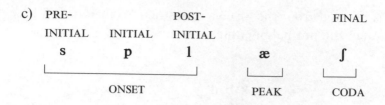

d)

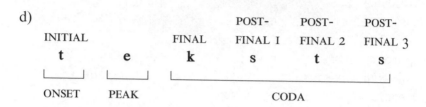

Chapter 9

1 ə pətɪkjələ prɒbləm əv ðə bəʊt wəz ə liːk
2 əʊpnɪŋ ðə bɒtḷ prɪzentɪd nəʊ dɪfɪkḷti
3 ðər ɪz nəʊ ɒltɜːnətɪv tə ðə gʌvn̩mənts prəpəʊzḷ
4 wi ɔːt tə meɪk ə kəlekʃn̩ tə kʌvə ði ɪkspensɪz
   (also possible: kḷekʃn̩)
5 faɪmli deɪ əraɪvd ət ə hɑːbər ət ði edʒ əv ðə maʊntɪnz
   (hɑːbr̩ possible).

Chapter 10

1 a) pro'tect   prə'tekt
   b) 'clamber   'klæmbə
   c) fes'toon   fes'tuːn
   d) de'test   dɪ'test
   e) 'bellow   'beləʊ
   f) 'menace   'menɪs
   g) disco'nnect   dɪskə'nekt
   h) 'entering   'entərɪŋ   ('entr̩ɪŋ)
2 a) 'language   'læŋgwɪdʒ
   b) 'captain   'kæptɪn
   c) ca'reer   kə'rɪə
   d) 'paper   'peɪpə
   e) e'vent   ɪ'vent
   f) 'jonquil   'dʒɒŋkwɪl

g) 'injury   ˈɪndʒəri   (ˈɪndʒr̩i)

h) co'nnection   kəˈnekʃən   (kəˈnekʃn̩)

Chapter 11

1 and 2

  a) 'shop ˌfitter   ˈʃɒp ˌfɪtə

  b) ˌopen 'ended   ˌəupn̩ 'endɪd

  c) 'Javaˈnese   ˌdʒɑːvəˈniːz

  d) 'birth ˌmark   ˈbɜːθ ˌmɑːk

  e) ˌanti 'clockwise ˌænti 'klɒkwaɪz

  f) ˌconfirˈmation   ˌkɒnfəˈmeɪʃn̩

  g) ˌeight 'sided   ˌeɪt 'saɪdɪd

  h) 'fruit ˌcake   ˈfruːt ˌkeɪk

  i) deˈfective   dɪˈfektɪv

  j) 'roof ˌtimber   ˈruːf ˌtɪmbə

Chapter 12

1   aɪ wɒnt ə tə pɑːk ðæt kɑːr əuvə ðeə

2   əv ɔːl ðə prəpəuzl̩z ðə wʌn ðət juː meɪd ɪz ðə sɪliəst

3   dʒeɪn ən bɪl kəd əv drɪvn̩ ðəm tuː ən frɒm ðə pɑːti
    (kʊd is also suitable)

4   tə kʌm tə ðə pɔɪnt wɒt ʃl̩ wi duː fə ðə rest əv ðə wiːk

5   həz enɪwʌn gɒt ən aɪdɪə weər ɪt keɪm frɒm

6   pədestrɪənz məst ɔːlwɪz juːz ðə krɒsɪŋz prəvaɪdɪd

7   iːtʃ wʌn wəz ə pɜːfɪkt ɪgzɑːmpl̩ əv ði ɑːt ðət əd biːn dɪveləpt
    ðeə

Chapter 13

1   In this data there is no evidence of **ŋ** contrasting with **n**, since **ŋ**
    never occurs except before **k** and **g**. So all phonetic **ŋ** consonants
    are phonemic **n**.

  a) **θɪng**

  b) **θɪnk**

  c) **θɪnkɪng**

  d) **fɪngə**

  e) **sɪngə**

  f) **sɪngɪng**

2   a) **saʊnd**
     b) **æŋgə**
     c) **kɑːnt**
     d) **kæmpə**
     e) **bɒnd**

3   /t/ is realised as [ɾ] when it occurs between vowels if the preceding vowel is stressed and the following vowel is unstressed.

4

	p	d	s	m	z
Continuant	–	–	+	+	+
Alveolar	–	+	+	–	+
Voiced	–	+	–	+	+

5   a) All the vowels are close or close mid (or between these heights).
     b) All require the tongue blade to be raised for their articulation, and all are in the alveolar or post-alveolar region.
     c) None of these requires the raising of the tongue blade – all are front or back articulations.
     d) All are voiceless.
     e) All are rounded or end with lip-rounding.
     f) All are approximants (they create very little obstruction to the airflow).

Chapter 14

1   a) A | bird in the | hand is worth | two in the | bush
     b) | Over a | quarter of a | century has e | lapsed since his | death
     c) Com | puters con | sume a con | siderable a | mount of | money and | time
     d) | Most of them have ar | rived on the | bus
     e) | Newspaper | editors are in | variably | under | worked

2   a)   b)

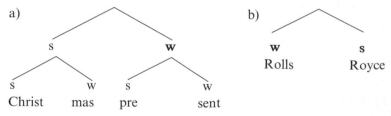

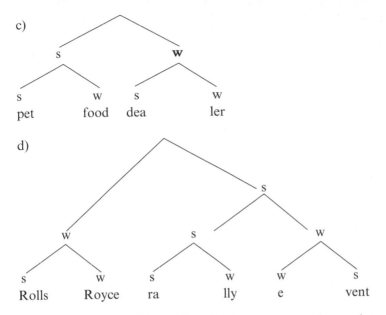

(The stress levels of 'Rolls' and 'Royce' are exchanged to avoid "stress clash" between 'Royce' and 'ra-'.)

3 a) wʌŋ kɔːz əv æsmərɪsspəʊstəbi æləʤiz
   b) wɒt ði ɜːbm̩ pɒpjəleɪʃn̩ kəʤuːz ɪz betə treɪnz
   c) ʃi æks pətɪkjəli wel m̩nə fɜːssiːn
   (The above represent just one possible pronunciation: many others are possible.)

Chapter 15

1 This train is for ˌLeeds, ˌYork ˌDarlington and ˌDurham
2 Can you give me a ˌlift
   ˇPossibly   Where ˌto
3 ˌNo   Certainly ˌnot   Go aˌway
4 Did you know hed been convicted of drunken ˌdriving   ˏNo
5 If I give him ˌmoney he goes and ˌspends it
   If I lend him the ˌbike he ˌloses it
   Hes completely unreˌliable

Chapter 16

1 (This is an exercise where there is more than one correct answer.)
   a) <u>buy</u> it for me
   b) <u>hear</u> it
   c) <u>talk</u> to him
2 a) 'mind the <u>step</u>
   b) 'this is the 'ten to 'seven <u>train</u>
   c) 'keep the 'food <u>hot</u>
3 a) 'Only when the ˬ<u>wind</u> blows

   b) ˌ<u>When</u> did you say

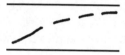

   c) 'What was the ˌ<u>name</u> of the place

Chapter 17

1   a) 'Which was the ˌcheap one did you say

    b) I 'only 'want to ˇtaste it

    c) ˌShe would have ˌthought it was ˰obvious

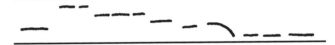

    d) There 'wasnt 'even a 'piece of ˌbread in the ·house

    e) ˌNow will you be·lieve me

2   a) opportˌunity

    b) ˇactually

c) ˌconfidently

d) magˌnificent

e) reˌlationship

f) afterˬnoon

Chapter 18

(The following are possible intonation patterns, but others could be correct.)

1   Its 'rather ˬcold
2   Beˈcause I 'cant aˌfford it
3   Youre ˌsilly then
4   Oh ˬplease
5   ˌSeven oˌclock ˌseven ˌthirty and ˌeight
6   ˮFour
7   Ive ˌgot to ˌdo the ˌshopping
8   ˬSome of them ·might

Chapter 19

1. a) <u>right</u> can I do the <u>shopping</u> for you
   b) <u>right</u> can I do the shopping for <u>you</u>
   c) first the professor explained her <u>theory</u>
   d) <u>no</u> first the pro<u>fes</u>sor explained her theory
   e) first she ex<u>plained</u> her theory
   f) <u>no</u> ten <u>past</u> three
   g) <u>no</u> <u>ten</u> past three
   h) <u>no</u> ten past <u>three</u>
2. a) he wrote the letter <u>sadly</u>
   b) he wrote the <u>letter</u> | <u>sadly</u>
   c) four plus <u>six</u> | divided by <u>two</u> | equals <u>five</u>
   d) <u>four</u> | plus six divided by <u>two</u> | equals <u>seven</u>
   e) we broke <u>one</u> | thing after another fell <u>down</u>
   f) we broke one thing after an<u>other</u> | that <u>night</u>

Chapter 20

1. This accent has a distribution for **ŋ** similar to BBC pronunciation (i.e. a case can be made for a **ŋ** phoneme), except that in the case of the participial '-ing' ending **n** is found instead of **ŋ**.
2. This accent has two additional long vowels (**eː** and **oː**) and, correspondingly, two fewer diphthongs (**eɪ** and **əʊ**). This situation is found in many Northern accents.
3. The fricatives **θ**, **ð** and **h** are missing from the phoneme inventory, and **f** and **v** are used in place of **θ**, **ð**. /l/ is realised as [w] where BBC pronunciation has "dark l". This is typical of a Cockney accent.
4. This data is based on the traditional working-class accent of Bristol, where words of more than one syllable cannot end in **ə**. The accent is rhotic, so where there is an 'r' in the spelling (as in 'mother') a **r** is pronounced: where the spelling does not have 'r', a /l/ sound is added, resulting in some loss of distinctiveness in words (cf. 'idea', 'ideal': 'area', 'aerial').
5. Here we appear to have three vowels where BBC pronunciation has two: the word 'cat' has the equivalent of **æ**, 'calm' has a vowel similar to **ɑː** while in the set of words that have **æ** in many Northern accents ('plaster', 'grass', etc.) an additional long vowel **aː** is used. This is found in Shropshire.

Answers to recorded exercises

Audio Unit 2

Exercise 2

1 æ in **bæn** 'ban'
2 ʌ in **hʌb** 'hub'
3 ɪ in **fɪl** 'fill'
4 ɒ in **mɒs** 'moss'
5 e in **led** 'led'

6 ʊ in **pʊt** 'put'
7 ʌ in **kʌm** 'come'
8 ɪ in **mɪd** 'mid'
9 ɒ in **bɒm** 'bomb'
10 e in **sel** 'sell'

Audio Unit 3

Exercise 3

1 iː in **siːt** 'seat'
2 ɑː in **dɑːk** 'dark'
3 ɜː in **bɜːd** 'bird'
4 ɔː in **fɔːt** 'fought'
5 ɑː in **pɑːt** 'part'

6 uː in **fuːd** 'food'
7 ɜː in **kɜːt** 'curt'
8 ɑː in **pɑːk** 'park'
9 iː in **niːd** 'need'
10 ɔː in **hɔːs** 'horse'

Exercise 5

1 ɜː in **hɜːd** 'heard'
2 ɒ in **sɒŋ** 'song'
3 ɔː in **sɔː** 'saw'
4 ʌ in **kʌm** 'come'
5 ɑː in **mɑːtʃ** 'march'

6 ʊ in **fʊl** 'full'
7 ɑː in **pɑːt** 'part'
8 ɒ in **dɒl** 'doll'
9 ʌ in **lʌv** 'love'
10 ɜː in **bɜːn** 'burn'

Exercise 7

1	ɪə in **fɪəs** 'fierce'	7	aɪ in **kaɪt** 'kite'
2	eə in **keəd** 'cared'	8	ɪə in **bɪəd** 'beard'
3	ʊə in **mʊəz** 'moors'	9	ʊə in **tʊəz** 'tours'
4	eɪ in **reɪd** 'raid'	10	əʊ in **bəʊn** 'bone'
5	aɪ in **taɪm** 'time'	11	ɔɪ in **bɔɪl** 'boil'
6	əʊ in **kəʊt** 'coat'	12	aʊ in **taʊn** 'town'

Audio Unit 4

Exercise 3

1	**p** in 'harp' **hɑːp**	6	**k** in 'ache' **eɪk**
2	**g** in 'rogue' **rəʊg**	7	**d** in 'ode' **əʊd**
3	**t** in 'eight' **eɪt**	8	**p** in 'rip' **rɪp**
4	**d** in 'ride' **raɪd**	9	**g** in 'sag' **sæg**
5	**b** in 'mob' **mɒb**	10	**t** in 'feet' **fiːt**

Exercise 5

1	'debate'	6	'guarded'
2	'copied'	7	'dedicated'
3	'buttercup'	8	'paddock'
4	'cuckoo'	9	'boutique'
5	'decayed'	10	'appetite'

Audio Unit 5

Exercise 3

1	**geɪt** 'gate'	11	**gæp** 'gap'
2	**kəʊt** 'coat'	12	**bɪəd** 'beard'
3	**bɪt** 'bit'	13	**kɑː** 'car'
4	**taɪəd** 'tired'	14	**peɪd** 'paid'
5	**biːt** 'beat'	15	**gʌt** 'gut'
6	**pəʊk** 'poke'	16	**daʊt** 'doubt'
7	**kɑːt** 'cart'	17	**təʊd** 'toad'
8	**kɔːt** 'caught'	18	**duː** 'do'
9	**paʊə** 'power'	19	**peə** 'pair'
10	**kɔːd** 'cord'	20	**dek** 'deck'

Exercise 4

1	'keep'	11	'duck'
2	'boat'	12	'cope'
3	'cup'	13	'dog'
4	'dirt'	14	'coward'
5	'bike'	15	'bake'
6	'cab'	16	'tied'
7	'gate'	17	'beard'
8	'cared'	18	'put'
9	'tired'	19	'bug'
10	'bird'	20	'doubt'

Audio Unit 6

Exercise 2

a) initial position b) medial position c) final position

a) initial position	b) medial position	c) final position
1 ʃ in ʃəʊ 'show'	6 v in əʊvə 'over'	11 ð in ləʊð
2 θ in θaɪ 'thigh'	7 ʒ in meʒə	'loathe'
3 z in zuː 'zoo'	'measure'	12 v in iːv 'Eve'
4 f in fɑː 'far'	8 s in aɪsɪŋ 'icing'	13 ʃ in æʃ 'ash'
5 ð in ðəʊ 'though'	9 ʃ in eɪʃə 'Asia'	14 f in rʌf 'rough'
	10 h in əhed 'ahead'	15 θ in əʊθ 'oath'

Audio Unit 7

Exercise 6

1	**juːʒʊəl** 'usual'	7	**vaɪələns** 'violence'
2	**rɪmeɪn** 'remain'	8	**emfəsɪs** 'emphasis'
3	**eksəsaɪz** 'exercise'	9	**dʒentli** 'gently'
4	**weərɪŋ** 'wearing'	10	**θɪŋkɪŋ** 'thinking'
5	**ɜːdʒənt** 'urgent'	11	**taɪpraɪtə** 'typewriter'
6	**mɪnɪməm** 'minimum'	12	**jɪəli** 'yearly'

Audio Unit 8

Exercise 6 (Spellings)

1	'scraped'	5	'crunched'
2	'grudged'	6	'thrones'
3	'clothes'	7	'plunged'
4	'scripts'	8	'quench'

Audio Unit 9

Exercise 5

1	**'gɑːdn̩ə** 'gardener'	6	**'sʌdn̩** 'sudden'
2	**'kɒləm** 'column'	7	**'kæləs** 'callous'
3	**'hændl̩z** 'handles'	8	**'θretn̩ɪŋ** 'threatening'
4	**ə'laɪv** 'alive'	9	**pə'laɪt** 'polite'
5	**prɪ'tend** 'pretend'	10	**'pʌzl̩** 'puzzle'

Audio Unit 10

Exercise 1

1	**'enɪmi**	6	**səb'trækt**
2	**kə'lekt**	7	**'elɪfənt**
3	**'kæpɪtl̩**	8	**əb'zɜːvə**
4	**kɑː'neɪʃn̩**	9	**'prɒfɪt**
5	**'pærədaɪs**	10	**entə'teɪn**

Exercise 2 (Spellings)

1	Shrewsbury	6	Birmingham
2	Polperro	7	Northampton
3	Aberdeen	8	Dundee
4	Wolverhampton	9	Canterbury
5	Aberystwyth	10	Basingstoke

Audio Unit 12

Exercise 3

1 'liːv ðə 'rest əv ðə 'fuːd fə 'lʌnʃ
2 'aːnt ðə səm 'letəz fər ə tu 'əupən
3 'weə də ði 'egz kʌm frɒm
4 'riːd ɪz 'bʊk ən 'raɪt səm 'nəʊts
5 ət 'iːst wi kən 'traɪ ən 'help

Audio Unit 13

Exercise 1 (Spellings)

1	Colchester	6	Holyhead
2	Carlisle	7	Framlingham
3	Hereford	8	Southend
4	Scunthorpe	9	Cheltenham
5	Glamorgan	10	Inverness

Exercise 2

1 'lestəʃə (Leicestershire) 6 kəʊl'reɪn (Coleraine)
2 dʌn'fɜːmlɪn (Dunfermline) 7 'hʌdəsfiːld (Huddersfield)
3 'stiːvnɪdʒ (Stevenage) 8 heɪlz'əʊɪn (Halesowen)
4 pen'zæns (Penzance) 9 'wɪlmzləʊ (Wilmslow)
5 'gɪlfəd (Guildford) 10 'baːnstəpl̩ (Barnstaple)

Exercise 3

1 'James de'cided to 'type the 'letter him'self
2 The 'plane was ap'proaching the 'runway at 'high 'speed
3 'Try to 'see the 'other 'persons 'point of 'view
4 You 'put your 'brakes on when the 'light 'turns to 'red
5 In a 'short 'time the 'house was 'full of 'children

Audio Unit 14

Note: When recordings of conversational speech are used it is no longer possible to give definite decisions about "right" and "wrong" answers. Some problems, points of interest and alternative possibilities are mentioned.

1 ə bjuːtʰf̩l̩ gɜːl (Careful speech would have had bjuːtɪf̩l̩ or bjuːtɪfʊl.)

2 wi siːm tə hæv ə defnət wʌn ðeə (Careful speech would have defɪnɪt, defɪnət or defn̩ət; notice that this speaker uses a glottal stop at the end of definite so that the transcription – phonetic rather than phonemic – defnəʔ would be acceptable. There is a good example of assimilation in the pronunciation of 'one there'; as often happens when **n** and **ð** are combined, the **n** becomes dental **n̪**. In addition, the **ð** loses its friction – which is always weak – and becomes a dental nasal, so that this could be transcribed phonetically as wʌn̪n̪eə.)

3 kʊd ɪt bi ə stuːl rɑːðð̩n̩ə teɪbl̩ (Careful speech would have rɑːðə ðən ə; the **ð** is long, so the symbol is written twice to indicate this.)

4 ə fɪθ ɪn (Careful speech would have fɪfθ; the transcription cannot, of course, show very fine details of articulation, but it is likely that though the sound one hears is most like **θ** there is some slight constriction between upper teeth and lower lip as well.)

5 eni pʰkjuːljærətɪz əbaʊt ðæt (The main elision is of the ɪ vowel in the first syllable of 'peculiarities': a less noticeable case is that instead of having **i** before the **æ** in this word the speaker has a non-syllabic **j**; note the glottal stop at the end of 'about'.)

6 æn haʊ mni straɪps ɒn jɔːz (Careful speech would have **meni**; it is perhaps surprising that the speaker has **æ** rather than **ə** in 'and'; jɔːz is a frequently found alternative pronunciation to juəz.)

7 wel ɪt əpɪəz tə bʌtn̩ ʌp ɪs gɒt θriː (The elision is in 'its'; careful speech would have ɪts or, since this speaker uses glottal stops quite frequently – notice one between 'it' and 'appears' and another at the end of 'got' – ɪʔs.)

8 ɔːðə wɒtʃəkɔːl ɪt ðə sɪl ('What do you call it' or 'what d' you call it' is used frequently when speakers cannot remember a word.)

9 **baɪ kɒləm ɪntʰ kɒləmz ɔːraɪt** (Careful speech would have **ɪntə** and **ɔːl raɪt**.)
10 **daɪəmən ʃeɪp pætʃ** (Careful speech would have **daɪəmənd ʃeɪpt pætʃ**)
11 **ænd aɪ ʃd θɪŋk frɒm ɪkspɪrɪəns f kɪtʃɪn naɪvz** (Careful speech would have **ʃʊd** or **ʃəd** and **əv**.)
12 **wɒt ʃ wi duː neks gəʊ daʊn** (Careful speech would have **ʃəl** and **nekst**.)
13 **ðiː tɒp f ðə bɒtl̩ ɪz pr̩dʒektɪŋ aʊtwədz ɪntʰ ðə ruːm** (Careful speech would have **əv, prədʒektɪŋ** and **ɪntə**; the **r** in 'projecting' is devoiced as well as being syllabic; notice the glottal stops, one before the **k** in 'projecting' and another before the **t** in 'outwards': the strong form of 'the' at the beginning is probably a sort of slight hesitation.)

Audio Unit 15

Exercise 3

1	ˇone	6	ˏsix
2	ˎtwo	7	ˎnow
3	ˏthree	8	ˇyou
4	ˆfour	9	ˆmore
5	ˎfive	10	ˏus

Audio Unit 16

Exercise 1

1 We could go by <u>bus</u>.
2 Of <u>course</u> its broken
3 The car was where Id <u>left</u> it
4 How much is the <u>big</u>gest one
5 I <u>knew</u> it would go wrong
6 It was too <u>cold</u>
7 <u>Here</u> it is
8 That <u>was</u> a loud noise
9 We could go from <u>Man</u>chester
10 Have you <u>fin</u>ished

Exercise 4

1   'What 'time will they ˌcome
2   A 'day re'turn to ˌLondon
3   The 'North ˌPole would be warmer
4   'Have you de'cided to ˌbuy it
5   I re'corded them on casˌsette

Audio Unit 17

Exercise 4

1   'Now 'heres the ˌweather ·forecast
2   You ˌdidnt say ˌanything about ˌrates
3   A ˌfew ˌyears ago they were ˌtop
4   'No-one could 'say the 'cinema was ˇdead
5   Is there ˌanything you ·wouldnt ·eat
6   'Have you 'ever con'sidered ˌwriting
7   ˌThat was ˌwhat he ˇclaimed to be
8   We 'try to do 'our 'shopping in the ˌmarket
9   But I ˌnever ·go there ·now
10 It ˌwouldnt be ˌdifficult to find ˌout

Audio Unit 18

Note: Since these extracts were not spoken deliberately for illustrating intonation, it is not possible to claim that the transcription given here is the only correct version. There are several places where other transcriptions would be acceptable, and suggestions about alternative possibilities are given with some items, in addition to a few other comments.

1   it 'looks like a 'French magaˌzine (slight hesitation between 'looks' and 'like')
2   the 'television 'is plugged ˇin
3   'does your 'colander have a ˌhandle ('does' possibly not stressed)
4   a ˌflap on it
5   'you tell me about ˌyours (narrow pitch movement on 'yours'; 'tell' may also be stressed)
6   'well ˌdark hair

7   ˌmore than ˌhalf ˌway

8   but er 'not in the ˌother ·corners

9   a ˌsort of ˌDaily ˌSketch ·format ·newspaper ('sort' possibly not stressed)

10   'on the ˌtop | 'on the ˌlid (both pronunciations of 'on' might be unstressed)

11   well theyre 'on alˬternate ·steps | theyre 'not on ˬevery ·step

12   'what about the ˌvent | at the ˌback

13   and a 'ladys ˌhandbag | ˌhanging on a ˌnail on the ˌwall

14   'you do the ˌleft hand ·bit of the ·picture | and ˌIll do the ˌright hand ·bit

15   were being 'very parˬticular | but we 'just havent 'hit upon 'one of the ˌdifferences ·yet (stress on 'just' is weak or absent)

16   and 'what about your teleˌvision | 'two ˌknobs | in the ˌfront |

Audio Unit 19

Note: transcription of natural speech involves making decisions that have the effect of simplifying complex phonetic events. The broad transcription given below is not claimed to be completely accurate, nor to be the only "correct" version.

ɪwəz 'rɑːðə ˌfraɪʔnɪŋ

bɪkəz ðə ðərə ˌskɔːz

ə ðiːz ˌbaɪs kl̩z

ju 'riːli ˌhæv tu

'hæv jə wɪts əˌbautʃu

'ɔːl ðə ˌtaɪm

bɪkəz ðə jə nəʊ ðə ðəɪ ˬstɒp ·sʌdn̩li

ɪts -ɔːkwəd

bkəz ðə ˌtræfɪk regjə·leɪʃn̩z

ɑː mɔː ˌɒnəd ɪn ðə ˌbriːtʃ

ðən ði əb ˌzɜːvəns

aɪm 'nɒt ɪn ˌnɒt riːli ·ʃɔː wɒt

ˌregjələɪʃn̩z ðər ˌɑː

fr̩ ˌɪnstəns

ðiː ə ˌtræfɪk ·laɪts

'red ˌred ·laɪts

du nɒt ə ˌplaɪ

fjɔː ˌtɜːnɪŋ ˌraɪt

wɪtʃ ˌmiːnz ðət
'ɪf jə 'kʌmɪŋ 'ʌp tu ə ˌtræfɪk ·laɪt
'sʌmwʌn ˌstɒpt
hu ˌwɒnts tə ˌgəʊ streɪt ˌɒn
ɔː ˌtɜːn ˌleft
ən 'juː wɒnt tə tɜːn ˌraɪt
ðen jupʊl ˌaʊt
ˌəʊvə ˌteɪk ðəm
ən ðen 'kʌt ə ˌkrɒs
ɪn ˌfrʌnt

Audio Unit 20

Exercise 1

1 I suppose the best thing is to try later.
2 If he's coming today there ought to be a letter around.
3 The world's greatest lawn tennis festival begins on Monday.
4 We've fixed for the repair man to come and mend it under guarantee.
5 The number's been engaged for over an hour.

Exercise 2

1 aɪ spəʊz ð bes θɪŋz tʰ traɪ leɪtə
2 ɪf ɪz kʌmiŋ tʰ deɪ ðr̩ ɔːt tʰ bi ə letr̩ r̩aʊnd
3 ðə wɜːlz greɪts lɔːn tenɪs festʰvl̩ bɪgɪnz ɒm mʌndeɪ
4 wɪf fɪks fə ðə rɪpeə mæn tʰ kʌm əm mend ɪt ʌndə gærn̩tiː
5 ð nʌmbəz bɪn ɪŋgeɪdʒ fr̩ əʊvr̩ ən aʊə

Recommendations for general reading

References to reading on specific topics are given at the end of each chapter. The following is a list of basic books and papers recommended for more general study: if you wish to go more fully into any of the areas given below you would do well to start by reading these. I would consider it very desirable that any library provided for students using this book should possess most or all of the books listed.

English phonetics and phonology

There are two major textbooks in this area (sometimes irreverently known as the Old Testament and the New Testament): the older one is D. Jones, *An Outline of English Phonetics* (1918; 9th edn, Cambridge: Cambridge University Press, 1975); the newer one is A. Cruttenden's revision of A. C. Gimson's *The Pronunciation of English* (London: Edward Arnold, 1994). The latter book is, not surprisingly, more up to date than Jones', and has the additional advantage of using almost exactly the same symbols as those used in this course. However, the Jones book contains much of value and of interest; both books are valuable sources of information for students who wish to go on to more advanced and detailed study after working through this course. A well-established and popular book at a much simpler level is J. D. O'Connor, *Better English Pronunciation* (2nd edn, Cambridge: Cambridge University Press, 1980).

Two other books that approach the subject in rather different ways are G. O. Knowles *Patterns of Spoken English* (London: Longman, 1987) and C. W. Kreidler, *The Pronunciation of English* (Oxford: Blackwell, 1989). H. Giegerich, *English Phonology: An Introduction* (Cambridge: Cambridge University Press, 1992) is more advanced, and contains useful information and ideas. There is a valuable collection of papers on English phonetics in S. Ramsaran (ed.), *Studies in the Pronunciation of English* (London: Routledge, 1990), many of which give an idea of how research in this field is developing.

General phonetics

There are several good introductory books: one is P. Ladefoged, *A Course in Phonetics* (3rd edn, New York: Harcourt Brace Jovanovich, 1993) and another is J. D. O'Connor, *Phonetics* (London: Penguin, 1991). A more recent book is M. Ball and J. Rahilly, *Phonetics: The Science of Speech* (London: Arnold, 1999). D. Abercrombie, *Elements of General Phonetics* (Edinburgh: Edinburgh University Press, 1967) is also good, but less suitable as basic introductory reading. J. C. Catford, *A Practical Introduction to Phonetics* (Oxford: Oxford University Press, 1988) is good for explaining the nature of practical phonetics. J. Laver, *Principles of Phonetics* (Cambridge: Cambridge University Press, 1994) is a very comprehensive and advanced textbook. A recent addition to this list is P. Ladefoged *Vowels and Consonants* (Oxford: Blackwell, 2000).

Phonology

Several books have appeared in recent years that explain the basic elements of phonological theory. F. Katamba, *An Introduction to Phonology* (London: Longman, 1989) is a good introduction. Covering both this area and the previous one in a readable and comprehensive way is J. Clark and C. Yallop, *An Introduction to Phonetics and Phonology* (2nd edn, Oxford: Blackwell, 1995). A lively and interesting course in phonology is I. Roca and W. Johnson *A Course in Phonology* (Oxford: Blackwell, 1999). The classic work on the generative phonology of English is N. Chomsky and M. Halle, *The Sound Pattern of English* (New York: Harper and Row, 1968); most people find this very difficult.

Accents of English

The major work in this area is J. C. Wells, *Accents of English*, 3 vols. (Cambridge: Cambridge University Press, 1982), which is a large and very valuable work dealing with accents of English throughout the world. A shorter and much easier introduction is A. Hughes and P. Trudgill, *English Accents and Dialects* (3rd edn, London: Arnold, 1996). See also P. Foulkes and G. Docherty, *Urban Voices* (London: Arnold, 1999) and P. Trudgill, *The Dialects of England* (2nd edn, Oxford: Blackwell, 1999).

Teaching the pronunciation of English

Good introductions are M. Celce-Murcia, D. Brinton and J. Goodwin, *Teaching Pronunciation* (Cambridge: Cambridge University Press, 1996), C. Dalton and B. Seidlhofer, *Pronunciation* (Oxford: Oxford University Press, 1994) and J. Kenworthy, *Teaching English Pronunciation* (London:

Longman, 1987). See also A. Baker, *Introducing English Pronunciation* (Cambridge: Cambridge University Press, 1982). A. Cruttenden's revision of A. C. Gimson's *The Pronunciation of English* (London: Edward Arnold, 1994) has a useful discussion of requirements for English pronunciation teaching in Chapter 13.

Pronunciation dictionaries

Most modern English dictionaries now print recommended pronunciations for each word listed, so for most purposes a dictionary which gives only pronunciations and not meanings is of limited value unless it gives a lot more information than an ordinary dictionary could. Two such dictionaries are currently available for British English. One is the 15th edn of the *Daniel Jones English Pronouncing Dictionary*, edited by P. Roach and J. Hartman (Cambridge: Cambridge University Press, 1997). Jones' work was the main reference work on English pronunciation for most of the twentieth century. I was the principal editor for this new edition, and have tried to keep it compatible with this book. The other dictionary is J. C. Wells' *Longman Pronunciation Dictionary* (London: Longman, 2000).

Intonation and stress

Two good introductions to intonation are A. Cruttenden, *Intonation* (2nd edn, Cambridge: Cambridge University Press, 1997) and E. Couper-Kuhlen, *An Introduction to English Prosody* (London: Edward Arnold, 1986). D. R. Ladd, *Intonational Phonology* (Cambridge: Cambridge University Press, 1996) is much more difficult, but covers contemporary theoretical issues in an interesting way. E. Fudge, *English Word Stress* (London: Allen and Unwin, 1984) is a useful textbook on word stress.

Bibliography

Abercrombie, D. (1965) 'RP and local accent', in D. Abercrombie, *Studies in Phonetics and Linguistics*, Oxford: Oxford University Press, pp. 10–15.

Abercrombie, D. (1967) *Elements of General Phonetics*, Edinburgh: Edinburgh University Press.

Abercrombie, D., Fry, D. B., MacCarthy, P. A. D., Scott, N. C. and Trim, J. L. M. (eds.) (1964) *In Honour of Daniel Jones*, London: Longman.

Adams, C. (1979) *English Speech Rhythm and the Foreign Learner*, The Hague: Mouton.

Albright, R. W. (1958) 'The International Phonetic Alphabet: its backgrounds and development', *International Journal of American Linguistics*, vol. 24.

Baker, A. (1982) *Introducing English Pronunciation*, Cambridge: Cambridge University Press.

Ball, M. and Code, C. (1997) *Instrumental Clinical Phonetics*, London: Whurr.

Ball, M. and Rahilly, J. (1999) *Phonetics: The Science of Speech*, London: Arnold.

Bauer, L. (1983) *English Word-Formation*, Cambridge: Cambridge University Press.

Bloomfield, L. (1933) *Language*, London: Allen and Unwin.

Bolinger, D. (1951) 'Intonation: levels vs. configurations', *Word*, vol. 7, pp. 199–210.

Bolinger, D. (1972) 'Accent is predictable (if you're a mind-reader)', *Language*, vol. 48, pp. 633–44.

Borden, G. and Harris, K. S. (1994) *A Speech Science Primer*, 2nd edn, London: Williams and Wilkins.

Brazil, D. (1994) *Pronunciation for Advanced Learners of English*, Cambridge: Cambridge University Press.

Brazil, D., Coulthard, M. and Johns, C. (1980) *Discourse Intonation and Language Teaching*, London: Longman.

Brown, G. (1990) *Listening to Spoken English*, 2nd edn, London: Longman.

Brown, G., Curry, K. and Kenworthy, J. (1980) *Questions of Intonation*, London: Croom Helm.

Brown, G. and Yule, G. (1983) *Teaching the Spoken Language*, Cambridge: Cambridge University Press.

Catford, J. C. (1964) 'Phonation types', in D. Abercrombie *et al.* (1964), pp. 26–37.

Catford, J. C. (1977) *Fundamental Problems in Phonetics*, Edinburgh: Edinburgh University Press.

Catford, J. C. (1988) *A Practical Introduction to Phonetics*, Oxford: Oxford University Press.

Celce-Murcia, M., Brinton, D. and Goodwin, J. (1996) *Teaching Pronunciation: A Reference for Teachers of English to Speakers of Other Languages*, Cambridge: Cambridge University Press.

Chen, M. (1970) 'Vowel length variation as a function of the voicing of the consonant environment', *Phonetica*, vol. 22, pp. 129–59.

Chomsky, N. and Halle, M. (1968) *The Sound Pattern of English*, New York: Harper and Row.

Clark, J. and Yallop, C. (1995) *An Introduction to Phonetics and Phonology*, 2nd edn, Oxford: Blackwell.

Couper-Kuhlen, E. (1986) *An Introduction to English Prosody*, London: Edward Arnold.

Cruttenden, A. (ed.) (1994) *Gimson's Pronunciation of English*, 5th edn, revised and edited version of A. C. Gimson's original book. London: Edward Arnold.

Cruttenden, A. (1997) *Intonation*, 2nd edn, Cambridge: Cambridge University Press.

Crystal, D. (1969) *Prosodic Systems and Intonation in English*, Cambridge: Cambridge University Press.

Crystal, D. (1997) *English as a Global Language*, Cambridge: Cambridge University Press.

Crystal, D. and Quirk, R. (1964) *Systems of Prosodic and Paralinguistic Features in English*, The Hague: Mouton.

Dalton, C. and Seidlhofer, B. (1994) *Pronunciation*, Oxford: Oxford University Press.

Dauer, R. (1983) 'Stress-timing and syllable-timing reanalyzed', *Journal of Phonetics*, vol. 11, pp. 51–62.

Davidsen-Nielsen, N. (1969) 'English stops after initial /s/', *English Studies*, vol. 50, pp. 321–8.

Denes, P. and Pinson, E. (1993) *The Speech Chain*, 2nd edn, New York: Anchor.

Dimitrova, S. (1997) 'Bulgarian speech rhythm: stress-timed or syllable-timed?', *Journal of the International Phonetic Association*, vol. 27, 27–34.

Foulkes, P. and Docherty, D. (1999) *Urban Voices*, London: Arnold.

Fox, A. T. C. (1973) 'Tone sequences in English', *Archivum Linguisticum*, vol. 4, pp. 17–26.

Fox, A.T.C. (1978) 'To "r" is human?', *Journal of the International Phonetic Association*, vol. 8, pp. 72–4.

Fromkin, V. A. (ed.) (1978) *Tone: A Linguistic Survey*, New York: Academic Press.

Fry, D. B. (1958) 'Experiments in the perception of stress', *Language and Speech*, vol. 1, pp. 126–52.

Fudge, E. C. (1969) 'Syllables', *Journal of Linguistics*, vol. 5, pp. 253–86.

Fudge, E. C. (ed.) (1973) *Phonology*, London: Penguin.

Fudge, E. C. (1984) *English Word Stress*, London: George Allen and Unwin.

Fudge, E. C. (1999) 'Words and feet', *Journal of Linguistics*, vol. 35, pp. 273–96.

Giegerich, H. J. (1992) *English Phonology: An Introduction*, Cambridge: Cambridge University Press.

Gimson, A. C. (1960) 'The instability of English alveolar articulations', *Le Maître Phonétique*, vol. 113, pp. 7–10.

Gimson, A. C. (1964) 'Phonetic change and the RP vowel system', in D. Abercrombie *et al.* (1964), pp. 131–6.

Goldsmith, J. A. (1990) *Autosegmental and Metrical Phonology*, Oxford: Blackwell.

Halliday, M. A. K. (1967) *Intonation and Grammar in British English*, The Hague: Mouton.

Harris, J. (1994) *English Sound Structure*, Oxford: Blackwell.

Hayward, K. (2000) *Experimental Phonetics*, London: Longman.

Hirst, D. and di Cristo, A. (eds.) (1998) *Intonation Systems*, Cambridge: Cambridge University Press.

Hogg, R. and McCully, C. B. (1987) *Metrical Phonology: A Coursebook*, Cambridge: Cambridge University Press.

Honikman, B. (1964) 'Articulatory settings', in D. Abercrombie *et al.* (1964), pp. 73–84.

Hughes, A. and Trudgill, P. (1996) *English Accents and Dialects*, 3rd edn, London: Edward Arnold.

Hyman, L. (1975) *Phonology: Theory and Analysis*, New York: Holt, Rinehart and Winston.

International Phonetic Association (1999) *Handbook of the International Phonetic Association*, Cambridge: Cambridge University Press.

Ioup, G. and Weinberger, S. (1987) *Interlanguage Phonology: The Acquisition of a Second Language Sound System*, Rowley, MA: Newbury House.

Jakobson, R. and Halle, M. (1964) 'Tenseness and laxness', in D. Abercrombie *et al.* (1964), pp. 96–101.

James, A. R. (1988) *The Acquisition of a Second Language Phonology*, Tübingen: Narr.

Jenkins, J. (2000) *The Phonology of English as an International Language*, Oxford: Oxford University Press.

Johnson, K. (1996) *Acoustic and Auditory Phonetics*, Oxford: Blackwell.

Jones, D. (1931) 'The word as a phonetic entity', *Le Maître Phonétique*, vol. 36, pp. 60–5.

Jones, D. (1956) *The Pronunciation of English*, 4th edn, Cambridge: Cambridge University Press. First published in 1909.

Jones, D. (1975) *An Outline of English Phonetics*, 9th edn, Cambridge: Cambridge University Press. First published 1918.

Jones, D. (1976) *The Phoneme: Its Nature and Use*, Cambridge: Cambridge University Press. First published 1950.

Jones, D., edited and revised by P. J. Roach and J. Hartman (1997) *Daniel Jones English Pronouncing Dictionary*, 15th edn, Cambridge: Cambridge University Press. First edition published 1917, London: Dent.

Katamba, F. (1989) *An Introduction to Phonology*, London: Longman.

Kenworthy, J. (1987) *Teaching English Pronunciation*, London: Longman.

Kingdon, R. (1958) *The Groundwork of English Intonation*, London: Longman.

Knowles, G. O. (1987) *Patterns of Spoken English*, London: Longman.

Kreidler, C. W. (1989) *The Pronunciation of English*, Oxford: Blackwell.

Labov, W. (1972) *Sociolinguistic Patterns*, Oxford: Blackwell.

Ladd, D. R. (1996) *Intonational Phonology*, Cambridge: Cambridge University Press.

Ladefoged, P. (1993) *A Course in Phonetics*, 3rd edn, Fort Worth, TX, London: Harcourt Brace Jovanovich.

Ladefoged, P. (2000) *Vowels and Consonants*, Oxford: Blackwell.

Lass, N. J. (ed.) (1996) *Principles of Experimental Phonetics*, St Louis, MO, London: Mosby.

Laver, J. (1980) *The Phonetic Description of Voice Quality*, Cambridge: Cambridge University Press.

Laver, J. (1994) *Principles of Phonetics*, Cambridge, Cambridge University Press.

Lee, W. R. (1958) *English Intonation: A New Approach*, Amsterdam: North Holland.

Lehiste, I. (1977) 'Isochrony reconsidered', *Journal of Phonetics*, vol. 5, pp. 253–63.

Lieberman, P. and Blumstein, S. (1988) *Speech Physiology, Speech Perception and Acoustic Phonetics*, Cambridge: Cambridge University Press.

Lisker, L. (1970) 'Supraglottal air pressure in the production of English stops', *Language and Speech*, vol. 13, pp. 215–30.

MacCarthy, P. A. D. (1952) *English Pronunciation*, 4th edn, Cambridge: Heffer.

Mitchell, T. F. (1969) Review of Abercrombie (1967), *Journal of Linguistics*, 5, 153–64.

Mortimer, C. (1984) *Elements of Pronunciation*, Cambridge: Cambridge University Press.

O'Connor, J. D. (1980) *Better English Pronunciation*, 2nd edn, Cambridge: Cambridge University Press.

O'Connor, J. D. (1991) *Phonetics*, London: Penguin.

O'Connor, J. D. and Arnold, G. F. (1973) *The Intonation of Colloquial English*, 2nd edn, London: Longman. First published 1962.

O'Connor, J. D. and Tooley, O. M. (1964) 'The perceptibility of certain word boundaries', in D. Abercrombie *et al.* (1964), pp. 171–6.

O'Connor, J. D. and Trim, J. L. M. (1953) 'Vowel, consonant and syllable: a phonological definition', *Word*, vol. 9, pp. 103–22.

Palmer, H. E. (1924) *English Intonation with Systematic Exercises*, Cambridge: Heffer.

Pike, K. L. (1943) *Phonetics*, Ann Arbor, MI: University of Michigan Press.

Pike, K. L. (1945) *The Intonation of American English*, Ann Arbor, MI: University of Michigan Press.

Pike, K. L. (1947) *Phonemics*, Ann Arbor, MI: University of Michigan Press.

Pike, K. L. (1948) *Tone Languages*, Ann Arbor, MI: University of Michigan Press.

Pring. J. (1976) 'More thoughts on the /r/-link business', *Journal of the International Phonetic Association*, vol. 6, pp. 92–5.

Procter, P. (1995) *The Cambridge International Dictionary of English*, Cambridge: Cambridge University Press.

Pullum, G. K. and Ladusaw, W. (1996) *Phonetic Symbol Guide*, 2nd edn, Chicago, IL: University of Chicago Press. First edition published 1986.

Radford, A., Atkinson, M., Britain, D., Clahsen, H. and Spencer, A. (1999) *Linguistics: An Introduction*, Cambridge: Cambridge University Press.

Ramsaran, S. (ed.) (1990) *Studies in the Pronunciation of English*, London: Routledge.

Roach, P. J. (1982) 'On the distinction between "stress-timed" and "syllable-timed" languages', in D. Crystal (ed.), *Linguistic Controversies*, London: Edward Arnold.

Roach, P. J. (1994) 'Conversion between prosodic transcription systems: "Standard British" and ToBI', *Speech Communication*, vol. 15, pp. 91–9.

Roach, P. J. and Hartman, J. (eds.) (1997) see Jones (1997).

Roach, P., Stibbard, R., Osborne, J., Arnfield, S. and Setter, J. (1998) 'Transcription of prosodic and paralinguistic features of emotional speech', *Journal of the International Phonetic Association* 28, pp. 83–94.

Roca, I. and Johnson, W. (1999) *A Course in Phonology*, Oxford: Blackwell.

Sapir, E. (1925) 'Sound patterns in language', *Language*, vol. 1, pp. 37–51.

Schmerling, S. (1976) *Aspects of English Sentence Stress*, Austin, TX: University of Texas Press.

Sharp, A. E. (1958) 'Falling–rising intonation patterns in English', *Phonetica*, vol. 2, pp. 127–52.

Sledd, J. (1955) Review of Trager and Smith (1951), *Language*, vol. 31, pp. 312–45.

Summers, D. (1987) *Longman Dictionary of Contemporary English*, 2nd edn. London: Longman.

Taylor, D. S. (1981) 'Non-native speakers and the rhythm of English', *International Review of Applied Linguistics*, vol. 19, pp. 219–26.

Trager, G. L. (1964) 'The intonation system of American English', in D. Abercrombie *et al.* (1964), pp. 266–70.

Trager, G. L. and Smith, H. L. (1951) *An Outline of English Structure*, Washington, DC: American Council of Learned Societies.

Trim, J. L. M. (1959) 'Major and minor tone groups in English', *Le Maître Phonétique*, vol. 112, pp. 26–9.

Trubetzkoy, N. S. (1939) *Grundzuge der Phonologie*, Transactions du Cercle Linguistique de Prague, 7. (English translation: *Principles of Phonology*, transl. C. A. M. Baltaxe, Berkeley, CA: University of California Press, 1969.)

Trudgill, P. (1999) *The Dialects of England*, 2nd edn, Oxford: Blackwell.

Wells, J. C. (1970) 'Local accents in England and Wales', *Journal of Linguistics*, vol. 6, pp. 231–52.

Wells, J. C. (1982) *Accents of English*, 3 vols., Cambridge: Cambridge University Press.

Wells, J. C. (2000) *Longman Pronunciation Dictionary*, 2nd edn, London: Longman. First published 1990.

Williams, B. (1996) 'The formulation of a transcription system for British English', in G. Knowles, A. Wichmann and P. Alderson, *Working with Speech*, London: Longman.

Windsor Lewis, J. (1975) 'Linking /r/ in the General British pronunciation of English', *Journal of the International Phonetic Association*, vol. 5, pp. 37–42.

Windsor Lewis, J. (1977) 'The r-link business: a reply', *Journal of the International Phonetic Association*, vol. 7, pp. 28–31.

Index

accents 2, 5, 100, 101, 208
  American 209, 3
  Australian 208
  BBC 209
  English regional 67, 209, 210
  Irish 5, 209
  models 6
  rhotic 63
  Royal Family 26
  Scottish 5, 209
  Welsh 209
acoustic phonetics 204
Adam's Apple 27
affixes 105
affricates 48, 54, 121–4
airstream, pulmonic 29
allophone 41
alphabet 39
alveolar ridge 9
approximants 62, 63
articulators 8–10
articulatory phonetics 8, 204
articulatory setting 148
aspiration 34, 41
assimilation 138–42
attitudinal function 184–90
auditory phonetics 204
autosegmental analysis 179–80, 181

BBC Pronunciation Unit 5
BBC pronunciation vii, 3, 4, 25, 67, 209
body language 188, 201
breath-group 150
breathy voice 52

Cardinal vowels 13, 17

cartilage 27, 28
centralisation 42
chart, English consonant phonemes 65
Chinese 11
clusters, consonant 71, 80, 127
  tables 72, 74
coarticulation 259
coda 76
communication 6
complex word stress 104–11
compound words 105
  stress 108–9
computer symbols 46
computer technology 206
contoids 17
connected speech 134–49
consonants 10, 27
  affricate 48, 54, 121–4
  alveolar 9
  ambisyllabic 78
  approximants 62, 63
  bilabial 10
  clusters 71, 80, 127
    tables 72, 74
  dental 10
  final 73
  fortis 35–6, 36–7, 54–6
  glottal 55, 56
  j 63–4
  l 61–2, 86
  labiodental 10
  lateral 61
  lenis 35–6
  m 89
  n 81, 88
  nasal 58–61

ŋ 66, 70, 89
phonemes in English, chart 65
post-initial 73
r 62–3, 89
retroflex 62
syllabic 76, 81, 86–90, 125–7
velar 9
w 63–4
see also diphthongs, fricatives,
    plosives
contractions 143
cover term 37

declination 176
diacritics 42, 46
dialect 2
dialectology 208
    diphthongs 21–3
    see also diphthongs, fricatives,
        plosives
discourse intonation theory 202
distinctive feature analysis 128–30
distribution 11
    complementary 41

electromyography 205
electropalatography 205
elision 81, 142–3
English consonant phonemes, chart 65
Estuary English 4, 5
experimental phonetics 184–7, 212
extended tones 180

fall-rise tone 154, 160, 171–3, 180
falling tone 152
feet 164
force of articulation 36–7
fortis consonants 35–6, 36–7, 54–6
frequency 151
fricatives 48–54, 49
    alveolar 51
    dental 50, 56
    glottal 29, 56
    groove 56
    labiodental 50
    post-alveolar 51
    slit 56
function words 112

function/s 183
functions of intonation 152–3, 183–203

generative phonology 101–2
glottal plosive 29
glottal stop 29
glottalisation 55–6
glottis 28, 30
groove 56

hard palate 9
heads 164, 173–6
hierarchical relationship 164
homorganic 49

Interlanguage Phonology 7
International English 7
International Phonetic Association 17,
    46
    Chart xi
intonation 2, 45, 81, 150–203
    autosegmental analysis 179–80
    form 152–3
        problems in analysing 176–9
        subordination 199, 202
intonation functions 152–3
    accentual 183, 193–5
    attitudinal 183, 184–90
        paralinguistic features 188
        prosodic 187
        sequential 187
    discourse 184, 197, 197–201, 202
    grammatical 184, 195–7
        question-tags 197
intonation languages 162
intonation unit 168
intrusive r 147

jaws 10
juncture 144

laboratory phonetics 204–8
larynx 8, 27–9, 36
lateral consonants 61
lax 25
lenis 35–6
level tone 152
linking 144–5, 147

Index

lip-rounding 15
lip-spreading 15
lips 10, 15
loudness 94
lungs 30

maximum onsets principle 77
minimal pairs 66
Minimum General Intelligibility 7
minimum syllable 70
morpheme 59
morphology 59
movement 94, 97
moving tone 152

nasal consonants 58–61
neutralisation 84, 127
nuclear stress 163

paralinguistic features 188, 190–1
peak 76
pharynx 9
phonation 31, 131, 191
phonation type 191
phonemes 1, 38–40, 79, 164
  English consonant: Chart 65
phonemic analysis 121–33
phonemic symbols ix–x
phonemic system 40, 44–5
phonetics 1, 8, 204–13
  experimental 184–7, 212
phonology 1, 44–5, 150, 204–13
  generative 101–2
phonotactics 71
pitch 94, 150, 167–8
  height 154–5
  perceptibility 151
  phonemes 158
plosion 32
plosives 32–5, 36, 127
  aspiration 34, 41
  closure 32
  compression 32
  English 32
  glottal 29
  position 33
  post-release phase 32
  release 32

polysyllabic words 104
post-alveolar approximant 62
pre-head 165
prefixes 105, 107
primary stress 96, 106
productive suffixes 105
progressive assimilation 139
prominence 94
pronunciation teaching 6, 206

question-tags 197

realisation 41, 142
Received Pronunciation (RP) vii, 3, 6,
  25
regressive assimilation 139
respiration 29–31
retroflex 62
rhotic accents 63
rhythm 134–8, 146
rise-fall tone 154, 160, 171–3, 180
rising tone 152
root 106
RP (Received Pronunciation) vii, 3, 25

schwa 17, 82–4, 127
segmental phonology 150
segments 38
semivowel 64
sense-group 150, 168
sentence stress 193
slit 56
soft palate 9
spectrogram 207
speech chain 204, 212
speech databases 207
speech synthesis 206
  by rule 120
spelling 83
stem 106
stress 2, 45, 93–103, 98
  levels 95
  nuclear 163
  perception 93
  primary 96, 106
  production 93
  rules 101
  sentence 193

shift 137
simple words 93–103
tonic 163, 201
variable 109
word vii, 96–100, 104–11
stricture 31
strong forms 81, 112
strong syllables 81–2
subglottal pressure 31
suffixes 105–7
suprasegmental phonology 45, 150
suprasegmental variables 166–9
syllabic consonants 76, 81, 86–90,
    125–7
syllabicity 126
syllables 45, 70–92, 98, 164
    division 77, 79
    nucleus 163
    onset 71, 77
    rhyme 76
    tonic 163, 177–8
symbols 5, 19, 41–4, 46
    phonemic ix–x

tail 165, 171–3
teeth 9
tense 25
ToBI 181
tonal rhyme 172
tones 152, 153–8, 180
    see also fall-rise, rise-fall
tone languages 153–4, 159
tone-group 168
tone-unit 159, 162–8, 179
    anomalous 179
    boundaries 178–9, 181
    simple 164
tongue 9
tonic stress 163, 201
tonicity 201
trachea 27
transcription 2, 36, 41–4

triphthongs 24

utterances 152, 164

variability 207
variable stress 109
variety 208–12
velum 9
vocal cords 28
vocal folds 28
vocal tract 8
vocoids 17
voice quality 191
voicing 27, 29–31
    onset 34
vowels 10–17
    back 12, 84
    Cardinal 13, 17
    close 12, 84
    diphthongs 21–3
    English 124–5
    front 12, 84
    glide 21
    lax 25
    length 94
    long 19–21
    open 12
    pure 21
    quadrilateral 13
    quality 94
    short 15–17
    tense 25
    triphthongs 24

weak forms 81, 112–20
weak syllables 81–2
    close back/front 84–6
    schwa 17, 82–4, 91, 127
word stress vii, 104–11, 105
word-class pairs 110

zero coda 73